ANCIENT FAIRY AND FOLK TALES

This anthology explores the multitude of evidence for recognisable fairy tales drawn from sources in the much older cultures of the ancient world, appearing much earlier than the 17th century where awareness of most fairy tales tends to begin.

It presents versions of *Cinderella*, *The Emperor's New Clothes*, *Snow White*, *The Frog Prince* and a host of others where the similarities to familiar 'modern' versions far outweigh the differences. Here we find Cinderella as a courtesan, Snow White coming to a tragic end, or an innocent heroine murdering her sisters. We find an emperor's new clothes where the flatterers compare him to Alexander the Great, or a pair of adulterers caught in a magic trap. Tantalising fragments suggest that there is more to be discovered: we can point to a Sleeping Beauty where the girl takes on the green colouring of the surrounding wood, or we encounter a Rumpelstiltskin connected to a mystery cult. The overall picture suggests a much richer texture of popular tale as a fascinating new legacy of antiquity.

This volume breaks down the traditional barriers between Classical Mythology and the fairy tale, and will be an invaluable resource for anyone working on the history of fairy tales and folklore.

Graham Anderson is Emeritus Professor of Classics at the University of Kent. He has written extensively on ancient folk and fairy tale, including *Fairytale in the Ancient World* (2000) and *Greek and Roman Folklore: A Handbook* (2006). His most recent publication is *Fantasy in Greek and Roman Literature* (Routledge, 2019). He is currently working on a study entitled *The Pepaideumenos and his World: Intellectuals in the Roman Empire*.

ANCIENT FAIRY AND FOLK TALES

An Anthology

Graham Anderson

LONDON AND NEW YORK

First published 2020
by Routledge
2 Park Square, Milton Park, Abingdon, Oxon OX14 4RN

and by Routledge
52 Vanderbilt Avenue, New York, NY 10017

Routledge is an imprint of the Taylor & Francis Group, an informa business

© 2020 Graham Anderson

The right of Graham Anderson to be identified as author of this work has been asserted by him in accordance with sections 77 and 78 of the Copyright, Designs and Patents Act 1988.

All rights reserved. No part of this book may be reprinted or reproduced or utilised in any form or by any electronic, mechanical, or other means, now known or hereafter invented, including photocopying and recording, or in any information storage or retrieval system, without permission in writing from the publishers.

Trademark notice: Product or corporate names may be trademarks or registered trademarks, and are used only for identification and explanation without intent to infringe.

British Library Cataloguing-in-Publication Data
A catalogue record for this book is available from the British Library

Library of Congress Cataloging-in-Publication Data
Names: Anderson, Graham, author.
Title: Ancient fairy and folk tales: an anthology / Graham Anderson.
Description: Abingdon, Oxon; New York: Routledge, 2019. | Includes bibliographical references and index.
Identifiers: LCCN 2019031939
Subjects: LCSH: Fairy tales—History and Critism. | Folklore—History.
Classification: LCC GR550 .A56 2019 | DDC 398.209—dc23
LC record available at https://lccn.loc.gov/2019031939

ISBN: 978-1-138-36178-2 (hbk)
ISBN: 978-1-138-36179-9 (pbk)
ISBN: 978-0-429-43244-6 (ebk)

Typeset in Bembo
by codeMantra

For Richard Stoneman

CONTENTS

Preface ix
List of abbreviations and cue-titles xi

1 Introduction: who's been telling *my* tale? 1

2 The classic fairy tale: *Cupid and Psyche* 17

3 Arts of variation: Cinderellas and Snow Whites 55

4 Otherworldly encounters 70

5 Siren women 87

6 Rewards and punishments I 99

7 Rewards and punishments II: three innocent slandered maidens 125

8 Tricksters 143

9 Traditional heroes, magic objects 155

10 Animal tales 167

11 Tiny people   178

12 Miscellaneous tales   184

Appendix 1: the Sleeping Beauty (ATU 410, The Petrified Kingdom)   *195*
Appendix 2: some fragmentary hints   *198*
Bibliography   *199*
Glossary of sources in Greek (G) or Latin (L)   *207*
Index of tale types   *209*
Index   *211*

PREFACE

There has been no lack of new writing about Fairy Tale over the past half-century. But amid the greatly increased provision of materials it is not unreasonable to describe Ancient Fairy Tale as still a Cinderella subject. I set out to remedy this at the end of the last millennium with a treatment entitled *Fairytale in the Ancient World*; two years later William Hansen produced a much more comprehensive handling in his presentation of International Tales, *Ariadne's Thread*. Both treatments endeavoured to establish the existence of a canon of traditional popular tales in Greek and Roman literature, and both were keyed as a matter of strong principle to what is now the Aarne-Thompson-Uther Index, so as to be easily accessible to professional folklorists and encourage the maximum access to comparative material. But the overall result has given rise to a lack: we do not have an annotated collection in translation of Greek and Roman fairy and folktales as such. Both Hansen and I had presented our respective repertoires through extensive summaries of tales: it is now useful to provide a collection of actual texts in translation, as Bryan Reardon's anthology has long done for the ancient novel. While this book was in its final stages Hansen brought out a comprehensive *Book of Greek and Roman Folktales, Legends and Myths* (2017): once again Hansen's scope is wider, emphasising originally oral anecdotes, jokes and the like, but his scholarly apparatus is this time designedly much more limited. Some 50 tales in the following collection do not appear in either of Hansen's volumes; the need for a further collection of classical fairy and folktales remains.

I have accumulated a number of debts along the way: more than a decade ago I presented a consultation paper at the Folklore Society on the scope of a projected anthology: I am grateful to all who took part and contributed useful suggestions. I owe a special debt to William Hansen, who has supplied me with offprints over a number of years, and to Nancy Canepa, Debbie Felton and Daniel Ogden, who invited me to join in complementary projects which have offered further stimulus. I have been grateful for the support of Jack Zipes over many decades, and of two anonymous referees who encouraged me towards a more expansive introduction. The book is dedicated to Richard Stoneman, close on 20 years after our first foray into Fairy Tale. I described my study then as a Bluebeard's castle of dismembered narratives; it has now seen their reassembly into witnesses that speak with their own voice.

Graham Anderson
University of Kent at Canterbury

ABBREVIATIONS AND CUE-TITLES

Aesopica	*Aesopica* ed. B.E.Perry, Urbana, IL
AJPh	*American Journal of Philology*
AT	Antti Aarne and Stith Thompson *The Types of the Folktale*, 2nd revision 1961, Helsinki
ATU	A. Aarne-S.Thompson and H.-J. Uther (2004), *The Types of International Folktales*, Helsinki
BP	J. Bolte and G. Polivka, (1913–32) *Anmerkungen zu den Kinder- und Hausmärchen der Brüder Grimm*, I-V, Leipzig
BSOAS	*Bulletin of the School of Oriental and African Studies*
CQ	*Classical Quarterly*
Dasent	G.W. Dasent (1910 repr. 1970) *East o' the Sun and West o' the Moon: Norwegian Folk Tales*, New York
DBF	K. Briggs (1970), *A Dictionary of British Folktales in the English Language*, I-II, London
EM	K. Ranke et al. (1977–2015) *Enzyklopädie des Märchens*, I-XV, Berlin
FFC	*Folklore Fellows Communications*, Helsinki
FGrH	F. Jacoby (ed.) (1923–1958), *Die Fragmente der griechischen Historiker*, Berlin and Leiden
Gantz	T. Gantz (1993), *Early Greek Myth: A Guide to Literary and Visual Sources*, Baltimore, MD
Hansen	W. Hansen (2002), *Ariadne's Thread: A Guide to International Tales found in Classical Literature*, Ithaca, NY
Imagines	Philostratus (Senior) *Imagines*
JAF	*Journal of American Folklore*
JHS	*Journal of Hellenic Studies*

LIMC	H.C. Ackermann and J.-R. Gisler, (eds) (1981–97) *Lexicon Iconographicum Mythologiae Classicae*, I-VIII, Zurich
Met.	(Apuleius, Ovid) *Metamorphoses*
ML	R. Christiansen (1958), *The Migratory Legends*, Helsinki
NH	Pliny the Elder, *Naturalis Historia*
PIR^2	*Prosopographia Imperii Romani*
RhM	*Rheinisches Museum für Philologie*
RSV	*Revised Standard Version*
TAPhA	*Transactions and Proceedings of the American Philological Association*
Thompson, S.	(1955–58) *A Motif-Index of Folk Literature*, I-VI, Bloomington, IN
VA	Philostratus, *Vita Apollonii Tyanensis*
VS	Philostratus, *Vitae Sophistarum*

1

INTRODUCTION

Who's been telling *my* tale?

The catchphrase above suggests that someone else has got there first: that familiar and much-loved stories we claim as 'ours'[1] may not necessarily be so after all; we may not find older tellings instantly recognisable in every detail, but that is in itself a reason for looking further back than we have been accustomed to do. The dwarves in *Snow White* who ask that sort of question we take for granted as characters in a fairy tale; but it will be useful to define what sort of material such a term has come to entail, and just how old we might expect some fairy tales to be.

As a working definition of a fairy tale I have adopted the following: 'a tale with a marked fantastic or magical content and a high moral standpoint'. Fairy tale belongs to the larger category of folktale, associated in the first instance with oral tradition. Within that broad grouping it differs from myth in not attempting explanation of creation or the world; it differs from legend in not offering historically believable material; and it differs from other non-magical folktale categories such as humorous tales and novellas in its framework of unbelievability.[2] It can include literary works of named authors as well as anonymous narrators: fairy tales are frequently presented even in literary settings as popular and traditional material being told orally to a listener or listeners. It is easy to think of examples where such categories overlap, and scholars may choose to see the story of the one-eyed ogre as fairy tale[3] as readily as folktale.

So much for definitions in isolation. Students of fairy and folktale can voice frustration at the diversity of formulations possible; and we can feel left with a sense of confusion worse confounded.[4] Of some half-dozen definitions collected by Stein[5] those of Bolte and Ranke are similar to the above; those of Stith Thompson and Vladimir Propp emphasise their own specific interest in motifs and functions[6] respectively. J.R.R. Tolkien invoked a background of what he called 'Faerie' for the ethos of the fairy tale.[7] Perhaps the least satisfactory characterisation is ironically one by Jacob Grimm himself, simply contrasting the poetic quality of the fairy tale with the historical aspect of legend. The level of documentation is now such that the Grimms' tales have acquired their own corpus of annotations, by Bolte and Polivka (1911–1932); and even Tolkien's celebrated essay has acquired its own text and commentary! But some attempt at precision is necessary, because in practice the terms relating to popular storytelling are often loose and based on verbal association. Supernatural forces are normal in fairy tale, but need not be fairies as such; and many tales include gods, but not acting in some higher mythical capacity. The term 'fairy tale' is generally used as an equivalent to 'magic tale'[8] (German *Zaubermärchen*) or 'wonder tale' (*Wundermärchen*), but normal English usage now prefers *Grimms' Fairy Tales* to *Grimms' Wonder Tales*. Folk tale and fairy tale are often treated as almost interchangeable, but a traditional riddle-tale like *King John and the Abbot* is a folktale without any claim to being a fairy tale, precisely because any wonder or magical element is missing. The term 'international tale' is a useful professional term when linking folktales to the Aarne-Thompson-Uther index of tales (*ATU*),[9] where magic tales occupy numbers 300–749; but again the term's currency outside the academy is much less than that of folktale as a matter of common usage. In the end I chose to emphasise fairy tale because I think it best links an ancient tale like *Cupid and Psyche* with the elaborately decorated *contes de fées* of 17th-century France,[10] and because fairy tales like those of Perrault or the Grimms are the kind of stories most likely to lie still partly submerged and undetected in the ancient world.[11]

Fairy tales of any period present some specific expectations of thematic content. We might expect family disharmony that calls for resolution: typically sibling rivalry is involved, like that of Psyche and her sisters, or even incest, as in some forms of *Cinderella*. A tale may involve a quest or the solution to a problem, like Psyche's implementation of tasks set by a future mother-in-law. Also important is the sympathy of the reader or listener for the protagonist. A supernatural agent, magic helper or magic object will somehow be expected to put matters right in the plot; and there will be rewards for the modest and virtuous, and punishments for those who are not. There are some distinctive motifs that seem to point to fairy tale quite inexorably: if anyone is turned into or out of a frog,[12] then fairy tale will be the first thing to suggest itself. If however someone turns into or out of a stag, the reader will be more likely to think of the story as myth[13]: such is the whimsical power of traditional association. We expect some typical tale elements, as when animal helpers assist the heroine to accomplish impossible household tasks, or a king offers half his kingdom for whatever it might be, or there is a surfeit of golden objects, or invisibility looms large. We are also prone to associate certain stereotyped phrases with the fairy tale: 'All the better to x you with…' is among the most distinctive; to say nothing of 'Once upon a time' and 'happily ever after', as well as 'Who's been sleeping in my bed?' There may be gruesome features, like Psyche's indirect murder of her sisters, and happy endings are not as assured as we tend to take for granted: Hippomenes and Atalanta undergo a transformation that denies them any sexual fulfilment, just as surely as Perrault's version does not save Red Riding Hood from being finally eaten by the wolf.

The fairy tale: towards a traditional history

Before adding in a range of earlier examples, it is useful to suggest a chronological overview of Western fairy tale. Two Renaissance collections mark the beginnings of the modern genre as generally conceived: Straparola's *Le piacevoli notti* (The Delectable Nights) (1550–1553) with 14 fairy tales among 73 tales; and Basile's *Lo cunto de li cunti* ('The Tale of Tales', otherwise known as the *Pentamerone*), consisting of 49 tales and a frame (1634–1636). Both authors present an audience listening to a cycle of tales, preserving the illusion of orality, and in Basile's case told by lower-class women. From the end of the 17th century come the significant markers of Charles Perrault's *Histoires ou contes du temps passé*, with its sub-title *Contes de ma mère L'oye* (*Mother Goose Tales*) and tales by Madame D'Aulnoy, who coined the term *Contes de fées* itself (1698)[14]; it is with her set of 15 tales that the resourceful manipulation of fairy tale motifs might be said to come of age, and no fewer than five of her narratives look back to *Cupid and Psyche* as a model. Perrault had just produced what have become canonic versions of *Cinderella*, *Puss in Boots*, *Sleeping Beauty* and others; whatever the previous history of these tales, they here appear against an aristocratic, court background which valued good manners and an ethos of opulence. There is noteworthy inventiveness in evidence: d'Aulnoy's Finette Cendron and her sisters touch on *Babes in the Wood*, and even a one-eyed cannibal giant tricked into his own oven, before their own Cinderella plot is completed. Such tales are the product of educated circles and set the pattern of fairy tales that are essentially literary, and authored by named individuals, in a world where Ancient Ovidian metamorphosis and Medieval romance effortlessly coalesce.[15] The fashion for fairy tale continued, notably in the hands of educated women writers such as Marie-Jeanne L'héritier and Rose de la Force,[16] till the substantial *Cabinet des fées* on the threshold of the French Revolution.

The tide now turned in favour of the notion of the oral tale collected from humble informants. By the early 19th century such tales could be collected along local or national lines for the most part, by individual scholarly initiatives, most notably those of the Brothers Grimm. In contrast to the educated output of the French salon-ladies, these tales were seen at least at the time as the preserve of the folk, the heritage of a nation's soul[17] through the spontaneous voice of the peasantry. This idealised state of affairs is now accorded a good deal of modification: the Grimms themselves edited and revised their collection *Kinder-und Hausmärchen* (*Children's and Household Tales*) seven times between 1812 and 1857; and at least some of their versions appear to have been influenced by literate versions of French inspiration.[18]

Since the Grimms the study of the oral tale has greatly developed, and a landmark was reached in 1910 with Antti Aarne's index of popular tale types, revised by Stith Thompson in 1928 and 1961 and much expanded by H.-J. Uther in 2004, under the title *The Types of International Folktales*. A series of monographs appeared until around 1960 by various researchers studying

4 Introduction: who's been telling *my* tale?

the motif-variations of individual tales according to the historic-geographic method.[19] Stith Thompson's revision of his motif-index of individual constituents of tales appeared in 1955–1958. The 'magic tales', otherwise fairy tales, are placed before religious tales, romances and stupid ogre stories in what is now the Aarne-Thompson-Uther classification, though these categories also contain a sprinkling of fairy/magic tales as well. And the massive *Enzyklopädie des Märchens* begun by Kurt Ranke in 1977 saw its final supplementary volume in 2015.[20] Of course the production of individually invented fairy tales taking only their starting-point from the traditional fairy tale has continued through the last three centuries, faster than scholarly study can keep up with them.

Here the history of the fairy tale might be allowed to rest, with occasional skirmishing over the 'invention' of the first fairy tale: Ruth Bottigheimer saw Straparola as the actual inventor of the genre, giving rise to substantial controversy, particularly over whether the fairy-tale genre developed through oral use of written texts.[21] But there remains a nagging doubt that the outline suggested so far cannot be the whole story. Two texts in particular stand out to challenge the above account: the 9th-century CE Chinese story of Yeh-Hsien which has been acknowledged as a fully-fledged Cinderella long before the European Renaissance, and one not truncated in any way[22]; and the substantial tale of *Cupid and Psyche* forming the centrepiece of the picaresque novel the *Metamorphoses* (*The Golden Ass*) by the Latin sophist Apuleius as early as the 2nd century CE.[23] Some classicists explain the latter piece in different terms, and it is indeed a richly multifaceted text[24]; but only its mannered Late Latin language would prevent its being passed off as a text from an 18th-century French *salonnière*. The fairy tale has been around for a good deal longer, and reached its literary maturity early.

To address the question of continuity between ancient and modern fairy tale repertoire two treatments appeared around the millennium: the present author and William Hansen independently produced studies setting out to show that the links from Antiquity to the Renaissance are much more extensive than usually assumed.[25] Not all the examples adduced were of complete tales, but at least it should now be no longer possible to claim that fairy tales as we know them are no older than the Renaissance.[26] (A recent radical claim in effect allowing fairy tales to be no older than the Grimms depends on redefining the genre to an unconvincing degree.[27])

In fact classicists and folklorists alike have long been aware that there are *some* continuities between Classical Antiquity and modern oral storytelling, both at the level of motifs and complete tales: Stith Thompson (1946: 278–281) listed a substantial number of significant motifs, including the single eye of the Phorcides (K333.2), the war between pygmies and cranes (F535.5.1), the lotus-eaters (D1365.1.1), and the sail signal on Theseus' ship (Z130.1). But groups of motifs can also be found, yielding at least the possibility of survival of larger tales: this appears to be the case with the story of the Argonauts, which furnishes analogues to the tale 'Six around the world/The land and water ship' (the outward journey) and 'the obstacle flight' (the return). So too the *Tale of the Two*

Brothers contains several motifs which turn up together in modern oral versions of this very ancient tale (guaranteed as such by an ancient Egyptian version as well as the Greek story of Peleus).[28]

Fairy tales in context

In a good number of instances we are lucky enough to have some notion of a context in which an ancient fairy tale is actually being told. Odysseus tells the stories of Polyphemus and Circe before an aristocratic audience in a place which Homer himself seems to present as a kind of fairy-tale island in its own right.[29] Other stories are told by the local bard Demodocus.[30] Prominent among the occasions is that of after-dinner entertainment. Indeed dinner-parties continue to be a traditional opportunity for storytelling throughout antiquity: our clearest allusion to the Frog Prince story comes in a bizarre Roman dinner party in Petronius' comic novel (1st c. CE), which also provides an allusion to the man who finds the goblin's cap to take him to a treasure.[31] A number of stories retold by Lucian's porte-parole Tychiades centre on the supernatural and are set by their frame narrator at a sickbed clearly meant to evoke discussion of the after-life, and looking back to Plato's *Phaedo*.[32] At the other end of the spectrum we find stories presented or dismissed as old wives' tales, told by female nurses to scare, enthral or reward their child charges, often to the disapproval of the reporter: imagination is implied to be dangerous or subversive.[33]

In terms of literary genre there is a wide range of formal classifications in which fairy tales are able to surface. Those I have included from the *Odyssey* can at no point be mistaken for heroic tales: Odysseus is no giant-killer like Heracles in the slaying of Cacus in the *Aeneid*, for example; in the Circe tale he has only to follow Hermes' instructions in order to turn the tables on the witch; and the tale of Ares and Aphrodite is at base a novella which just happens to be in verse in the middle of an Epic. Some fairy tales find themselves in slightly artificial company in Ovid's *Metamorphoses*, where they are part of a Hellenistically styled catalogue poem, and may seem to be distorted to include an explanatory cause or a metamorphosis. Others however only survive in the barest of mythographers' summaries, or antiquarian travelogues, where their impact as fairy tales runs the risk of being all but lost. Sadly, we should expect to have a great many more if we had more substantial remains of Athenian Satyric drama, where the satyrs themselves as mischievous and often comic supernatural creatures may well have provided their fair share of otherworldly beings to interact with humans in distress. Most intriguing are those fairy tales which appear embedded in larger works of fiction, with varying degrees of recognisability. One at least, *Chione*, appears to be a *Snow White* novel, but the remains are still very fragmentary.[34] Such a development is parallel to the efflorescence of fairy tale across the 17th/18th centuries in France, where the fairy tale could indeed attain to novel proportions. We can also be aware of traditional material being earthed into historiography, with or without the credulity of the historical narrator himself. Without an actual ancient term for fairy tale (other than Greek *mythos*, a not-necessarily-reliable tale) we have no ancient anthology to correspond to the kind of compilation found in Straparola, Basile or Perrault, though it might be suggested that Ovid and other compilers such as Antoninus Liberalis,[35] an assembler of metamorphoses in the 2nd century CE, come at least close at times to such an enterprise.

Fairy tales and children

A good many fairy tales do seem to be directed towards a younger audience: most obviously *Cupid and Psyche* is told as an *anilis fabula* – an old wives' tale – to a young girl; and we hear a number of instances where tales are told to distract, reward, caution or otherwise influence children.[36] More unusual is the setting of Philostratus the Elder's first set of *Imagines* (Greek *Eikones*), where the author takes a child round a picture-gallery and explains paintings with a notably mythical or fairy-tale subject-matter.[37] But a passage in Aristophanes' *Wasps* indicates an unsophisticated old man as also a likely teller of (apparent) fairy tales; it may be that for lack of any education in between, it is the tales that he heard as a child that he regards as suitable for re-telling.[38]

Symbol and social agenda

Fairy tales offer an Aladdin's cave of material for students of human nature and social history alike, but there are a good many pitfalls along the way. Undoubtedly fairy tales target genuine family problems such as the death of a mother and her replacement by a stepmother, or the issue of sibling rivalry and the need to socialise children out of cruel and selfish behaviour. It is all very well to claim that the adventures of fairy tale heroes and heroines encourage the resilience of the growing child,[39] but it might just as readily be suggested that they encourage the child to wait for the fairy god-person to manage difficult family situations. There will also be assumptions that are to say the least questionable: that nasty people are physically ugly, and kindly ones correspondingly beautiful. We must be ever wary of imposing the notion that all fantasy tales must have some kind of 'meaning' that can be unlocked and can be proven: it is perfectly possible to see competition between generations in tales where a humbly born hero threatens to supplant a king, but it may be going too far to see the king himself as a Freudian father-figure. Where we can see such motifs as incest we can expect it to be explicit, as in those *Cinderella* variants where the heroine flees from a father who wishes to marry her.[40] We could be persuaded that stories of frog or snake bridegrooms and the like are motivated by attempts to prepare innocent young girls for the first sight and experience of male genitals; or indeed that the preoccupation with fitting feet into shoes has a similarly sexual connotation.

It is worth noting that the social agenda of a specific fairy tale may change over time: a society conscious of child abuse may feel that *Little Red Riding Hood* is or may be read as a warning against strangers in lonely places, but in the ancient version of Euthymus and Lycus it is the whole community that has to expose the girl to 'marriage' with the wolf-spirit, and the whole dynamic of the story is correspondingly different.[41] There is also a widespread assumption that folktales in general concern the very humble in society, though it may chart their social rise. This does not bear examination: in the five Cinderella- or Cinderella-related tales featured here, each girl starts at a different point on the social ladder: Rhodopis is a slave, Aspasia lowborn but free, Chloe a foundling aristocrat, Aseneth an aristocrat throughout and Aphrodite a goddess!

Sometimes social position is built into the tale: it is required that the person who tells the truth in *The Emperor's New Clothes* should be someone with no social position to lose, hence an old woman from up country in the case of Pyrrhus flattered as the image of Alexander the Great; in the late Medieval Count Lucanor version the whistle-blower is a negro, for whom it is not important whether legitimately born or not.[42] Sometimes occupation will play a significant part: Jack Zipes has underlined the essential economic role of spinning in the tale of Rumpelstiltskin.[43]

How do ancient examples alter our perception?

It is often in relation to popular assumptions about the psychological meaning and social history of tales that ancient examples can hope to offer if not correctives, certainly cautions about what we can take to be the essentials of a tale. The first thing one tends to notice is that the Ancient World is a great deal less tolerant to heroines: those impregnated by gods are not seen in Antiquity as rape victims, but as girls who must immediately curb their pride and arrogance.[44] We note too the insistence in the Polyphemus tale of the punishment for the giant's crime of neglecting Zeus and the laws of hospitality,[45] a matter of rather less consequence in versions after the end of Antiquity. We are also accustomed to think of traditional fairy tale as being very unspecific ('once upon a time in a certain country…'), where a Greek mythographer handling the same material will routinely tie a specific hero to a specific parentage and a specific city. In some cases the world below seems to be presented differently: the underworld is sometimes peopled in modern folktale by trees with silver, gold and diamond branches[46]: Virgil famously used the golden bough in the singular in just such a context.[47] Underground one is to expect trees of precious metals and jewels.

How old are fairy tales?

It does not take much acquaintance with the tales of the Ancient Near East to realise that classical versions of fairy tales are in most cases unlikely to be the first of their kind. The adultery of Ares and Aphrodite on a divine level as early as Homer's *Odyssey* is little different from the human case of Ubainer's wife and her paramour from the Egypt of the previous millennium: a magic crocodile to hold the adulterer under water serves the same function as the invisible bonds supplied by Hephaestus.[48] Sumerian sacred tales already anticipate a fair proportion of the essentials for Cinderella-type narratives, even if we cannot produce the whole template from any one text[49]; and the ancient Egyptian *Tale of Two Brothers* supplies more of the modern international tale than what has survived from the Graeco-Roman world of the story of Peleus and Thetis.[50] The Old Testament also affords a number of folklore-based episodes: Abel's murdered remains cry out to God from the ground; Jacob is an accomplished trickster; Daniel fulfils the qualification for an *Emperor's New Clothes* story when he foresees the nakedness of Nebuchadnezzar; or the pharaoh defaults on payment for plagues, and so God kills the Egyptian firstborn sons to the same effect as the Pied Piper. We are wise to suspect or even assume that we are unlikely ever to know when we have chanced on the very first telling of any specific fairy tale. It may take no more than the belief in supernatural involvement in human domestic affairs to generate such a story.

Oral or written?

Ancient examples do not have a great deal of light to shed on the transmission of our materials. All our surviving specimens must have been written down at some point; otherwise we should not have them at all. We know that sometimes as humble a genre as the fable was versified for added elegance. Yet the Homeric poems are generally acknowledged to be examples of a tradition of oral composition, and so the tales of Polyphemus and Circe, Nausicaa, and Ares and Aphrodite are seen as among the products of it. The prose example in the Medieval Turkish *Book of Dede Korkut* is even more clearly suffused with oral mannerisms: ('What did he recite? Let us see, O my Khan, what he recited...'). At the other extreme Apuleius' version of *Cupid and Psyche* could scarcely be more clearly the product of a literate culture decorated with rhetorical mannerisms learned in a school. A near contemporary of Apuleius, Dio of Prusa, actually offers us an account of a female wise woman and oral storyteller he says he met on his travels in rural Greece: but the story she tells, a version of the so-called Allegory of Prodicus, is once again a highly contrived literary artefact.[51] Time and again we are confronted with the mixture of oral and written: Lucian's ghost stories underline very well the interplay between superstitious intellectuals talking off the cuff. The issue has tended to generate more heat than light between oral folklorists and students of literature, but we are not likely to be far wrong if we suspect a mixture of oral and written transmission for the majority of tales.

The historical progression of tales

It is difficult to attempt any continuous history of ancient to modern fairy tale, because the gaps in what has survived are so great. If we were to set out even to provide a history of *Cinderella*, for example, we have a huge gap between the first 'modern' telling in Basile's *La Gatta Cenerentola* and the 9th-century Chinese version long wrongly thought to be the earliest known; we could now hope to add a miscellany of classical Greek versions, not all of which quite encompass the whole tale; or assemble the pieces of a group of Sumerian Inanna-texts that are closest to Basile, with their distinctive date-tree dowry/trousseau tree motif. But without any notion of how and when versions of the tale travelled (if indeed they had to wait till historical times to do so) the operation is next to meaningless. We should of course also be aware that in even the modern history of the tale it is by no means clear how much one anthologist could have known of the work of his predecessors, with Basile's collection in particular inaccessible in Neapolitan Dialect until translated into Italian in the 19th century. Yet it is equally clear that for example the Egyptian *Tale of Two Brothers* should have remained in the oral repertoire to re-emerge in the modern tale, and that *The Poor Man of Nippur* can be confirmed as having done the same. The assumption of continuous tradition should be the norm rather than the exception.

The selection and categorising of tales

Given the flexibility of definition we should allow for fairy tales, and the diversity of materials and contexts where they occur, it is worth reflecting on the reasons for adopting the present arrangement of tales, which in the end has had to be an arbitrary choice among many. My overall objective here has been to suggest a sequence that offers variety and readability, and which serves to make the relationship between ancient and modern fairy tales as clear as can be expected.

Cupid and Psyche

I have made *Cupid and Psyche* the starting point, as it offers the single best illustration of what an ancient fairy tale could attain, both in scale and artistry: otherwise few examples outside Homer and Ovid come close to it in the control of detail, and they are in verse. At first glance it might appear that the author has stitched together elements of *Beauty and the Beast* (the supposedly 'animal bridegroom'), *Cinderella* (the wicked jealous siblings) and *Snow White* (the near-deathly sleep dispelled by the bridegroom); but the very similar story of Semele establishes that the skeleton of the tale is earlier than Apuleius (analogues in Hittite tales suggest how much earlier at least); and the story is part of the core repertoire of international tales known both to Basile in the 17th century and the Grimms in the 19th century. Central to the action is the innocent young girl who is actually forced into a marriage, which the rest of the tale is contrived to retrieve (the so-called 'search for the lost husband'). Characteristic components of the fairy tale are already in place: it centres on the unseen bridegroom, with a sight taboo duly attached; the ever-vulnerable heroine persecuted by the bridegroom's mother, embodying the problem of family relationships; and the supposedly lethal tasks which can only be accomplished with assistance from the natural world and the supernatural husband himself. The divine characters behave like fairy tale movers rather than religious forces; and Psyche does little on her own initiative, other than tidy the shrines of Ceres and Juno, who are both powerless to help her; and bizarrely, to contrive the deaths of her treacherous sisters. From the outset, the matter of unquestioning obedience to the gods is in place: there is no escape from the dictates of the oracle which enjoins Psyche's marriage. Most characteristic in the story is the atmosphere of opulence: in particular Cupid's palace with its invisible servitors attains a level of fantasy which the tales of Perrault and the contemporary coteries of French female storytellers will reclaim only a millennium and a half later.

Arts of variation: Cinderellas and Snow Whites

It is useful at an early stage to appreciate how traditional tales change with transmission from one storyteller to the next, and from one geographical area to another; or how much an educated writer creating a literary version may introduce a new twist to a familiar tale. Within the ancient world we have the sense that tales may somehow turn out 'the same but different'. It may come as a jolt that Rhodopis is a slave and a courtesan, if we were simply expecting bullying by jealous stepsisters as the basis for a persecuted heroine. We have to think of the implications of a slave-owning society, and one where tales are not always aimed at a child audience, but are allowed to contain 'adult' material. Again, we think of 'flight from the ball'; but what happens in a society where there are no such events? Aspasia offers further mutations, including forced attendance at a royal drinking-bout, and use of a token test to acknowledge the groom's mother's status rather than identify the bride; Asenath's washing of Joseph's feet has the same effect of establishing marital subservience. Longus' pastoral tale makes free use of a range of Cinderella motifs, including helpful animals and rustic deities: here golden slippers are used to identify the social status rather than the identity of the bride.

Snow White variants can be no less unpredictable. We are so used to the magic mirror on the wall that we do not expect the heroine's jealous rival simply to be named 'Diviner' (Manto), or the chaste helper to be a single herdsman rather than three giants or seven dwarfs: Xenophon of Ephesus' novel has to keep to what is possible in the real world. Nor do we expect an unhappy ending, with Ovid's heroine killed by Artemis and immolated, yet her name Chione itself clearly enough identifies her as the Snow Girl; to say nothing of the exposure of Pygmalion's bride as a marble statue that comes to life (rather than a girl in a glass case), offering a happily-ending second half of the tale.

Otherworldly encounters

Actual practitioners of magic serve naturally as the protagonists of fairy tale, sometimes combined with erotic themes and often featuring barbarian outsiders to the Greek world. Nor was Apuleius alone in cultivating supernatural tales in an educated medium: the eminent sophist Hadrian of Tyre acquired a reputation for actually practising magic because of his tales of magicians, which are unfortunately lost.[52] Tales range from simple detection of an unburied corpse actively haunting a house, to those of return from the dead, taking in corpses who reclaim their lost property on the way, or unnaturally long sleeps. Familiar favourites include *The Sorcerer's Apprentice*, with its supernatural and duplicating servants, and a rather minimalist version of *Rip van Winkle*, this time with the little people missing. The ancient tale of Alcestis, thanks to Euripides' dramatic version, actually remains better known than the modern popular tale.

Siren women

Women living apart or in female-only communities could easily be cast as dangerous outsiders: the operations of Circe are presented at the very outset of classical literature, in what has clearly the credentials of an international tale. The instances of metamorphosis of men into beasts are not confined, however, and St. Augustine's notice of two cases he encountered in Italy emphasises the popular character of the belief, writ large in two novel-length versions in Apuleius' *The Golden Ass* and a Greek epitome of the same story.[53] It is worth noting that for all its detail the Homeric tale of Circe leaves us asking why exactly the witch-figure should wish to transform Odysseus' crew in the first place: the two tales from St. Augustine suggest an answer (transformation into draft animals suggests rather that they should be raised as transport).

Rewards and punishments

This is a broad and miscellaneous group, but is justified by the strong moral dimension which ensures punishment for undetected murder, after often magical means of detection. It also includes the tale of Hippomenes and Atalanta, bizarrely punished for sacrilege and prevented from a normal sexual fulfilment. The two tales of Erysichthon offer good illustrations of a vengeful fairy readily equivalent to the classical nymph. The category also contains tales in which an initial reward is cancelled out by the greed of an unthinking recipient, perhaps *the* fairy tale which best represents one of the core features of the genre: the world of make-believe and 'if only' can be realised, and then brought down to earth again, by ordinary human failings.

Tricksters

There is an argument for placing tricksters in the realm of folktale rather than the narrower field of fairy tale, but the one-eyed giant ogre situates the Polyphemus-story firmly in the latter camp as well, and the king who offers the clever thief his daughter's hand in marriage would also place Herodotus' tale of Rhampsinitus in the same area. Homer's tale of Odysseus and Polyphemus can be seen as a lavish version of the story in terms of its detail, and we note also that there is actually no magic or supernatural aid at all in the outwitting of the giant, but only the protagonist's own skill. The tale as Odysseus tells it is probably incomplete, however, as there is only a trace of the magic self-announcing ring motif which figures in the medieval Oghuz Turkish version[54] and elsewhere. It should be emphasised that trickery is seldom absent for too long from most examples of fairy tale or its mythical counterpart: even the innocent Psyche practises murderous deception without turning a hair. Unfortunately we have no surviving detailed version of the trickster-cycle surrounding Sisyphus and Autolycus, the former of whom actually tricks Death himself into being locked up.

Traditional heroes, magic objects

In fairy tales of this broad category we can expect a number of standard features: that the hero begins at some social disadvantage and is subject to threat or persecution; and that magical or supernatural intervention is necessary to enable him to survive death threats and achieve marriage or some similar social success. Both Bellerophon and Perseus underline the fact that little actual heroism is required, rather than astute precautions, as in such matters as cutting out wild beasts' tongues to prevent false claims by rivals. The tales of Melampus and the frenzied women and Hippomenes and Atalanta feature heroic pursuits, in the latter case with golden apples supplied by Aphrodite. The treatments of the Argonauts in Apollonius Rhodius' *Argonautica* afford little prominence to the special skills of the crew: where these are limited to some half-dozen in the popular versions there is room for all of them to show off their magic endowments of extraordinary sight, hearing or the like. Also, the scattering of the limbs of Medea's brother Apsyrtus is a far cry from the magic comb giving rise to a forest that we find in the oral fairy tale tradition. Euthymus' rescue of a girl from a wolf-spirit offers an ancient form of the longer version of *Red Riding Hood*, where the wolf is defeated and drowned. Gyges' magic ring is the nearest we seem to find for Aladdin's Lamp, perhaps unsurprisingly against a West Asian background.

Animal tales

Aesopic fables can seldom be subsumed within fairy tale: one accepts the initial premise of talking animals, but otherwise the majority of stories proceed as simple parables of social hierarchy or survival. The tale of Demicoq ('Half-Chick') on the other hand presents an animal with a capacious all-absorbing backside in popular versions, and in Lucian's polite literary presentation an animal able to subsume multiple identities by transmigration. By contrast the story of Alope seems to offer a compressed and elliptical working of *Puss in Boots*, with the frequent alternative protagonist the fox. The effect is the same, but the ogre is here actually the fox's father, as the pauper who inherits a kingdom is her son. This removes the criticism levelled at the modern tale that the hero prospers unjustly through the cat's dishonest trickery. In this ancient version the heroine is in fact the rightful heir to the ogre's territory.

Little people

It seems natural enough that stories aimed at or at least told to children should include the doings of tiny folk, and a number of categories could be distinguished in classical antiquity: these include the *Pēcheis* ('Cubits') that are said to be children of the Nile, *Erōtes* as depicted in classical art, *Daktyloi* ('Tom Thumbs'), or persons with names like Pygmalion ('little fist') or the like. In some cases only the name seems to indicate stature, while the bearer seems otherwise to be of normal size; but *Erōtes* in particular must be of a size to ride plausibly on swans or dolphins.

Indispensable to the ancient nursery is a whole collection of bogeywomen used to scare children into good behaviour (Akko, Alphito, Empousa, Gello, Lamia, Mormo); their general association is with the loss, or indeed the eating, of children; unfortunately we lack substantial ancient narratives about them, no doubt because their nursery connections rendered them trivial in the eyes of the highly educated.

Miscellaneous tales

Two tales deal with language: a cautionary tale is concerned with interpreting symbols in accordance with wishful thinking; and understanding animal speech is presented as a reward for pious action. The inversion of status offers the essence of *The Emperor's New Clothes*. Once more we need to adjust our vision to recognise Pyrrhus' court flatterers not as praising the royal clothes, but the king's likeness to Alexander the Great. Two anecdotes deal with extraordinary perception, of a woman's touch and a feather. Deceptive appearances figure in an unusual presentation of a familiar favourite; we have the repugnant brine-encrusted figure of Odysseus talking matrimony to a princess before Athene transforms his own appearance to a handsome stranger – complete with lost ball and location at the world's end; we are at least in the broad territory of the familiar frog prince. The last exhibits are two tantalising tales sharing in common the problem that they appear to be connected with the celebration of mysteries, which makes it very difficult to collect much testimony about ancient versions, though in both instances we can build up a case from circumstantial evidence. There are two nuggets of tradition about gold-related mysteries which seem to set the scene for the story of Rumpelstiltskin without actually telling it; an analogous story presented in dramatic form in Lucian's *Fugitivi* does give the significant name Cantharus (Scarab-beetle) for the mysterious and cantankerous helper and kidnapper of women, but its dramatic form obscures the outlines somewhat. Central to an ancient Bluebeard version is the person of the Athenian Princess Procris, who in fact survives *two* Bluebeard figures in the first instance, while Eumolpus, a son of Poseidon who demands the sacrifice of sisters and institutes mysteries celebrating a girl kidnapped underground, seems to continue the connexion with Eleusis. *The Sleeping Beauty* is among the most difficult tales to reconstruct from ancient remains: but the Basile tale of Sun, Moon and Talia seems to confirm its identity.

Scope of the present anthology

In the following collection I have translated some 70-odd different traditional tales, the great majority of which can reasonably be presented as fairy tales of the kind Perrault and the Grimms have produced, even if their *ATU* credentials lie outside those they describe as 'magic tales'. I have not included more than a couple of Aesopic animal fables, which constitute a separate genre; historical legends appear only if they offer a clearly fairy tale content; myths similarly only if the gods in them seem to behave in such roles as magic helpers or bad fairies. A number of ordinary folktales have also been included. The primary motive is to alert students and scholars, classicists or folklorists and the general reader to what is out there, and for that heritage to be enjoyed as well as studied.

There have had to be some economies of scale. I have not succumbed to the temptation of including most or all of *The Golden Ass*, which is already well served with translations; I have aimed in the notes to draw attention only incidentally to traditional commentary-type details which any reader has to know, and refer to standard commentaries where available. The proliferation of accessible commentary in recent years has made this task easier than it might have been, and most readers will not need to go too far back beyond Hansen's magnificent *Ariadne's Thread* of 2002.

Just as within modern collections of variants of individual tales there are some exhibits more instantly recognisable than others, so in the case of ancient examples. Among those readily identifiable I should place most *Cinderellas* and *Snow Whites*, *The Dancing Princesses*, *The Stupid Ogre*, *The Sorcerer's Apprentice* and a good many others. Odysseus as *The Frog Prince* requires rather more adjustment of focus, as may *The Pied Piper*, while *Rumpelstiltskin*, *Bluebeard* and *Puss in Boots* present more debatable cases. But where a reader cannot accept the classification suggested, we can still be left with examples which are clearly fairy tales; their difficult relationship with modern tales as we know them may serve to remind us of how many alternative versions and 'missing links' may have been lost.

Notes

1 For the concept of 'ownership' of fairy Tales, Haase in Tatar (1999), 353–364.
2 Cf. Swann Jones (1995), 8.
3 He has a walk-on part in Madame D'Aulnoy's *Finette Cendron,* where he meets the fate of the witch in Hansel and Gretel (Zipes, 1989, 409f.).
4 E.g. Zipes (2000), xv.
5 Ibid., 167f.

6 Proppian functions (Propp, 1968, 25–65) are of limited value because of their vagueness and excessive elasticity.
7 *On Fairy-Stories* (1947), 32 in the Flieger-Anderson pagination (2008).
8 Short list of 'magic tales' in Hansen (2002), 13f.; cf. Gerndt s.v. *Zaubermärchen, EM* 14, 1182–1188 (on varied approaches to Structure and Function, 1184–1185). Gerndt emphasises the importance of *Zaubermärchen* in relation to other types, but there is no call for over-rigid hierarchies.
9 See below at n. 19.
10 Cf. Marina Warner (1994), xivf, taking her starting-point from Perrault.
11 Such titles as *The Classic Fairy Tales* (Opie and Opie, Tatar) or the several 'Companions to the fairy tale' (Zipes, Ellis-Davidson and Chaudhri, Tatar) use the label without risk of ambiguity. Cf. also Gerndt above n. 8.
12 Cf. Zipes (2008), 'What makes a repulsive frog so appealing?', 109–143.
13 I.e. with reference to the story of Actaeon (Ovid *Met*. 3. 193–199).
14 For fairy tale it may be important to bear in mind the derivation of French *fées* from Latin *fata*: we should note how often fairies or fates do attend the birth or the wedding of an individual, and what fate or fortune will rest upon it, as in the tale of Meleager, Ovid *Met*. 8. 451–455.
15 See especially Zipes (2012), 32–37.
16 Conveniently collected by Zipes (1989).
17 Cf. Von Hendy (2002), 62ff, I am grateful to an anonymous referee for this reference.
18 So Bottigheimer in Zipes (2000), 204.
19 On the method, Krohn (1926); Stith Thompson (1946), 430–446. The rationale itself is sound, but the difficulty lies in the relative lack of early examples for analysis.
20 I have generally included *EM* references to individual tales. These are on the whole invaluable for tracing the earliest Late Medieval or early modern appearances of specific tales; and for disentangling bifurcating versions over time. They do justice to ancient tales where an ancient example happens to be the best-known version, as in the case of Polyphemus or Alcestis; but otherwise they do not always deal adequately with the earliest classical examples. Kawan's treatment of *Schneewitchen* too readily dismisses the extant fragments of a *Chione* romance from the classical period (Anderson 2000, 50f.), while Wehse's discussion of Cinderella does not pick up the full implications of Herodotus' treatment of Rhodopis.
21 Bottigheimer (2002, 2009). For overview of the issue, Ben-Amos in *JAF* 123 (2010), 426–446 ('The Revolution That Was Not'); Jorgensen's review of Bottigheimer (2009), *JAF* 125 (2012), 508–510 (bibliography 509); Zipes, (2012), 157–173. On 'Magic Tales and Fairy Tale Magic', Bottigheimer (2014), with Jorgensen's review in *Journal of Folklore Research*, October 24th 2017.
22 Translation in Dundes (1982), 75–77.
23 Edition and Commentary by E.J. Kenney (1990).
24 As an oriental myth (Reitzenstein) or a religio-philosophical allegory (Walsh).
25 Anderson (2000, 2003); Hansen (2002).
26 Further support from Ziolkowski (2007), drawing on Medieval Latin predecessors of Grimms' tales.
27 So W. de Blécourt (2012); see the review by Zipes (2012), 175–189.
28 For Fable, Holzberg (2002).
29 Homer, *Odyssey* 9.1–10.396.
30 *Odyssey* 8.72–82; 266–366.
31 Petronius *Satyrica* 77.6; 38.8.
32 Lucian's *Philopseudeis*, on which see now Ogden (2007). I accept Macleod's emendation that the title is plural ('Lovers of Lies').
33 For the term *anilis fabula*, Apuleius *Met*. 4.27.
34 Anderson (2000), 46–57.
35 For the latter, see now the annotations of Celoria (1992).

36 Useful references in Anderson (2000), 2–9.
37 Philostratus: Fairbanks (1931); Kalinka-Schönberger (1968). The author of the *Imagines* may or may not be identical to that of the *Lives of the Sophists* and the *Life of Apollonius*.
38 Aristophanes' *Wasps* 1174ff.
39 Cf. Bruno Bettelheim (1976). I am grateful to A.M. Gray for discussion of this much over-quoted book.
40 I.e. the variants at Aarne-Thompson-Uther 510B.
41 At Pausanias 6.6.7–11.
42 Lucian *Adversus Indoctum (The Ignorant Book Collector)* 21; Count Lucanor, Tale 31.
43 Zipes (1993), 43–60.
44 E.g. Chione, Ovid *Met.* 11.318–323.
45 *Odyssey* 9.275–279; 369f.
46 E.g. *The Twelve Dancing Princesses*, Opie and Opie (1980), 250f.
47 *Aeneid* 6.124–155.
48 Ubainer: Parkinson (1997), 106–109.
49 Anderson (2000), 39–41.
50 Anderson (2000), 184.
51 Dio *Or.* 1.52–84.
52 Philostratus *VS* 590.
53 See Scobie (1983).
54 For a possible trace of this elsewhere in Antiquity, cf. Petronius, *Satyrica* 48.7, with M.S. Smith's note ad loc.

2
THE CLASSIC FAIRY TALE
Cupid and Psyche[1]

Apuleius, *Metamorphoses*, 4.28–6.24[2]

Cupid and Psyche has a fair claim to vindicate the case for the existence of Fairy Tale in Antiquity. Its scale is like that of some 18th-century French tales, with their preoccupation with expensive dresses, manners and furnishings, and a generally elite society. Its author is highly educated, just as was Charles Perrault in the late 17th century, and no-one reading the tale unaware of its context is likely to imagine that its supposed reporter Lucius happened to be in the form of an ass when himself listening to the account told as an Old Wives' Tale! Two similar tales of the salvation of Semele after her similarly rash curiosity underline the perils of sleeping with a god and boasting about it.

Cupid and Psyche

(4.28.1) In a certain city there were a king and queen.[3] They had three beautiful daughters: the elder two were very pleasing to look at,[4] but people thought that human praise was enough to do them justice; however the youngest was so conspicuously and so superlatively beautiful that human speech did not suffice to describe her beauty or indeed to praise it enough. And so many citizens and a stream of visitors were brought together in an eager throng by the report of this amazing sight. They were dumbfounded by admiration of her unrivalled beauty, and raising their right thumb and forefinger to their lips they would worship her outright as though she were the goddess Venus herself. And already the nearby cities and neighbouring regions had heard that the goddess born of the deep blue sea and raised by the dew of its foaming waves was mingling amid the throng of mankind and distributing her favour far and wide, or at least that through the seeding of heavenly dews it was not the sea but the land that had produced a young Venus of her own in the full bloom of her virginity. Hence the unbounded belief grew day by day, as her fame extended already to the neighbouring islands and a great part of the mainland and most of the provinces. Already many people made long journeys and crossed the ocean, flocking together to see the glory of the age. No-one sailed to Paphos, no-one sailed to Cnidos or even to Cythera[5] for a sight of the goddess Venus. People abandoned her rites, profaned her temples, cast her couches to the ground and gave up her ceremonies; no garlands adorned her statues, and her empty altars were disfigured with ashes gone cold. People prayed instead to the girl, and sought to placate the power of this mighty goddess in human form; the name of Venus, no longer present, was propitiated at the girl's morning walk with sacrifices and banquets: and already as she roamed the streets the crowds prayed to her with garlands and single flowers.

(4.29.5) The real Venus was furious at this outrageous shift of divine honours to the cult of a human girl[6]; she could not contain her indignation, but tossed her head and went into a foul rage as she rehearsed to herself:

> Just look at the ancient mother of the natural world, the first origin of the elements: here is Venus, the nourisher of the whole earth[7]: I am treated with only a share of my majesty, shared with a mortal girl, and my name, set in heaven, is being profaned with earthly filth! No doubt I shall sustain the uncertainty of sharing my worship with a deputy, and a mortal girl will carry round the likeness that belongs to me. In vain did that shepherd whose fairness and integrity Jupiter approved prefer me to these great goddesses for my outstanding beauty.[8] But this woman, whoever she is, will not enjoy like this these honours of mine she has usurped: now I shall ensure that she will be sorry for this very beauty without a licence.

(4.30.4) And at once she called her winged son, that notorious and reckless boy who flouts public decency with his wicked ways,[9] and armed with flame and arrows runs amok through other people's houses, destroying everyone's marriages, and gets off with it, and commits such dreadful crimes and does no good whatsoever. This lad already impertinent – it was in his own character to take liberties – she goaded still further by her words and brought him to the city, and pointed Psyche out to him – for that was the girl's name[10]; she laid before him the whole tale of her beautiful rival, moaning and seething with indignation, and said:

> I entreat you by the bonds of your mother's love, by the sweet wounds of your arrow, by the honey-sweet burning of your dreaded torch, exact full vengeance for your mother's sake. And severely punish her insolent beauty, and do this one thing willingly in return for everything: let this detestable

girl be possessed with the most ardent passion for the basest of men, someone condemned by fortune for his low rank, his poverty, his insecurity – someone so low that she cannot find anyone more miserable.

(4.31.4) With this she plied her son with long, close kisses with open mouth, and returned to the nearest shores of the sea. As she placed her rosy feet on the tips of the heaving waves, already on the damp surf there was an amazing calm; and – the very thing she had begun to want – there immediately appeared her watery retinue, as if she had previously given instruction. The daughters of Nereus were there, singing their chorus, and Portunus, with his thick sea-coloured beard, Salacia, weighed down with her lap of fish, and tiny Palaemon, an outrider on his dolphin; and already far and wide hordes of Tritons leaping on the sea.[11] One gently blew his resounding horn, another with an awning of silk shielded her from the heat of her enemy the sun, a third offered a mirror beneath the eyes of her mistress, while others paired together, swimming beneath her chariot. Such was the train that went with Venus as she made for the ocean.[12]

(4.32.1) In the meantime, Psyche, although she realised she was so beautiful, took no benefit from it. Everyone gazed at her, everyone sang her praises, and yet no-one, no king, no prince, no common man even approached to seek her hand in marriage. They admired her divine appearance, to be sure, but all admired her like a statue brought to perfection by a sculptor. Some while back her elder sisters, whose moderate beauty none had celebrated like her own, had been betrothed to royal suitors and had already won prosperous marriages,[13] but Psyche remained at home, an unmarried virgin: she wept over her lonely and abandoned state, her body going to waste, her mind hurt; and she hated the beauty that had enthralled the world. And so her unhappy father feared that divine jealousy was at work against his afflicted daughter, and in fear of the wrath of the gods he consulted the most ancient oracle of Milesian Apollo, and with prayers and sacrifices sought marriage and husband for his unfortunate daughter from that great deity.[14] And Apollo, Greek and Ionian as he was, obliged the writer of our Milesian[15] tale with a response in Latin.

> Place the girl, O king, on the peak of the lofty mountain
> Arrayed in the garb of her funeral bridechamber;
> Nor expect a son-in-law of mortal race
> But a fierce and savage beast, an evil viper
> which flits on wings over all the air and wearies all things,
> weakening them with its fiery flame[16];
> Jupiter himself trembles at him, he terrifies the gods,
> The rivers draw back in fear, and the darkness of the Styx.

The king, happy once upon a time, accepted the utterance of the holy prophecy, and listless and sad returned home and unravelled the instructions of the unlucky oracle to his wife. There was mourning, weeping and lamentation for days on end. But already the foul execution of her dire fate pressed upon them; already the accoutrements for the fierce rites of the unhappy bride were laid out; already the light of the torch grew dim with black smoke and ash, and the sound of the wedding flute changed to the mournful Lydian mode; the joyful wedding song concluded with mournful wails, and the bride-to-be wiped her tears with her very bridal outfit. Thus the whole city too joined in the sad fate of the stricken household, and immediately public business was suspended to accord with the city's grief.

(4.34.1) But it was necessary to obey the divine instructions, and they demanded that poor little Psyche should submit to her preordained punishment. And so the rites of her savage bedchamber were carried out in the greatest sorrow, and the bride was led forth escorted by the whole nation[17] as a living corpse; the tearful Psyche was accompanied not to her wedding but to her funeral rites.[18] And while her distraught parents, reeling from such a terrible disaster, delayed the execution of their dreadful crime, their daughter herself encouraged them[19] with these words:

> Why do you torment your unhappy old age with continual weeping? Why do you weary your spirit, or rather mine, with all your laments? Why do you spoil the faces I should worship with pointless tears? Why do you tear my eyes by tearing yours? Why do you tear apart your white hair? Why do you beat the breasts that I hold sacred? These are the chief rewards for you of my outstanding beauty. Now do you realise too late that you are struck by the deadly blow of wicked jealousy? When nations and peoples were celebrating us with divine honours, they named me the new Venus with one accord; then you ought to have mourned and wept. Then already you should have wept for me as if I were lost. Now I realise, now I see that I have been lost for the name of Venus alone. Take me and put me on the rock my destiny has determined. Not soon enough[20] can I go through this all too happy marriage of mine; not soon enough can I see my noble bridegroom. Why do I postpone it; why do I shrink from his arrival, when he is destined to destroy the whole world?

(4.35.1) With this the girl said no more, and now firmly stepped in time with the accompanying procession. They made their way to the preordained rock on the high mountain, and all left the girl in place on the highest peak. There they left the bridal torches that had lit their way, now extinguished by their tears, and made their way home with heads downcast. And her wretched parents, defeated by their daughter's dreadful misfortune, shut up their palace and secluded themselves in the darkness, and gave themselves up to everlasting night.[21] But as for Psyche, fearful and trembling as she was and weeping on the summit of her rock, the gentle breeze of Zephyr's soothing breath blew the borders of her dress back and forth, breathed into its folds and gently lifted her up[22]; he carried her with his quiet breath gradually down and down the slope of the high rock and quietly sat her down after her fall on the flower-studded meadow in the bosom of the valley below.

(5.1.1) Psyche lay sweetly relaxed in the tender grass on her couch of dewy turf. And with all her anxiety at rest, she fell into a sweet sleep. And now that she had had her fill of refreshing rest she rose in a calm frame of mind. She saw a grove planted with mighty tall soaring tress; she saw a spring of water clear as glass. In the middle of the grove beside where the spring tumbled down, there was a royal palace,[23] built not by human hands, but by divine arts. Already you could see from the first entrance that you were looking at the resplendent and beautiful pleasure pavilion of some god. For columns of gold supported a coffered ceiling above, carefully hollowed out in citron-wood and ivory; all the walls were covered with silver chasing, as wild beasts and other animals met the visitor's gaze. Indeed it was an amazing man or rather a demigod or even a god who had brought the wildness out of so much silver with the subtlety of his great art. Moreover even the floors were divided into various sorts of pictures in mosaics cut from precious stones: twice blessed and more those who trample on precious stones and jewellery! And now the rest of the priceless house extended far and wide: and all the walls, built of solid gold, flashed with a brilliance of their own, so that the house offered its own daylight even without the sun – so brilliant was the glitter of the rooms, the colonnades, and even the doors. Nor did the other furnishings fail to measure up to the magnificence of the house, so that it seemed right to say that mighty Jupiter had fashioned a heavenly palace to mingle with mortals.

(5.2.1) Enticed by the delight of such quarters Psyche came closer, and when she grew more confident she crossed the threshold, then in her delight at so beautiful a spectacle, she looked carefully at every detail; on the other side of the mansion she saw lofty storehouses perfectly constructed and brimful of great treasure. Nor was there anything that was not there. But apart from her amazement at so great a store of riches, what was most amazing was that this treasure of the whole world was not protected by any chain, bar or guardian. And so she viewed this with so much delight. There was a disembodied voice[24]:

> Mistress, why are you amazed at such a great store of wealth? All this is yours. And so go to your own room and relieve your weariness on your very own bed, and take a bath whenever you like. We whose voice you hear are your servants: we will wait diligently upon you; and once you are refreshed you will enjoy a royal banquet without delay.

(5.3.1) Psyche realised that she was blessed with divine providence; she listened to the advice of the disembodied voice, and first in sleep then by a bath she put an end to her weariness. At once there appeared beside her a semi-circular seat; she supposed from the dining layout that this was for her refreshment. She gladly reclined at table. And at once there were course upon course of various foods and nectar-like wine, supplied by no servant, but blown to her only by some mysterious breath. And yet she could see no-one, but only heard the words being uttered, and had only voices for her table servant. After a sumptuous banquet someone came in and sang invisibly and another played the lyre, which was likewise invisible. Then she heard the voices in harmony of a great many singers, so that there was an invisible choir in evidence.

(5.4.1) When these pleasures were at an end, the evening persuaded Psyche to lie down. And already night was well on when a gentle sound reached her ears. Then, as she was all alone, she feared for her virginity, and in fear and trembling she was afraid of the unknown more than whatever ill might befall. And already her unknown husband was there, came to her bed, and made Psyche his wife, and promptly departed before dawn.[25] And at once the voices in attendance in the bedchamber looked after the new bride <and consoled her for> the loss of her virginity. And this was how things were for some time. And as nature had duly arranged, the new experience she grew accustomed to, so that it became a source of delight; and the sound of the unknown voice consoled her in her solitude.

Meanwhile her parents aged with their unrelenting grief and misery; and as the tale spread further afield, her elder sisters came to know the whole story, and at once they too were consumed with grief: they left home and rivalled each other's efforts to see and speak to their parents. (5.5.1) That night her husband spoke to his darling Psyche (for with her hands and ears she felt his presence totally, only not with her eyes):

> Sweetest Psyche, dear wife, Fortune in still crueller form is threatening you with dreadful danger: I solemnly enjoin you to guard against her with ever-increasing caution. Already your sisters, disturbed by the belief that you are dead, are following your footsteps, and will soon reach the mountain-top: should you hear their mourning, you are not to answer or even so much as look; otherwise you will give me the greatest suffering, and bring total destruction on yourself.[26]

She assented and promised to follow her husband's judgement; but as soon as that night was over, the poor girl spent the whole day in tears and laments, repeating that even now she was totally destroyed: she was shut up in this bountiful prison and deprived of human company and conversation, and even when her own sisters were mourning on her own behalf, she could not come to the rescue or even see them at all. She refused to bathe or eat or refresh herself in any other way, but sank into sleep in floods of tears.

(5.6.1) Without delay, a little earlier than usual her husband came to her bed and finding her still weeping, embraced her and pleaded:

> Is this what you promised, my very own Psyche? What am I, your own husband, to expect from you, what hopes do I have? All day and all night long you do not stop tormenting yourself, even in the arms of your

husband. Then act now as you please, and obey the ruinous dictates of your heart. Only remember my grave warning, when you begin too late to regret it.

Then Psyche begged her husband, and threatened suicide to force him to agree to what she wanted: she was to see her sisters, soothe their grief and talk to them. So he indulged the wish of the new bride, and besides let her give them all the gold or jewels she wanted. But time and again he warned her and repeatedly not to heed the ruinous advice of her sisters to enquire about her husband's appearance, nor with sacrilegious curiosity to cast herself down from such dizzy heights of fortune so that she should be robbed of his embrace ever after. She thanked her husband, and now with her mind more at ease, she said:

> May I die a hundred times rather than be deprived of you, my sweetest of husbands! For I love you and whoever you are I am besotted with you as I love my own life; even Cupid himself I could not compare with you.[27] But this also I beg you to grant: instruct your servant Zephyrus to bring my sisters here as he brought me.

And pressing him with seductive kisses and plying him with soothing words, and enclosing her compelling limbs <round him> she added still more endearments: 'my honey, my husband, the very soul of your dear Psyche!'. Unwillingly her husband gave in to the powerful force of her whispered words of love, and said he would do everything she asked; and as dawn was already drawing nigh he disappeared from his wife's embrace.

(5.7.1) But the sisters kept asking the site of the rock where Psyche had been abandoned, and were quick to arrive; there they kept up their wailing and their beating of breasts, so that the rocks and crags resounded with the echo. And now they called on their hapless sister by her own name, until Psyche, out of her mind at the penetrating sound of their lament, rushed out of the palace: 'Why', she said,

> are you distressing yourselves needlessly with unhappy laments? Here I am, the very victim you are grieving over! Lay aside your doleful cries and at last dry your cheeks, wet with continual weeping, since at last you can embrace <the sister> you were mourning.

Then she called for Zephyrus and told him her husband's order. Without delay he obeyed the command and at once conveyed them safely with the gentlest of breaths. And now they took their fill of mutual embraces and rushed to kiss one another, and the tears they had held back now returned out of sheer joy. 'You are welcome to enter my hearth and home and refresh your tortured souls in your sister Psyche's company'. With this she revealed to their eyes and ears the bountiful riches of the golden palace, and the huge staff of servants' voices.

She refreshed them bountifully with the most beautiful bath and the elegance of her supernatural table, so that they took their fill of the copious riches of their divine affluence; they already nourished envy deep in their hearts. At length one of them would not stop asking all too keenly and inquisitively who was the master of all this heavenly wealth, or who or what was Psyche's husband. But Psyche did not rashly disobey her husband's command in any respect, or drive them from her inner heart, but made up that he was a handsome youth,[28] his cheeks growing with a downy beard; he himself was immersed for the most part in hunting in the countryside and on the mountains. And to make sure she would not betray her silent thoughts by some slip of the tongue, she immediately gave them over to Zephyrus to carry back, after loading them with golden products and jewelled gems.

(5.9.1) When she had done this deed, these wonderful sisters[29] at once set off home, already burning with the poison of their mounting envy, and created a commotion as they went on and on to each other; in fact the one began:

> To think how blind and savage and unfair Fortune is! Does she really approve that we sisters of the same parents should suffer such different fates? We who are the elder, yielded up as maidservants to foreign husbands, refugees from our home and our own country to live far from our parents as exiles; but she, the youngest,[30] born last from parents long past their prime, should come into possession of such enormous wealth and a god for a husband, she who does not even know how to make use of such a store of good things. You, sister, saw all the precious necklaces, the shimmering garments, the sparkling gems, and most of all, all the gold trodden everywhere underfoot. But if her husband too is as handsome as she claims, there is no girl now happier in the whole world. But perhaps as they come to know each other and their affection grows stronger, her divine husband will make her a deity as well.[31] That is how things are, I swear it: that is how she was behaving and comporting herself. Even as we speak she looks upward, and already has the air of a goddess, this girl who has voices as her servants and gives the winds their orders. But as for me, my wretched lot is a husband older than my father,[32] balder than a pumpkin, and weaker than any mere boy, who stands guard and keeps the whole house locked up with bolts and chains.

(5.10.1) The other sister took over:

> As for me, I have to suffer a husband folded over and bent with disease in the joints, and so very rarely able to fulfil my needs. And I spend most of my time massaging his twisted fingers hardened into stone, burning my delicate hands with stinking poultices and horrid plasters: I do not play the part of a dutiful wife, but instead perform the drudgery of a nurse. And you, sister, for your part should consider how patiently, or rather slavishly – for

> I shall speak my mind frankly – you can bear this, for I at any rate am unable to suffer any longer such blessed fortune fallen to the undeserving. For do you remember how proudly, how arrogantly she dealt with us and betrayed her boastful spirit with the sheer display of boundless ostentation? And from what huge wealth she reluctantly threw us a tiny amount, and bored with our company lost no time in ordering us to be driven, blown, and whistled off? As I am a woman, and indeed as I live, I swear to bring her down to ruin from all her riches. And if as is proper, you too have been stung by her contempt for us, let us both look for a courageous plan. And now let us not show these contemptible gifts to our parents or anyone else, or rather let us not even claim to know anything about her survival. It is enough that we ourselves have witnessed what we wish we had not, without broadcasting her great good fortune to our parents and all the nations of the world. For people are not rich if no-one knows it. She will find out that we are her sisters, not her servants. And now let us go back to our husbands and return to our homes, poor as they are but decent, and at last let us arm ourselves by thinking more urgently and more determined to come back and punish her arrogance.

(5.11.1) This wicked plan the bad women thought a good one: they hid all their precious gifts, dragged out their hair and tore their cheeks, just as they deserved, to resume their pretended mourning. And so they rekindled their parents' grief all over again, and dashed their hopes, took off to their homes swollen with raging jealousy, as they planned a wicked ploy, or rather a murderous one against their innocent sister. Meanwhile Psyche's unknown husband once more warned her in his familiar night's conversation[33]:

> Don't you see how great the danger that is threatening you? Fortune is engaging you at long range, and unless you take very strong-willed precautions, soon combat will be fought at close quarters. Treacherous little she-wolves are trying hard to lay traps for you, especially to persuade you to discover my face, which, as I have often warned you, once you have seen it you will never see it again.[34] And so if these dreadful hags come with vicious intent, as I know they will, you must not even speak to them, and if you cannot bear that because of your genuine naivety and tenderness of heart, at least you are not to hear anything about your husband, nor give them any answers. For soon we shall have an addition to our family[35], and this womb, till now a child's, is carrying for us a child in turn[36]: if you conceal our secrets in silence it will be divine, but if you declare it, it will be mortal.

(5.12.1) At the news Psyche bloomed with happiness and applauded at the consolation of divine offspring; she rejoiced at the glory of their future child and exulted in the dignity of a mother's name. As the days increased and the months passed by she anxiously kept count, and as she taught herself to bear her unfamiliar burden she was amazed that from a quick little prick there should be such a great yet delicate increase (*tantum incrementulum*) in her fertile womb.

But already those pests, those foulest of Furies, breathed vipers' poison and were at sea, hastening with unseemly haste. Then once more the fleeting husband gave Psyche this warning[37]:

> Now you are looking at the final day, the last chance. Already your own sex is against you, your own flesh and blood are the enemy. Already they have taken up arms and shifted camp and drawn up their battle-line and sounded the trumpet; already with their swords drawn your own wicked sisters are after your throat. What a disaster is forcing itself on us, my sweetest Psyche! Have pity on yourself, on both of us; with careful restraint free your home, your husband, yourself and that tiny one of ours from the misfortune of innocent ruin. Nor should you see or listen to those wicked women, whom you should not call by the name of sister after their internecine hatred and their tramping on the ties of blood, when like sirens perching on their crag they fill the rocks with their voices of doom.

(5.13.1) Psyche made her reply as she fought against her sobs and tears:

> For a long time, I think, you have weighed the proofs that I have been loyal and said little, nor any the less now shall my stiff resolve win your approval. Once more only order our servant Zephyrus to perform his duty, and in place of the holy sight of you that is denied to me at least let me have a sight of my sisters. I swear by your perfumed locks that hang all over, by those tender, smooth cheeks so like my own, by your breast warmed by heat unseen, so may I at least recognise your face in this little son; I pray you to answer the prayers of an anxious suppliant and allow me to enjoy my sisters' embraces, and refresh with joy the heart of your devoted Psyche. Nor do I ask for anything more (of the sight of) your face; at this time not even the darkness of night can blind me; I hold you, and that is my light.

Her husband was enchanted by her words and her tender embrace; he wiped away her tears with his own hair, promised he would do it, and quickly forestalled the light of the coming day.

(5.14.1) The pair of sisters and fellow-conspirators without so much as visiting their parents went straight from their ships and made for their accustomed rock with headlong speed, and without waiting for the wind to carry them threw themselves with presumptuous rashness down the cliff. And Zephyrus, unwilling as he was, did not forget the royal command, but took them in the bosom of his fresh breeze and restored them to the ground.[38] But without delay they at once rushed through the palace and embraced their quarry, pretending to the name sister but hiding the richness of their treachery under a face of gladness, as they flattered her:

> Psyche, no longer the tiny little one you were before, already you too are a mother; how much goodness you are bringing us in your tiny little pocket! What joy you will bring to gladden our whole house! How glad we will be to raise this wonderful child! If, as must be the case, he matches the beauty of his parents, he will be born an absolute Cupid!

(5.15.1) Thus with pretended affection they gradually insinuated themselves into their sister's heart. And at once she sat them down to refresh them after their weary journey, looked after them with a warm heart and delighted them with the refinements of the dining hall, with that amazingly rich food and those delicacies. She ordered the lyre to play, and it did so; for the flutes to sound, and they sounded; for the choir to sing, and it sang. And all of these soothed their audience's hearts with their sweetest strains, with no-one in sight. The mischief of these wicked women was not softened or put to rest by the honeyed sweetness of the music; but bringing their conversation towards the intended trap of their wiles, they sought to know under a pretext what sort of man her husband was, who his parents were and what his calling. Then Psyche, too naive and forgetful of what she had said before, made up a new tale, that he was a wealthy merchant in middle age, with a sprinkling of white hair. But she paused only a little time to describe him, before returning them to their aerial carriage loaded with opulent gifts.

(5.16.1) But as they made their way home, airborne on the gentle breath of Zephyrus, they went at each other:

> What, sister, do we say about that silly girl's amazing lies? First he was a young man only just growing a beard, with the down in bloom: now he is middle-aged with shining white hair. Who is this man transformed in a short interval into sudden old age? You will certainly find, sister, that either that dreadful woman is making up a lie, or that she is unaware of her husband's appearance. And whichever is the truth, she must be ruined as soon as possible through her wealth. But if she is unaware of her husband's face, she must have married a god and is bearing us a god with her pregnancy. But if she will be hailed as the mother of a divine child – may it not be so – I shall hang myself right away from a hangman's noose. And so meanwhile let us return home to our parents, and weave a yarn of the same deceitful colour as the beginning of our conversation.

(5.17.1) This inflamed them: they greeted their parents with cool propriety, and squandered the night in sleepless torment. In the morning they flew off and touched down in agitation, protected as usual by the wind; they forced themselves to weep by rubbing their eyelids, and called the girl in their wily way:

You for your part sit happy and blissful in your ignorance of such enormous mischief, unaware of our danger; but we are ever wakeful on your behalf, unceasingly alert, and dreadfully alarmed by your misfortune. For we are aware, and cannot conceal from you as partners in your grief and ill-fortune, that a huge snake, crawling in many coils, with its neck bloody with deadly poison, and gaping with deep maw, is secretly sleeping with you. Now remember the Pythian oracle, which proclaimed you were destined to wed a wild beast. And many farmers and hunters around the region and all the dwellers nearby have seen him returning from feeding and bathing in the shallows of the nearby river. And they all say that he will not be long, gently fattening you, but once your full womb has brought your pregnancy to fruition, he will devour you, now that you are richer in fruitfulness.[39] In response to this you must now decide whether you prefer to agree with your sisters anxious for your very life, and by avoiding death live secure from danger with us, or be buried in the entrails of the most savage beast. But if the loneliness of this singing region or the fetid intercourse of a secret love and the poisonous embraces of a serpent are what delight you, at least we your dutiful sisters will have done our part.

(5.18.4) Then poor, dear Psyche, like the simple and childlike girl she was, was terror-struck at such grim words. She was beside herself: she completely forgot all her husband's warnings and her own promises, and rushed herself into the depth of calamity and trembling; and ghastly with pallor she could only manage a whisper from half-opened lips:

Dearest sisters, you are steadfast in the discharge of your duty, as is right, but those who confirm such things to you do not appear to me to be lying. For I have never seen the face of my husband, nor have I any idea where he is from, but I only endure a husband of whom I know nothing, and who utterly shuns the light, catching his voice in the night, and I acknowledge that you are right to say it is some beast. For he always terrifies me greatly against looking at him, and warns me of the great ill of desiring to see his face. Now if you are able to offer any hope of safety to your sister in danger, now at this moment come to my aid; but a following neglect will detract from the benefits of your previous foresight.

(5.19.5) Then these wicked women, already coming upon their sister's mind with its gates wide open, threw aside the covert devices of their secret siege-craft, drew their swords of deceit, and took over the panic-stricken thoughts of their simple sister. So the one finally said:

Since our ties of kinship do not allow us to countenance any sort of danger when you are at risk, we will show you the one way which leads to safety, for time and again we have thought it out. Take a very sharp knife, and sharpen it even more by stroking it with your palm, and hide it secretly on your own side of the bed. And trim a lamp, fill it with oil, and as it burns with a clear light hide it with some sort of cover from a little jar to block its light, and do take the utmost care to conceal all you have prepared. And after he comes to his bed as usual, trailing the furrow of his path and stretched out, and begins to breathe in deep sleep, wrapped in the beginning of heavy slumber, slip out of bed on bare feet with tiny steps on tiptoe one by one, and free your lamp from the guardianship of blind darkness. By consulting the lamp[40] to find the opportunity for your glorious feat, boldly with your double-edged weapon, first raise your right hand high, and with as strong an effort as possible sever the join of the deadly serpent's head and neck.[41] And we will not fail to help you, but as soon as you save yourself by his death, we shall be waiting anxiously and will fly to you, and we shall take you away with all that wealth of yours, and will join you to a human husband in a marriage you would wish for.

(5.21.1) With these words they inflamed their sister's inner feelings, already burning fiercely in her heart, and immediately deserted her, leaving the place of such a dreadful crime in dire fear themselves, and stretched out on the usual force of the winged breath they threw themselves forward in flight over the rock and at once took ship and sailed off. But Psyche, left alone except that she was not alone but agitated by hateful Furies, was driven in her mourning back and forth like waves of the ocean, and no matter how steadfast her determined resolve, already she applied her hands to the crime, though still uncertain in her mind. She wavered and was torn by the many emotions of her plight.[42] She made haste, she put off, she dared, she hesitated, she was unsure, she was angry; and finally in one body she hated the beast and loved the husband. But as evening already dragged on the night, she laid out the means of carrying out her dreadful crime with precipitate haste; night arrived, her husband came, and after first engaging in the games of Venus,[43] had fallen into a deep sleep.

(5.22.1) Then Psyche, weak though she was in body and mind in all other ways, nonetheless grew more courageous, with the support of savage fate: she brought out the lamp, seized hold of the blade, and took the courage of the other sex. But the moment she cast the light to reveal the secrets of her bed, she saw the gentlest and sweetest of all wild creatures, Cupid himself,[44] the beautiful god in a beautiful sleep. At the sight of him the light of the lamp felt joy and brightened, and the blade felt ashamed of its sacrilegious point.[45] And yet Psyche was awestruck at the amazing sight; she lost control, as weak, pale, worn out and trembling, she let her legs give way and tried to hide the blade, but in her own bosom; and she would have done so, had not the blade, fearing to commit so dreadful a crime, fallen and flown from her rash hands. Already she felt weary, her safety lost, yet as she gazed again and again at the beauty of his divine face, she felt her spirits return. She looked at the inviting head of golden hair, drenched in ambrosia, the milk-white neck, the ruddy cheeks overrun with bunches of hair becomingly held back, some hanging in front, others behind. And already the lamplight was flickering at their excessive brilliance. And across the shoulders of the flying god there shone wings dripping with the florid sparkle, and although the wings themselves were resting, the down at the edge, gentle and delicate, playfully and restlessly shimmered; the rest of his divine body was smooth and shining; Venus had no need to be ashamed of giving birth to such beauty. And before the feet of the couch lay his bow, quiver, and arrows, the soothing weapons of a mighty god.

(5.23.1) Psyche was ever so curious, and could not resist going through her husband's weapons and handling them over and over in amazement. She took an arrow from the quiver and tried the very point by pricking her thumb on it; but even now her trembling hand applied too much force and she pricked too hard, so that she pierced the surface of her skin and wet it with tiny drops of rose-red blood. And so in her innocence Psyche through her own action fell in love with Love.[46] Then burning ever more with her desire for Desire, she lay over him: she gazed at him distractedly, and quickly drenched him with an impulsive spread of kisses, afraid he would wake. But while she was aroused by such a height of pleasure, as the passion surged from the wound in her heart – the lamp, whether out of treachery or guilty envy, or because it desired to touch so attractive a body and kiss it as best it could, poured from its spout a drop of burning oil onto the god's right shoulder. Well! To think that a bold and impulsive lamp, a wicked slave of love, should burn the very master of all fire, since some lover was no doubt the first to invent lamps to be able to enjoy desire still longer, even at night! That was how the god was burned: he jumped up, saw that his trust was betrayed and tainted, and flew off without a word from the kisses and embraces of his all too unhappy wife.

(5.24.1) But Psyche at once took hold of his right leg with both hands as he flew up, a pitiful appendage to his flight aloft; she held on and accompanied him as long as she could through the cloudy regions until at length she tired and fell to the ground. Nor did her divine lover desert her as she lay on the earth, but he flew to a nearby cypress tree and from its lofty top he spoke to her, bursting with emotion:

> Poor innocent Psyche, I forgot the instructions of my mother Venus: she ordered me to bind you fast with desire for the lowliest wretch alive and commanded you to be consigned to the most degrading marriage. But instead I flew to you as your lover. But I did this lightly, I know, and renowned archer that I was, I wounded myself with my own weapon and made you my wife, so that I suppose I should appear to you as a beast and you should cut off my head, a head which bears those eyes that love you. Time and again I warned you always to be on your guard against this; I kept warning you out of kindness. But those wonderful counsellors of

yours will soon pay me the penalty of their treacherous advice; but you I shall only punish by leaving you.[47]

And with the end of his speech he threw himself up in the air on his wings.[48]

(5.25.1) Psyche for her part lay stretched on the ground; she watched her husband's flight as long as she could keep him in view, and tormented her mind with dreadful lamentation.[49] But when the distance had parted her husband from her, sped away on the oarage of his wings, she threw herself from the nearby river-bank. But the gentle river, in honour no doubt of the god who is used to scorching even the very waters, and afraid for himself, at once with his innocent current laid her up on a grassy bank. Then it so happened that Pan, the rustic deity, was sitting near the brow of the river-bank with Echo in his arms, the mountain deity, and was teaching her to repeat all sorts of tiny utterances[50]; next to the bank his goats were playfully ranging at will, cropping the greenery by the river. The goat-like god, somehow not unaware of her plight, called Psyche to him, stricken and exhausted, and soothed her with gentle words:

> Little child, I for my part am a rustic and a herdsman, but have learned much through the benefit of great old age and much experience. But if my guess is right, and wise men I am sure call it divination, you are labouring under too great a burden of love, as I infer from your hesitant and often vacillating footsteps, and from your body's pallid look and your continual panting, and also from your failing eyes. And so listen to me, and do not again destroy yourself by throwing yourself down or by any other sort of self-sought death. End your grief, put aside your misery, and rather venerate Cupid, mightiest of gods, and win him over with submissive service, youthful, playful and pleasure-loving as he is.[51]

(5.26.1) When the shepherd-god said this, Psyche did not answer, but simply paid her respects to her saving deity and went on her way. But when she had wandered a good deal of the way with struggling steps, she came without knowing it by some path as day was already fading to a certain city, in which the husband of one of her sisters was the ruler. When she realised this Psyche was anxious to be announced to her sister; she was soon brought in and they exchanged embraces and greetings. She told her sister, inquiring why she had come: 'You remember your advice, when you persuaded me that I should destroy with a double-edged blade the beast which slept with me under the false title of husband, before he should swallow my poor boy in his voracious throat? But the moment I saw his face in my accomplice the lamp as I had agreed to do, I saw a marvellous, an absolutely divine vision, the son of Venus herself in person, I tell you Cupid himself, drowsing in gentle slumber. And while I was excited by the spectacle of such a great boon, and was confused by the sheer excess of pleasure, I found myself so troubled that I could not enjoy it, and by the worst of ill-luck, to be sure, the burning lamp spurted a drop of oil on his shoulder. He was at once shaken out of his sleep by the pain of this, and when he saw me armed with iron and fire, he said:

> You for your part leave my bed after so grave an offence and have all your property away with you, while I will now marry in formal ceremony your sister, and it was your name he mentioned. And right away he told Zephyrus to blow me beyond the boundaries of his mansion.'

(5.27.1) Psyche had scarcely finished speaking when her sister, driven by the goads of mad lust and malevolent envy, put together spontaneously a lie to deceive her husband, pretending that she had heard news of her parents' death, and at once sailed off and went straight away to the familiar rock, and although another wind was blowing, nonetheless all agog with delusive hope, she said 'Receive me, Cupid, as a worthy wife, and you, Zephyrus, sustain your mistress'; and she jumped headlong with a great leap. But she was unable to arrive at the hallowed spot, not even in her death. For she perished, among the rock crags, her limbs tossed and scattered and just as she deserved, her innards torn and offering a feed to the birds and beasts. Nor was Psyche's second vengeance slow in coming: for she once again arrived in her wanderings at another city, in which her other sister lived just like the first. She too was just as eagerly induced by the same sisterly ruse, and hurried as a rival to wicked wedlock, and at the rock she fell to a like death.[52]

(5.28.1) In the meantime, as Psyche went from country to country in her determined search for Cupid, he for his part lay in his mother's own bedroom, groaning with the injury from the lamp.[53] Then that pure white bird, the tern, which swims over the ocean waves on its wings, dived down swiftly to the deep bosom of the ocean. There he found Venus bathing and swimming; he perched beside her and told her that her son had been burned and was in agony from the intense pain of his wound, and not assured of recovery. And already rumours were circulating from mouth to mouth among all nations, and there were different malicious reports staining the whole family of Venus with scandal:

> He is off to consort with whores in the mountains, while you have gone off to swim in the sea, and because of this there is no pleasure, no grace, no delight. But instead everything is squalid, barbarous, and repulsive. There are no marriages, no friendly partnerships, no love between parents and children, but only a great ghastliness and the foul stench of sordid pairings.[54]

This news the wordy and all too inquisitive bird would prattle in the ears of Venus, tearing her son's reputation to shreds. But Venus was beside herself and suddenly cried out:

> Then that fine son of mine has now acquired some girlfriend? You must divulge it, my only devoted servant, the name of the girl who has led on

my innocent and unprotected son, whether she belongs to the Nymphs, or the ranks of the Hours or the chorus of the Muses, or belongs to my own servants the Graces.[55]

Nor did that talkative bird remain silent, but replied, 'Mistress, I do not know, but I think he is besotted with a girl – as I remember rightly, by the name of Psyche.' Then Venus in her indignation roared aloud: 'Is his true love Psyche, the very impostor of my beauty, the rival for my name? No doubt this burdensome child thought of me as the procuress who arranged his introduction to the girl?'.

(5.29.1) With these protests she hastily emerged from the sea and at once made for her golden chamber. She found her sick son, just as she had heard, and already she bawled out right from the very doorway:

> These are upright actions, well suited to your parentage and your own fine character, that at the very outset you should trample on the commands of your mother, or indeed your slave-mistress; not only did you not torment my enemy with a low-life love, but you, child that you are, joined her in your wicked adolescent embraces, so that I should have to put up with my enemy as a daughter-in law! But that you presume, you horrid worthless seducer, that only you can breed children, and that I am too old to conceive, then I should like you to know that I will give birth to a much better offspring than you, or rather so that you may feel the insult more I shall adopt one of my household slaves, and endow him with those wings, and torches and bow and the very arrows and all my equipment, which I had not given to you to treat like this[56]: for there is nothing from your father's estate to provide you with it.

(5.30.1) But you were badly brought up from your childhood. You have sharp fists and have struck out time and again at your elders with no respect, and your own mother, me I tell you, you show me up every day, you parent-killer, and too often you have struck me, and you despise me I suppose as a woman without a man, and you have no fear of your stepfather, strongest and mightiest of warriors as he is.[57] Of course not, since all too often to torment me you have been in the habit of supplying him with girls for his affairs. But now I shall see to it that you are sorry for this game, and that you feel the bitter acid taste of this marriage of yours. But at this moment, after being made a fool of, what am I to do? Where am to turn to? How am I to take control of this snake-in-the-grass (lit. lizard). Am I to seek support from my enemy Sobriety,[58] whom on account of the excess of this very son of mine I have so often offended? But I absolutely shrink from conversation with so unrefined and ill-kempt a woman. Yet the consolation of revenge is not to be underestimated, wherever it comes from. I must ally myself closely with her and no other: she will give that good-for-nothing a really nasty talking to, take his quiver apart, disarm his

> arrows, unstring his bow, put out his torch, and for that matter correct his own person with still sharper remedies.[59] Then I might believe that I have been compensated for my injuries, when she has shaved off the hair which I have stroked to a golden sheen with these very hands of mine, and cut the wings which I have nourished with nectar from my own breast.

(5.31.1) With this she threw herself out of doors, full of hate and an anger that belongs only to Venus. But Ceres and Juno encountered her at that moment, and they asked why her face was swollen, and why she restrained such attractive shining eyes under her lowering brow. But she answered:

> I suppose you arrive at just the right moment to assuage the desire that burns in this breast of mine. But hunt down for me Psyche, I beg you, with all your might: she is on the run and has taken to flight. For no doubt you must be aware of the notorious tale of my family and the deeds of my son, unworthy of the name.

Then they, not unaware of what had happened, tried to soothe Venus' savage rage:

> My lady, what has your son done wrong that you should impugn the pleasures of his high spirits, and that you should wish to destroy the girl he loves? What charge is it against you if he has smiled so freely at a winsome girl? Surely you are aware that he is a man and a young one, or at least have you forgotten how old he is now? Or, because he is so good at carrying his years, he always seems to you no more than a boy? Besides you yourself are a mother and a woman with her wits about her: will you always enquire closely into what your son gets up to, and find fault with his excess, and criticize his love-affairs, and find fault with your own wiles and pleasures in your good-looking son? For in any case what god or mortal will allow you to disseminate desire to peoples all over, when you grudgingly restrain love in your own family and debar the public discharging of women's weaknesses?

This was how they flattered the absent Cupid, with ingratiating support for his cause, in fear of his arrows. But Venus was indignant that her injuries should be treated so light-heartedly,[60] and she cut them short and sped off in another direction and made for the sea.[61]

(6.1.1) Meanwhile Psyche would wander back and forward, and day and night she was intent on searching for her husband, and the more sick at heart she was, the more eager to propitiate his anger with a slave's entreaties, if it was not possible to soothe him with the endearments of a wife. And when she saw a temple on the top of a steep hill, she said, 'But perhaps it is here that my lord is living?', and immediately she quickened her pace and made for it: hope and wishful thinking incited her speed, slowed by all her continual struggles. And now she made the effort and scaled the higher slopes, and drew near to the sacred couch. She saw ears of corn in a heap, and others bent into a crown, and ears of barley. There were sickles and all sorts of harvesting tools, but all lying scattered in a careless jumble as in summer, thrown down from the workers' hands. Each of these Psyche carefully sorted and divided into their proper places,[62] no doubt supposing that she ought to neglect the shrines and worship of none of the gods, but to invoke the kindness and pity of all of them.

(6.2.1) Kindly Ceres came upon her anxiously and busily attending to this and immediately she exclaimed at length:

> Well, Poor Psyche? All through the world Venus in a fit of fury is hunting you in an intense search, and intends to punish you with the severest punishment, demanding revenge with the full strength of her divinity; and yet you are at this moment looking after my property and thinking of anything but your own safety.[63]

Then Psyche fell at her feet, her hair wetting the feet of the goddess with copious tears; and sweeping the ground with her hair and joining many entreaties together she asked the goddess' favour:

> I beseech you by your fruitful right hand, by the gladdening rites of the harvest, by the silent secrets of the caskets, by the winged chariot of your dragon retinue and the furrows of the Sicilian turf, and the chariot that snatched Proserpina and the earth that held her, and her descent to her lightless wedding and her return to the discovery of the light,[64] and all the rest that the siren of Attic Eleusis conceals in silence[65]: come to the aid of the spirit of your pitiful suppliant Psyche. Allow me even for a very few days to lie concealed amid your heap of corn ears, until the savage wrath of so great a goddess is soothed by the passage of time, or at least until my energy, worn out by continual suffering, is gently nurtured by an interval of calm.

(6.3.1) Ceres replied:

> Certainly I am moved by your tears and prayers and I wish to help you, but I cannot suffer the ill-will of my kinswoman,[66] with whom moreover I have an old bond of friendship, and who is besides a fine woman. So leave this temple at once; be grateful that I have not arrested you and put you under guard.[67]

Psyche was rejected contrary to her hopes and smitten by double misery, as she retraced her steps: when she caught sight of a skilfully built shrine in a half-lit grove in the valley before her; and not wishing to miss out any way, even a doubtful one, of improving her hopes, but to seek the grace of any god, she approached the sacred threshold. She saw precious gifts and cloths inscribed with gold lettering attached to the branches of trees and doorposts, which bore witness to the name of the goddess they had been dedicated to, and the graciousness of her help. Then kneeling and embracing the warm altar with her hands, she wiped her tears away and prayed:

> (6.4.1) 'Sister and wife of mighty Jupiter, whether you reside in your ancient shrine at Samos, which alone has the glory of your birth, your infant crying and your nourishment, or whether you spend your time in your blessed abode in lofty Carthage which worships you as a virgin riding the sky on the back of a lion,[68] or whether you preside over those famous walls of the Argives beside the banks of the Inachus,[69] which remembers you as already the Thunderer's consort and the queen of the goddesses, whom the whole of the East venerates as Zygia and all the West as Lucina[70]: may you be Juno the Saviour in my hour of direst need and free me from fear of imminent danger, worn out by all the great sufferings I have endured. And as I am told, you are accustomed to come of your own accord to those in peril in their pregnancy'.[71]

As she prayed in this way, Juno presented herself at once with the august dignity of her divine presence and immediately declared:

> How I should wish, I swear, to nod assent to your prayers. But against the will of Venus my daughter-in-law, whom I have always loved as a daughter,[72] shame does not allow me to override her. And then again I am prevented by the law which forbids the protection of other people's runaway slaves without the consent of their master.[73]

(6.5.1) Psyche was terror-struck at this further shipwreck of her fortune, and no longer able to find her winged husband she laid aside all hope of saving herself, and reasoned with herself like this:

> Now what other aid can I try or apply to my misfortunes, since not even any of the goddesses can help me, even when they want to? So caught in such a net, which direction am I to take? Where can I find shelter or shadows where I am to hide from the inevitable eyes of mighty Venus? Rather then must I not take a man's courage and bravely renounce my shattered hope and give myself up voluntarily to my mistress, and soothe her savage attacks with submissiveness, even at this late hour?[74] Who knows whether the man I am searching for is to be found there in his mother's house?

And so she prepared herself for uncertain submission,[75] or rather for certain death, and thought about how to begin her coming entreaty.

(6.6.1) But Venus renounced her search for terrestrial remedies and looked to heaven. She ordered the chariot to be made ready that Vulcan the goldsmith had carefully brought to perfection with his intricate workmanship and had given her as a wedding present before the initiation of the bridal chamber[76]: an object conspicuous for what the file had trimmed off and precious even for the gold it had lost. From the many that had their quarters round their mistress' house four doves came forward. They gladly stepped out and twisted their painted necks to take the jewelled yoke, and picked up their mistress and happily flew off. The chariot was escorted by playful sparrows[77] chirruping noisily, and other birds sweetly singing and announcing the arrival of the goddess to the sound of their honeyed strains. The clouds parted, heaven opened for his daughter, and the topmost Aether joyfully received the goddess, nor did Venus' household of singers fear an encounter with eagles or savage hawks.[78]

(6.7.1) Then Venus immediately made for the royal citadel of Jupiter and haughtily demanded the loan she needed – the service of the loud crier Mercury. Jupiter nodded his dark brow,[79] then she triumphantly left the sky at once with Mercury in her train, and anxiously told him:

> My Arcadian brother,[80] doubtless you are aware that your sister Venus has never done anything without Mercury's being there, nor does it escape you for how long now I have been unable to find my elusive handmaid. So there is nothing for it but for you as herald to publish abroad the reward for finding her.[81] See then that you are quick to carry out my command, and clearly set forth the signs by which she may be recognised, so that if anyone commits the crime of concealing her against the law, he cannot defend himself with the excuse of ignorance.

As she said this she handed him a paper[82] with Psyche's name and all her details. When she had done so she immediately returned home.

(6.8.1) Nor did Mercury fail to obey her. For he ran far and wide across the face of all nations discharging the duty of making the proclamation she had ordered:

> If anyone can retrace or reveal the whereabouts of a runaway princess, a slave of Venus called Psyche, he is to report to the crier Mercury behind the Murtian turning-point of the circus,[83] and will receive from Venus herself as a reward seven sweet kisses and one with a thick coating of honey from the thrust of her flattering tongue.

When Mercury made this announcement the desire for such a great reward aroused the zealous rivalry of all the world. And it now completely removed from Psyche any will to delay. And already as she approached her mistress' doors she was met by one of Venus' household, Habit as she was called, who immediately exclaimed as loudly as she could:

> At last, wickedest of maids, are you beginning to realise you have a mistress? Or in your usual shamelessness do you also pretend to be unaware

what great efforts we have put out in our search for you? But fortunately it is my hands you have fallen into, and now you are held fast in the grip of Orcus,[84] no doubt to pay immediately the punishment for all your insolence.

(6.9.1) And she boldly took hold of Psyche's hair with her hand and dragged her in without any resistance. And when Venus saw her led in and at her mercy, she came out with the broadest cackle, as people do when roused to a fury, and shaking her head and scraping her right ear,[85] 'At last', she said,

you have seen fit to pay your respects to your mother-in-law?[86] Or have you come instead to call on your husband, whose life is at risk from the wound you gave him? But have no fear, for now I shall welcome you as a good mother-in-law should,

and she went on, Where are my handmaids Anxiety and Misery? When she had called them in, she handed Psyche over to them for torture. But they followed their mistress' command and after lashing poor dear Psyche with whips and tormenting her with other tortures, they brought her in again to face her mistress. Then Venus once more put on her smile and said,

And just look how she tries to make me sorry for her with the enticement of a swollen belly, with which no doubt she is to make me a grandmother[87] with her amazing offspring. Happy indeed am I, who in the very flower of my youth will be called grandmother and the son of a worthless slave will hear himself called grandson of Venus. And yet I am silly to speak in vain of a son: for the marriage is not an even match and moreover took place in a country estate with no witnesses, without the groom's father's consent. Such a wedding cannot appear legitimate,[88] and through it this bastard will be born, only however if I allow you to bear the child at all!

(6.10.1) With these taunts she lunged at Psyche: she tore her clothes to shreds, tore apart her hair, shook her by the head and laid into her hard. She also took wheat, barley, millet, poppy-seed, chickpeas, lentils and beans, mixed them all together, and scrambled them into a single heap, then said to Psyche:

You seem to me to be so base a slave that you can only gratify your lovers by busy drudgery: so now I myself will try out your worth. Separate this jumbled heap of these seeds and sort them all out properly into separate heaps, and before this evening let the work be done and carried out.[89]

And when she had assigned her the heap of such an amount of seeds, Venus went off to a wedding-banquet. Nor did Psyche strive to set her hand to that confused and inextricable mass, but dumbfounded by the awesomeness of the command she was struck dumb with consternation. Then that tiny little country creature the ant, sure of the scale of her difficult task, took pity on the mistress of the mighty god, and horrified at the cruelty of her mother-in-law, she rushed to call together and assemble the whole order of ants round about: 'Have pity, agile offspring of earth the mother of all, have pity on the wife of Love, the lovable girl in danger, and come to the rescue with all speed!'[90] Others rushed forward, and others again, wave upon wave, and with the utmost eagerness each of them sorted the whole heap a grain at a time, separated them, and distinguished the types, before smartly disappearing from view.

(6.11.1) But at the beginning of the night, Venus came back from the wedding feast[91] soaked in wine, reeking of perfume and garlanded all over with a brilliance of roses. When she saw the diligence of that amazing feat she said: 'This work, vilest slave, is not your doing, nor the work of your own hands, but is the work of the boy who fancies you but to the cost of both of you': she tossed Psyche a lump of coarse bread and went off to bed. Meanwhile Cupid was alone, shut in a single room within the house under lock and key, in part to stop him worsening the wound with his impulsive indulgence, in part to stop him getting together with his love.[92] And so although under the same roof the lovers were separate and apart, and spent a miserable night. But when Dawn was on her steed, Venus called Psyche and said to her:

> You see that wood with the river running by, and the long stretches of banking, with the bushes down below, overlooking the neighbouring spring? There sheep with shining fleeces of genuine gold wander and graze without a shepherd. From there I command you to bring me at once, no matter how you obtain it, a hank of that precious wool.[93]

(6.12.1) Psyche willingly set out, not that she really expected to perform the task, but hoping for a respite from her miseries by throwing herself down into the river from a rock. But at that point from the river a green reed,[94] nurse of sweet music, inspired with a gentle whisper of the sweet breeze, gave her this prophecy:

> Psyche, troubled with all your sufferings, you are not to pollute my sacred waters with your truly pitiful death, nor may you approach these fearsome sheep at this hour, while they are used to be driven wild by dire madness, taking their heat from the burning sun, and with their sharp horns and stone-hard foreheads and often too with their poisoned bites,[95] are used to rage and cause the death of mortals; but until midday has abated the heat of the sun and the flocks have settled in the cool breeze of the river, you can hide unnoticed under that great towering plane-tree which drinks the same river-current as I do. And once their fury has abated and the sheep's minds are relaxed, you must shake the branches in the nearby grove, and you will find the woollen gold, which sticks all over in their entwined stems.

(6.13.1) In this way the simple, kindly reed told the stricken Psyche how to save herself. Nor did she fail once instructed to pay attention to its valuable advice,[96] but she performed the instruction, easily stole the wool, and brought back to Venus her lap full of the softness of the tawny gold. And yet she did not receive a favourable report for her efforts, at least from her mistress, for the danger of her second labour. With knitted brow and a bitter smile Venus told her:

> I am not unaware that it was your adulterous husband who did this too. But now already I will be sure to test whether you are endowed with a truly courageous spirit and are really prudent. Do you see the summit of that steep mountain overhanging that loftiest of crags, from which dark waters from a black fountain flow, and shut into the vessel of a neighbouring valley, water the Stygian marshes, and feed the deafening flows of Cocytus?[97] Bring back from that very spot, from the deep gush at the head of the fountain at once in this tiny urn a draught of freezing water.

With this she handed her the little vessel hollowed from crystal, showering her with still more threats.[98]

(6.14.1) But Psyche, eager to quicken her pace, made for the topmost summit, at least hoping there to find an end to her life of utmost misery. But as soon as she came near the summit prescribed by Venus, she saw the deadly difficulty of her awesome task. For there was a great rock of enormous proportions, wild, slippery and inaccessible, pouring out horrid cascades from the jaws of stone in its midst. The water at once gushed from the gap of a sloping opening, and fell headlong, concealed in the eaten-out course of a narrow channel, and fell unseen into the nearby valley.[99] And to left and right from the hollows in the rocks she could see savage snakes with long necks crawling forth with their eyes devoted to waking vigilance, their pupils on guard in perpetual wakefulness. And now the very waters defended themselves with a voice of their own.[100] For they said: 'Leave' and 'What are you about? Take care', and 'What are you doing? Beware!', and 'Flee!' and 'You'll die!' And so Psyche was petrified by the very impossibility of her task, and although her body was there, her senses were elsewhere: and totally overwhelmed by the awesome scale of a danger from which she could not escape, she could not even find the final consolation of tears.

(6.15.1) Nor did the misery of this innocent soul escape the august gaze of kindly providence. For that royal bird of loftiest Jupiter, the snatching eagle,[101] suddenly was at her side with his wings outspread; he remembered his duty of old, when led on by Cupid he had stolen the Phrygian cupbearer[102] for Jupiter. Now he bore timely aid, and worshipping the god's divine spirit he brought help to his wife in her distress, deserting the roads of Jupiter on high, and flew down before the girl's face. 'But you', he said,

> innocent as you are and inexperienced in such matters, do you expect that you will steal so much as a single drop or get hold of it any other way

from this holiest and no less awesome of springs? You are aware that even to the gods, and even Jupiter himself, those waters of the Styx are fearful even to mention, and that what you mortals swear by the spirits of the gods, they themselves are accustomed to swear by the Styx? But lend me the tiny urn;

and at once he snatched if from her, held it and hurried off; and balancing on his mighty span of wings, between the jaws and the triple-forked tongues of the dragons he veered left and right, took the waters though they were unwilling and warned him to withdraw before suffering harm. He pretended that he was searching at the command of Venus and that his service was on her behalf, so that it was a little easier for him to gain access.

(6.16.1) Psyche gladly accepted the little urn filled in this way and returned it quickly to Venus. Not even then could she win the approval of the cruel goddess. For she smiled a destructive smile and threatened Psyche with still greater and more dangerous tasks, as she spoke to her: 'Already you seem to me to be some powerful and thoroughly accomplished witch, who have obeyed such orders of mine so quickly. But still you must serve me, my little one. Take this casket' – she gave it to her –

> go at once to the Underworld and the baneful deities of Hell itself. Then give Proserpina the casket, and you are to say to her: "Venus asks from you a little of your beauty – at least enough for the short space of a day.[103] For as she is looking after her ailing son, she has used up all she has and exhausted her supply". But come back in good time, as I must put it on before I visit the theatre of the gods.

(6.17.1) Then Psyche sharply realised that her luck had run out and that the veil was off, and understood that she was being clearly driven to a speedy end. How could it be otherwise, when she was being forced to go of her own accord to Tartarus and the Shades on her own two feet? Nor did she hesitate further, but made her way to some tower of great height, to throw herself down from that very place. For in this way she thought she would be able to go straight down to the Underworld by the best possible route. But the tower burst suddenly into voice[104]:

> Why, poor wretch, do you wish to kill yourself by your headlong fall, and why do you succumb rashly to the final dangerous trial? For if your spirit should once become detached from your body, you will assuredly go straight to the bottom of Tartarus, but from there you will be unable to return by any means. (6.18.1) Listen to me. Sparta, a noble city of Achaea, is situated not far from here. Look beside it for Taenarus, concealed off the beaten track.[105] There they point out the breathing-place of Dis, and the gaping gates of its impassable road. Cross the threshold, entrust yourself

to it, and you will go by a direct channel to the very palace of Hades. But you must not enter so far into these dark regions without equipment, but bring with you in each hand a cake of barley-meal soaked in honey-wine, while in your mouth carry two coins. And now that you have covered a good part of the deadly road you will encounter a lame ass loaded with wood, and a lame driver, who will ask you to hand him over some sticks that have fallen off the load, but without uttering a word you must pass by in silence. And without delay, you will arrive at the river of the dead, whose harbourmaster Charon at once demands the crossing-fare before he ferries travellers in a boat of skins to the further bank. So even among the dead avarice is alive. Nor does so mighty a god as Charon, the collector for Dis,[106] do anything for nothing, but a poor man on the brink of death has to look for his travel expenses and should he not have a bronze coin to hand no-one will allow him to die. To this unkempt old man you will give one of the coins you are carrying for his fare, but on condition that he takes it with his one hand from your mouth. And in like manner, as you cross the sluggish river, an elderly corpse swimming[107] over it will raise his decaying hand and beg you to haul him aboard the boat, but you must not be turned aside influenced by pity, as this is not allowed. (6.19.1) When you have gone a little way beyond the crossing, old women weavers setting up their loom will ask you to help them for a moment,[108] but neither are you allowed to be part of this. For all this and much besides will happen through the traps set by Venus, so that you let go one of your cakes. Nor should you take lightly the loss of that mere barley-cake: for if one of them is lost you will never see the light of day again. For a great dog with three-fold huge heads, a monstrous and formidable creature barking with its thunderous throats at the dead, vainly terrifying those whom he can offer no harm – this creature guards the empty house of Dis ever watchfully, and he stands before the very threshold and gloomy halls of Proserpina. This dog you must muzzle with the prize of one of your barley-cakes; then you will pass him easily and gain access at once to Proserpina herself,[109] who will receive you courteously and kindly, so as to persuade you to take a soft seat and a sumptuous meal. But you must sit on the ground and ask for cheap bread and eat it, then having announced the purpose of your visit and received what is offered you should return. Bribe the savage dog with the remaining cake and then give the greedy boatman the coin you had kept back; cross the river and retracing your previous steps return to the light of the chorus of heavenly stars. But amid all the rest I solemnly warn you to observe this above all: you should not wish to open or inspect the casket you bring,[110] or with too much curiosity try the hidden treasure of divine beauty.

(6.20.1) So did the perceptive tower fulfil its task of prophecy. Nor did Psyche delay; she made for Taenarus, duly took the coins and the cakes, and ran down to the lower world. She passed in silence the stumbling donkey-driver and gave the coin to the ferryman, ignoring the request of the dead swimmer and rejecting the crafty pleas of the weaving-women, and with the horrid rage of the hound put to rest with the barley-cake, she penetrated the home of Proserpina. She did not accept the delicate seat her hostess offered, nor the sumptuous meal, but sitting low before her feet and content with coarse bread, she delivered Venus' request. And at once she took the casket filled and sealed in secret; she deceived the dog with the trick of the second cake and muzzled its barking; she paid the ferryman with the remaining coin, and returned from the Underworld with much more vigour. She returned to the shiny light she knew and hailed it, and although she was hurrying to bring her task to an end, her mind fell victim to rash curiosity and she said: 'Look what a fool I am, to be the carrier of divine beauty, and not pour out even a tiny little of it for myself! And so perhaps to delight my beautiful lover'; (6.21.1) and with that she undid the casket. There was nothing in it, not any beauty, but a deathly and truly Stygian sleep,[111] which at once revealed by the opening of the lid took hold of her and went through all her limbs as a thick cloud of slumber. It held her in her tracks just where she was on the path, and she lay immobile, nothing but a sleeping corpse.

But Cupid, his wound now closed, was regaining his strength and could not bear the continual absence of his dear Psyche: he slipped through the topmost window of the room where he was held; his wings were refreshed by a good rest, and flying forward much faster, he ran towards his dear Psyche. He carefully rubbed away the sleep and carefully replaced it in its hiding place in the casket, and woke her with a tiny harmless prick of one of his arrows,[112] and said 'You see, once again you had perished, poor darling, through the same curiosity as before. But in the meantime you discharge diligently the task which was ordered you by my mother's bidding, and I will see to the rest'. With this her nimble lover took to the air, while Psyche at once brought back Proserpina's gift to Venus.

(6.22.1) Meanwhile Cupid, utterly consumed by love, fearing his mother's unexpected severity and looking ill, returned to type. And on his swift wings he went right to the summit of the sky and prayed to mighty Jupiter and pleaded his cause. Then Jupiter took Cupid by the cheek and brought it with his hand against his own cheek and kissed him and said to him:

> Although you, my son, have never given me the honour decreed by the acknowledgement of the gods, but have wounded with constant blows this breast of mine[113] by which the laws of the elements and the motions of the stars are disposed, and have fouled it with frequent misadventures of earthly lust, and although against the laws, even the Julian law,[114] and public morals, you have harmed my reputation and good name with shameful adulteries, by foully changing my serene countenance into snakes, fire, wild beasts, birds and beasts of the field,[115] nonetheless remembering my moderation and that you grew up in my hands I shall bring it all to fruition;

> whilst however you must know to look out for your rivals, and if there is any girl on earth supreme in beauty, you must reward me with her in turn in exchange for my present good deed.

(6.23.1) With this he ordered Mercury to call all the gods to a council right away, and if any one absented himself from the assembly of the celestials, to pronounce that he would incur a penalty of 10,000 sesterces. The heavenly theatre[116] was full as a result of this threat, and Jupiter, sitting on his lofty throne above the throng, made the following announcement:

> Conscript gods in the record of the Muses, this youth I am sure you all know, and that I reared him with my own hands. I have decided that the hot-blooded drives of his first flush of youth must be restrained by some kind of curb; it is enough that he attracted scandal through daily tales of adulteries and all manner of impropriety. All opportunity is to be removed and the wantonness of youth is to be bound up in the fetters of marriage. He has chosen his girl and taken her virginity. Let him keep her and take her and embrace Psyche in his arms and ever have enjoyment of his love.[117]

And to Venus he turned and said,

> Nor must you, my daughter, take it badly, nor fear for your mighty lineage or status because of marriage with a mortal. Now I shall make it not an ill-matched but a legitimate marriage, and one in accord with civil law.

And then through Mercury he ordered Psyche to be rushed to the spot and brought up to heaven, and given a cup of ambrosia. 'Take this, Psyche', he said, 'and be immortal, nor shall Cupid stray from his bond with you, but this marriage will bind both of you for ever'.

(6.24.1) And without delay, a lavish wedding banquet was provided: the husband held Psyche in his lap as he reclined on the couch of honour; as did Jupiter with his spouse Juno, and then all the gods in due order. Then Jupiter was served a cup of nectar by the country boy who served as his personal wine-waiter while the others were served by Liber; Vulcan cooked the dinner; the Hours spread a red hue over all with roses and other flowers, the Graces scattered perfumes, the Muses performed their musical songs; Apollo sang to the lyre, the lovely Venus danced, in step to the sweet music, having arranged a suitable spectacle, with the Muses singing the chorus and playing their flutes, while satyrs and a tiny Pan sang to a shepherd's pipe.[118]

So was Psyche duly married to Cupid; and in the fullness of time she gave birth to a daughter we call by the name of Pleasure (Voluptas).[119]

Another 'lost husband': two versions of Semele[120]

Diodorus 4.2.1ff. /Apollodorus 3.5.3 (ATU 425B)[121]

(Diodorus) Cadmus settled <in Thebes> and married Aphrodite's daughter Harmonia, and they had daughters Semele, Ino, Antinoe and Agave, as well as a son Polydorus.[122] Zeus was captivated by Semele and made love to her in secret and in silence. She thought the god had no regard for her and so she asked him to make love to her as he did to Hera. So Zeus came in a manner appropriate to a god, with the full blaze of his thunder and lightning, but Semele was pregnant and could not endure the great majesty of Zeus' presence, but gave birth prematurely. (Apollodorus) But Dionysus brought her back up from Hades[123] and ascended with her into heaven.

Nonnus, Dionysiaca 7.141ff.

(Semele) brushed the forgetful wing of sleep from her eyes, and sent her mind in a wander after a dream's image with a variety of oracles. It seemed to her that she saw a lovely-leafed tree in a garden, loaded with burgeoning unripened fruit watered with the son of Cronus' fostering dews, when suddenly a flash from heaven fell through the sky, flattening the whole tree, but leaving the fruit untouched… and Semele was the tree. The girl leapt up terrified from her bed,[124] and told her father of the fire that blasted the leafy tree, and King Cadmus shook when he heard of the tree burned by the father, and called the divine announcer (Tiresias), son of Chariclo, and told him that morning his child's blazing dreams. When he heard the oracular voice of Tiresias he sent out his daughter to the accustomed temple of Athena, to sacrifice to Zeus the hurler of bolts a bull, the image of Lyaeus who also bears horns, and a goat destined to be the enemy of the vintage as it cut down the vines.

From there she went before the city to kindle the altar for Zeus, the lord over lightning. As she stood beside the victims she sprinkled her bosom with blood; the girl was drenched in blood, and great streams of blood soaked her hair, and her clothes were crimson with the dripping bull's blood. And swiftly making her way beside the deep rush-beds of the river Asopus, the river of her native place, the girl with the discoloured robes plunged in to wash garments soaked and stained by the great spatter of blood. There she washed her body clean, and naked with her maids the girl ran through the water using her hands as paddles… (190) Nor did she escape the all-seeing eye of Zeus… (316ff.) The fastenings of the palace door opened of their own accord as he passed through, and he held Semele fast in the amorous bond of his arms. One moment he gave a bull's lowing voice with horned head above human limbs, in the image of Dionysus with his bull's horns; at another he took on the shape of a thick-maned lion; now he was a panther, as the begetter of a fierce son, the driver of panthers and holder of lions' reins.[125] Or again as a bridegroom he bound his hair snooded with snake-coils and vine-leaves, winding the purple ivy round his hair, the plaited adornment of Bacchus. And a coiling serpent crawled over the trembling bride's rosy neck with its gentle lips, and going down into her bosom it girdled the circling of her firm breasts as it hissed a wedding hymn, pouring forth the sweet honey of a bees' happy swarm, not the venomed arrow of a viper.[126] Zeus prolonged his receptive rite, and as if beside the winepress he exclaimed *Euos*, as he fathered the son who was to love the cry…and after the bedding he greeted Semele with loving words, as he cheered his bride with hopes for the future. 'My lady, I your bridegroom am the son of Cronus…'.[127] (8.178ff.) And Hera left the cave of the Dictaean rock with its swinging shields and the cavern of the goddess who brings about childbirth,[128] and came with guileful intent to Semele's chamber, puffing in her jealousy. She took on the shape of a honey-tongued old woman, the loving nurse that Agenor himself had chosen and supported. This was the woman Hera looked like when she stepped into the house, fuming at Semele and Cypris and Dionysus who had yet to see the light, and arriving at the chamber of the recent wedding she turned her gaze to the opposite wall, so as not to see the bed of Zeus; and Pisanassa the servant of Semele, the maiden of Tyrian descent, sat her on a seat, and Thelxinoe spread rugs over the gleaming chair. There the goddess sat alongside her, weaving her schemes.[129] And she found the girl heavy with the burden of ripening increase, and the birth, not yet reaching the month of delivery; her pallid cheek, and the paleness of her once rosy limbs, told of a womb unsealed. And the treacherous Hera's false form trembled with a feigned palsy as she sat, and the old woman nodded forwards to the ground on her bent shoulders. With difficulty she found her excuse: she gave a groan, wiping the well-pretended tear from her cheek, and she uttered her false words with her voice, enchanting the mind:

> Tell me, queen: Why these pale cheeks? Where has all your beauty gone? Who has grudged you your beauty and dimmed the sparkle of your rosy cheeks, and who has changed the rose colour to that of quickly fading anemones? And why do you languish in this downcast state? Have you too heard those shameful rumours that people are broadcasting? A curse on the tongues of women, root of all evil! But tell me, and do not hide anything: Who laid violent hands on your girdle? Which of the gods has polluted you, which has robbed you of your virginity?… (247) And if, as you claim, the son of Cronus is your bridegroom, let him come to your bed with the thunder of desire, helmeted with marital lightning, so that someone may say "Hera and Semele both enjoy the thunderings of the bridegroom". Jealous though she be, Zeus' consort will not give you trouble, for your grandfather Ares will not permit it…

… (264) With this she left the house, with the girl still troubled: she was envious of Hera's still unmatched marriage and resented the son of Cronus… (286) And Semele was weighed down heavily in her newly suffering heart, longing for the lightning to accompany their love with its flashes. She made her complaint to her husband, wishing for the fireworks of Hera's bed:

> By the rich nuptials of Danae[130] I beg you, grant me this gift, horned[131] spouse of Europa! For I am ashamed to call you the husband of Semele, when I see you only as a dream… (320) You go to Hera's bed in your divine form, lighting up your bride with nuptial lightnings, but for Semele you approach as a serpent (*drakōn*) or a bull. She hears the resounding Olympian thud of love, Semele hears the bastard bellow of a sham bull with only the shadow of a shape. Zeus comes to my bed noiselessly and cloudless, but as cloud-gatherer[132] he makes love to haughty Hera. My father flees the scandal of a daughter's disreputable marriage; your (very own) Cadmus is confined to his palace and avoids where people walk, ashamed to show face in public, because everyone pours scorn on your secret marriage, and criticizes Semele for her secret husband. You have given me a fine wedding gift – women's sneers! And the chorus of handmaids finds fault with me, and above all I fear the coarse tongue of a prattling nurse…(340) Not yet have I seen the face of the real son of Cronus, the gleaming flash of the eyelids, nor the light of his face, nor the blinding sheen of his beard. Not yet have I seen your Olympian form, but I expect a panther or a lion, I do not see a god as my husband. I view you as mortal when about to give birth to a god….

(348) So did Semele beg to meet her own fate: for the short-living bride aspired to be the equal of Hera, and hoped for the sweet spark of a gentle thunderbolt. But father Zeus listened and put the blame on the jealous Fates, and pitied Semele's untimely death. But he saw the selfish anger of the unsoftening Hera over Dionysus. And he ordered Hermes to seize the infant son of Thyone[133] blasted by the fire, from the flaming bolt… (407) And Zeus soothed the mind of the jealous Hera: he calmed the wild burden of threatening hatred, and let fiery Semele be transposed to the vault of the stars; she shared her home with the inhabitants of heaven.

Notes

1 Swahn (1955); Binder-Merkelbach (1968); Walsh (1970), 190–223; Wright (1971), 273–284; Megas, *EM* 1 (1977), 464–472; Kenney (1990); Anderson (2000), 61–69; Hansen (2002), 100–114.
2 *Cupid and Psyche* deserves pride of place as showing beyond reasonable doubt that the literary fairy tale had already come of age in the ancient world. There is little in content to say that this text belongs to Antiquity rather than the Renaissance, when even the pagan gods, as opposed to fairies and elves, would not look out of place. The sense of royal courts and opulence, the black-and-white moral values of wickedness punished, virtue rewarded, true love and happy ending are already there, together with a whole apparatus of magic effects, and the attention to a predominantly female world, suitable to an old wives' tale and its female captive audience; all this

might as easily belong to the artificial world of the French *Précieuses* in the 17th and 18th centuries.

Other views of the story have been held by classicists, most notably those seeking origins in oriental cult-myth (Reitzenstein) and Platonic Allegory (Kenney, among others), Apuleius having been himself a writer on Platonism. To the former can be added a number of analogues in Hittite myth about an ill-tempered god Telepinus, his demand for a wife, his anger at some kind of disobedience and a number of rituals performed to get him back and bring about the wedding (Anderson 2000, 63–67). These would correspond to Psyche's own tasks and provide better motivation. The cultic context would suit the tale well, as a tale told to a woman in labour to distract from the pain: one thinks of the pregnant Psyche faced with the threat of delayed delivery.

3   The heroine need not have elevated social status: the version of Basile (5.4, 'The Golden Root') has a poor man with three daughters.
4   Folk versions are sometimes less kind: 'The two eldest were proud and ugly but the youngest was the gentlest and most beautiful creature ever seen (Briggs, *DBF* 1970 A1, 458, 'The Red Bull of Norroway').
5   All three cult-centres of Aphrodite.
6   Many such tales tend to emphasise the arrogance of the woman (e.g. those of Chione, Semele). Apuleius takes care to emphasise the modesty and good nature of Psyche throughout.
7   The Lucretian echoes here pave the way for sly humour: the primeval majesty of the mother of creation is assigned to a very human, jealous, caricature.
8   In the Judgement of Paris, in which Venus bribed the judge.
9   The traditional casting of Eros/Cupid as delinquent from Archaic Greek literature onwards.
10 Psyche 'soul', with the name delayed with the casualness of the oral storyteller. There is certainly an unmissable allegorical element here, though how far this is simply ornamental is still a matter for debate.
11 A traditional cast-list of minor marine deities, presented as a retinue for Venus when travelling by sea.
12 The first of several purple passages relating to the movements of divine beings.
13 In accordance with their ambitions: 'I will have no-one lower than a king'…the second would take a prince or a duke even (Briggs, *DBF* A1, 458, 'the Red Bull of Norroway').
14 In folk-versions the divination for the bride may require nothing more than a spay-wife or the like ('What do you see?'. '…A great Black Bull…'. 'Thon's for you') (Briggs, 'The Black bull of Norroway', *DBF* A1, 156).
15 Milesian tales carried with them a reputation for salaciousness; the tale of the Widow of Ephesus (Petronius, *Satyrica*, 111f.) typifies the genre.
16 They and the *lector* of *The Golden Ass* are not meant to interpret this as Eros/Cupid, traditionally a 'dangerous' figure in ornamental Graeco-Roman literature. One might think in particular of the snake-lover which purports to seduce Olympias at the beginning of the *Alexander Romance*. The 'bestial' nature of the husband is variously interpreted: he has a whole range of animal guises in Nonnus' version of the Semele story.
17 In the novels the superlative beauty of the heroine is engaged with the reactions of the whole city (as much in the popular narrative of Xenophon of Ephesus as in the more sophisticated writers).
18 Compare the human sacrifice motifs in the story of Perseus and Andromeda, the exposure of Hesione, or the story of Lycus and the girl.
19 Psyche's mood varies in Apuleius from 'positive' initiative here through to abject suicidal resignation: Apuleius, and Silver-Age writers generally, have a taste for extremes of emotion.

20 Psyche's willingness to give herself when all others are delaying may be a hint of versions where the heroine has actually promised herself to be the bride of a monster (see 'The Red Bull of Norroway', Briggs *DBF* (1970), A1, 458).
21 The shutting up of the palace reappears e.g. in Perrault's version of *Sleeping Beauty*.
22 The Zephyr will act as celestial transport throughout: cf. the ornamental role in divine love-affairs in e.g. Lucian, *Dialogi Marini*, 15. In Dasent, 29ff. first the East then the more powerful West Wind, then South then North act as transport during the wanderings to find the Stepmother's abode. Some versions, particularly Italian, start with access to the underground palace by uprooting a plant; in Basile 5.4 Parmetella discovers a palace whose prince promptly proposes, with gold and silver around (cf. the trees of silver in Hades, as in *The Twelve Dancing Princesses*, Opie and Opie (1980), 250f.
23 The bridegroom's abode is often sumptuous: so Dasent, 23:

> The white bear gave a knock, and a door opened, and they came into a castle, where there were many rooms all lit up, rooms gleaming with silver and gold; and there too was a table ready laid, and it was all as grand as grand could be. The white bear gave her a silver bell, and when she wanted anything, she was only to ring it, and she would get it at once.

24 Sometimes the retinue is actually visible: Basile's Parmetella (5.4) is given a diamond coach drawn by winged horses complete with liveried monkeys. The disembodied voices so characteristic of Apuleius' version may be intended as a reinforcement of the invisibility of the bridegroom. They also serve to emphasise the isolation of Psyche herself.
25 The delicacy of Apuleius' narrative obscures the fact that this is at the very least a forced marriage, if not an actual rape: the 'invisible bridegroom' motif is of course incompatible with any notion of the mutual passion of the couple. The husband is not always invisible; Parmetella encounters a black youth who offers marriage which she accepts. The taboo is the same in this instance: he turns white during the night, a sight she must not see.
26 The first of Cupid's warnings against the jealous sisters. Sometimes the taboo is broken immediately: Parmetella is overcome by curiosity the second night of their marriage. The nature of the taboo varies greatly in the folktale tradition. Sometimes the bridegroom's advice might be not to talk with her mother alone (Dasent, 24), to whom she tells the whole story of the invisible groom, 25; the mother suspects a troll); or not to talk more than three words with her father, Grimm, 127: so Zipes (1987), 452.
27 An 'Ovidian' touch: in a conversation with a god, the divine party refers to himself, or the girl refers to him, in the third person, as yet unaware that she is actually addressing him (e.g. Jupiter smiled to be compared with himself by Callisto in *Metamorphoses*, 2.429f.).
28 As of course he turns out to be.
29 The ugly sisters, as in Cinderella tales. The sibling rivalry of jealous sisters does not figure in the Greek novel as currently known, but is familiar enough in the mythographic record: see especially Aglauros infected by jealousy for her sister Herse, lover of Hermes in Ovid *Metamorphoses*, 2.797–832.
30 Underprivileged younger siblings are the characteristic underdog heroines of fairy tale, but not always: the early Chinese Cinderella Yeh-Sien is an *older* sister.
31 As once more will prove to be the case, by which time envy will long ago have been the death of the sisters.
32 Ancient marriage conventions often allow a substantial age gap: the Younger Pliny's third wife would have been married in her teens to a husband in his late 30s or more.
33 The second warning of impending downfall.

34 Again the feel of a fairy tale motif: the fantasy as so often depends on the breaking of a taboo.
35 It is the husband who is first aware of the pregnancy, perhaps because divine intercourse is unfailingly fertile, but Psyche may preserve the genuine ignorance of the young and closeted aristocratic girl.
36 Pregnancy is a relatively rare component in Western fairy tale, with its preoccupation with virginal progress to the goal of marriage (likewise in the Greek novel, where only Chariton uses the motif prominently).
37 The third warning of impending downfall.
38 This trust in Zephyrus will be the eventual undoing of both.
39 Again a fairy tale motif of fattening to devour, as in the Empousa story, below c.5.
40 Lamps were endowed with personification as witnesses, especially in Hellenistic epigram: cf. Apuleius *Metamorphoses*, 2.11; Lucian *Cataplus*, 27.
41 Kenney notes some inconsistency here: the sisters genuinely seem to expect a serpentine husband, otherwise Psyche would have needed to be tricked into killing the supernatural husband in the dark.
42 There is something of Ovid's Althaea here (*Metamorphoses*, 8.465–474, where however it is the murder of a son that is in question).
43 Again a humorous twist, since uniquely they are his mother's domain.
44 An *ecphrasis* of Cupid, skilfully broken with the confused and panicking reaction of Psyche: here not quite Eros as the traditional Hellenistic putto.
45 For the naïve personification, cf. Ovid *Metamorphoses*, 8.513ff. (reluctance of Meleager's life-token to burn).
46 With slight inconsistency, as her love for her husband is already established.
47 Parmetella's husband simply swears at her: his sufferings will now last for 7 years.
48 In some versions the hero is more explicit at this point: the white bear explains having been bewitched by his stepmother, and is now to be forced to marry a bride with a nose three ells long in the castle East of the Sun and West of the Moon (Dasent, 26f.).
49 Sometimes the magic palace disappears at this point (Dasent, 27), with no complication of the sisters having to be killed).
50 For Pan and Echo it is perhaps a facetious touch to turn Pan into a counsellor on love: normally he is a shameless sexual opportunist with the nymphs: cf. Lucian *Dialogi Deorum*, 2.4.
51 At this point the heroine has to receive instructions from one or more 'supernatural helper' figures as to how to win back her injured husband. Parmetella is equipped by a fairy with several of a variety of objects (spindles, figs, iron shoes) and a single honey-jar, and told how to avoid the impending dangers. Submissive service is the key to the tasks section of the story: the young bride is to have a prolonged initiation into domestic tasks, in stark contrast to the comforts of her fully automated palace.
52 The murder of the sisters gives rise to some inconsistency. As Kenney notes, it rids the plot of the two unjust plotters and tormentors as soon as they have forced Psyche to betray her husband, thus gratifying the reader's thirst for rough justice. But it scarcely fits the character of Psyche herself, who is naturally generous and forgiving.
53 In the folk tradition he is often held by a witch or ogress, whose ugly daughter he is being forced to marry. One notes in the Hittite Telepinus texts that it is the bee who discovers the absent deity.
54 The Hittite tale already has the motif of failure of fertility:

> Mist seized the windows; smoke [seized the house]. In the fireplace the logs were stifled; [at the altars] the gods were stifled, in the sheep pen the sheep were stifled, in the cattle barns the cattle were stifled. Therefore barley (and) wheat no longer ripen. Cattle, sheep, and humans no longer become pregnant. And those already pregnant cannot give birth.

(Hoffner, 14f.)

55 I.e. minor superhumans and so respectable liaisons. In Hellenistic poetry and its sophistic prose successors there is often a comically bad relationship between Aphrodite/Venus and Eros/Cupid, as her disobedient and delinquent son.
56 Aphrodite/Venus threatens Eros'/Cupid's arrows as early as Apollonius Rhodius' *Argonautica*, 3.95ff. (and cf. Lucian *Dialogi Deorum*, 23).
57 I.e. Ares/Mars, as a (genuine) war-god.
58 A game of allegories has a characteristically Ovidian feel, where the opposites need each other but are disinclined to meet directly (e.g. Ceres and Hunger in the Erysichthon story, *Metamorphoses*, 8.785f.)
59 For the threats, cf. the contemporary Lucian, *Dialogi Deorum*, 20. There are also echoes of Apollonius of Rhodes' presentation of Athena and Hera seeking the help of Venus, *Argonautica*, 3.93–97.
60 One is reminded of her speedy and silent departure after being caught in bed with Ares (*Odyssey*, 8.362–366).
61 Throughout the chapter there are echoes of Moschus *Idyll*, 1 (*Erōs drapetēs*, where Aphrodite sets up a hue and cry for her son as a dangerous and delinquent 'Missing person'). Here she is preparing to hunt down Psyche, but her wayward son's attributes are evoked once more.
62 The sorting here seems a doublet of the grain-sorting which requires magic help in due course. Such episodes serve symbolically to domesticate the young bride with household tasks (cf. Snow White's tidying of the cottage for the dwarfs).
63 The two episodes where Psyche is 'moved on' by Ceres and Juno appear to refashion episodes where the folktale has the heroine stay with a supernatural/magical helper who actually does help by providing e.g. a means to defeat a false bride: Briggs, *DBF* A1, 459; 'The Red bull of Norroway' (Dasent, 32).
64 Psyche stresses the analogy between herself and Proserpina, readily realised in a myth analogous to the current tale.
65 I.e. the still not fully revealed mysteries of Demeter/Ceres at Eleusis.
66 Ceres is a daughter of Saturn, Venus of Jupiter, and so Ceres is Venus' aunt.
67 Other goddesses are wary of antagonising Venus, who is still capable of making them in turn fall in love unsuitably.
68 In fact the local deity Tanit.
69 I.e. as the goddess of Argos, ruled by Inachus who gave his name to the river.
70 Zygia: as the goddess who yokes in marriage; Lucina: as the goddess who presides over childbirth.
71 The fulsome flattery embodies typical prayer formulation, enumerating cult-titles and sites of the deity addressed, in the hope of finding the form most pleasing to the recipient.
72 The affection is disingenuous, after the Judgement of Paris.
73 By a rescript of Marcus Aurelius and Commodus: Apuleius thinks in terms of current Roman Law.
74 The desperate rhetorical expostulations are characteristic of the lamenting heroines of the Greek novels, e.g. Chariton, 3.7.5.
75 In this instance Psyche also adopts the stereotypical pose of the passive heroine which has so offended feminist re-workers of fairy tale.
76 Cf. his presentation in *Iliad*, 18.369–379.
77 Suitable birds of Venus, given their reputation for sexual insatiability.
78 Such scenes of departing celestial chariots are already well established in Homeric Epic and here add to the glitz and glamour of the overall décor.
79 A conventional Epic touch, cf. *Iliad*, 1.528.
80 His favourite residence is Mount Cyllene in Arcadia.
81 Once more a reminiscence of Moschus' *Erōs drapetēs*.
82 A rare glimpse of literate update in ancient mythological machinery.
83 Where the goddess Murcia had a shrine, and which was associated with prostitutes. The association is evidently with Venus Myrtia (myrtea): Kenny cites Varro *de lingua latina*, 5.154; Pliny *NH*, 15.121. See also Ogilvie on Livy, 1.33.5.

84 Orcus, i.e. Hades.
85 Scraping the right ear, as a gesture of annoyance.
86 Venus now plays the role of fairy tale stepmother/mother-in-law...
87 Not the least source of irritation: Venus has been made to 'feel her age' since the beginning.
88 Only now is doubt cast on the legitimacy of the union: but it may not have been clear-cut: Venus objects to the informalities of the countryside.
89 Sometimes the lost bridegroom may set a task with the persecutor's approval: (to wash the three drops of tallow off his shirt, Dasent, 34). Basile's Parmetella has to sort twelve sacks of vegetable seeds by evening, or be eaten. Ants sort the seed, sent by the now-freed husband ('Thunder and Lightning').
90 In the fairy/folk tradition it is sometimes a cannibal ogress who has to be placated (in Parmetella's case, Basile, 5.4, 123 Penzer).
91 As if this should be an official duty of Venus: perhaps facetiously, as she is as much the patroness of extra-marital affairs.
92 Is Psyche aware of Cupid's presence here? Kenny compares the frustration of closely proximate lovers in the novels: Chariton, 5.24, 6.2.11; Longus, 3.9.5; Achilles Tatius, 4.1.
93 Task two: Parmetella has to fill twelve mattresses with feathers by nightfall: Her husband tells her to call out that the King of the Birds is dead: birds drop feathers in grief. Walsh sees Psyche's version as least 'folkloric' here (though he notes an approximation in a North African version before opting for a mythological borrowing from Argonautic themes). But these are themselves steeped in folktale tradition. In general the mythological parallels seem not conspicuously striking, whether from Apollonius, *Odyssey*, 4, or Virgil's *Georgics*.
94 The use of a reed as informant is at least as old as *Gilgamesh*, where it passes on the warning of the flood to Utnapishtim; Kenney notes the same function in the story of Midas' ears.
95 Sheep with poisonous bites seem an unusual variation, given the range of others available. Conflation of Apollonius' guardian dragon and the golden fleece seem far-fetched to me: they suggest determination to relate oddities to accessible classical literature at all costs, and folk/fairy tale does not in general work like that.
96 One of the didactic mannerisms of fairy tale: the heroine must be seen to be obedient.
97 Cocytus: as the river of wailing.
98 Ludwig Bieler took both the third and fourth tasks to be doublets of 'the quest for the waters of life' (Binder-Merkelbach, 334–369); against, Wright, arguing that the fourth task is not such a quest.
99 For a description of the falls of the Styx at Nonacris, Pausanias, 8.17.6.
100 The personification of the waters here seems unusual in either classical literature or folktale tradition.
101 In the Hittite texts it looks for the vanished Telepinus, but is otherwise not involved.
102 I.e. Ganymede, snatched by an eagle up to Olympus or by Zeus in the guise of an eagle, e.g. Lucian, *Dialogi Deorum*, 10.1.
103 This is the task of fetching an object from a sister witch: 'Forbidden' caskets figure prominently in the hinterland of ancient fairy tale: apart from Pandora, the daughters of Cecrops break a similar taboo with still more lethal results: Gantz, 236f. In a corresponding task given to Parmetella, she has to placate seven spinning-women, sisters of the prince, attracting them with the honey corresponding to the sop to Cerberus here, and exacting an oath before she accepts their invitations. Parmetella has to go to the Ogress' sister to bring back a box of musical instruments; she has to give the 'sop to Cerberus' to feed a runaway horse, and stop a banging door. But she breaks a taboo not to open the box, and loses the instruments, which the husband has to replace.

104 The talking tower, like the lethal sheep, seems an odd detail, and might make better sense in a fuller context elsewhere.
105 Underworld journeys have stereotyped tolls, inevitably including those of Charon and Cerberus; for a much fuller list, cf. the twelfth tablet of *Gilgamesh*, with the corresponding taboos for the Sumero-Akkadian hero.
106 For the literary traditions on Charon, Terpening (1985), 25–123.
107 Not a feature of the literary tradition, any more than the stumbling donkey driver.
108 Parmetella encounters seven weaving-women, from whom she is to exact an oath before complying with their request. As expected these are a prominent cliché in the folk-tradition.
109 And so encourage the unwary traveller to repeat her own original error of eating in the underworld.
110 The problem with Psyche, as with Lucius in the frame-tale of *The Golden Ass*.
111 A Snow White moment, duly relieved by 'the prince'.
112 Corresponding to the kiss of the prince.
113 For the playful relationship with Zeus/Jupiter, cf. especially Achilles Tatius, 1.1f.
114 Augustus' *Lex Julia* of 18BC made adultery a criminal offence.
115 For the standard metamorphoses for seduction, e.g. Lucian, *Dialogi Deorum*, 6.
116 Cf. the celestial council in Ovid *Metamorphoses*, 1.167–245. Such a gathering also occurs in the Hittite Telepinus texts.
117 By contrast, in Parmetella's version the husband is to marry an ogress, but the latter confesses to selling kisses to a shepherd when Parmetella refuses to kiss the groom. Since Venus plays the part of the ogress, the motif of a rival bride is difficult to operate here. In folktale versions the Venus figure may burst with envy (Dasent, 35); this kind of extreme reaction necessarily disappears here.
118 There is no final formula of the kind 'I was at the wedding but didn't get a taste of the beer'; but the happy ending is clearly in place, in contrast to the frequent scenario in Graeco-Roman mythological tales, which punish the couple after the wedding, as in the case of Hippomenes and Atalanta, who commit sacrilege in a temple and are turned into wild beasts
119 In the folktale tradition the heroine may already have children, with the contacts with the heroine's family tied to the birth of successive offspring.
120 The two handlings illustrate a mere mythographic summary in contrast to a full-blown late antique Epic version replete with 'literary' apparatus.
121 Semele does not originally sleep with an invisible Zeus; he is seen, but only in a form suitable for mortal eyes.
122 For the misfortunes of Cadmus' line, Gantz (1993), 467–473; on Semele, 473–477.
123 Through the grotto of Lethe (Plutarch, *Moralia*, 565f.), or the temple of Artemis at Troezen, (Pausanias, 2.31.1f.)
124 A similar anticipatory dream precedes Europa's seduction by Zeus in Moschus, 2.1–12. The dream corresponds to the unnamed king's warning from the oracle in *Cupid and Psyche*: the bride's father has in effect to accede once more to his daughter's forced marriage.
125 Zeus routinely seduces mortal women under animal guises, but not normally the same woman with a series of transformations: serial metamorphosis is rather the hallmark of sea deities like Proteus or Thetis.
126 The snake as in Psyche's oracle; also, in legendary tradition, Nectanebus' shape for seducing Olympias in order to beget Alexander the Great in the *Alexander Romance*.
127 By contrast, Cupid does not announce his identity in *Cupid and Psyche*.
128 The cavern on mount Dicte is the birthplace of Zeus, and the shields were used to conceal the baby's cries from his cannibal father; the goddess of childbirth was Eilythuia.

129 For a similar scene, most likely the model for this one, compare the visit of Athene and Hera to the house of Aphrodite to plan the love of Jason and Medea (Apollonius, *Argonautica*, 3.36–110).
130 Seduced by Zeus disguised as a shower of gold, begetting Perseus.
131 In the guise of a bull.
132 Nephelēgetera, a Homeric epithet.
133 Her new, divine name, as noted also by Diodorus.

3
ARTS OF VARIATION
Cinderellas and Snow Whites

The variants of *Cinderella* underline the adaptability of the most popular heroines, both in substance and in narrative length. The first two examples come as mere narrative outlines, but the stories of Aspasia, Asenath and Chloe have considerable literary ambitions. Aelian offers a naïve and sentimental didacticism, and expands his tale well beyond the limits of the miscellaneous memorabilia in the rest of his collection: like the handling of Rhodopis it has the trappings of historiography. The anonymous Asenath-author produces a combination of Jewish piety and Hellenistic romance; and Longus uses a mixture of pastoral and novel structure to reset essentials of Cinderella against a country background. Known fragments of a *Snow White* novel (*Chione*) should make it less surprising that Xenophon of Ephesus annexes most of the popular tale to serve a cheaply emotional pulp-fiction plot, while Ovid presents us with what seems like two halves of a *Snow White*: an unhappily ending version including rape as well as murder; and instead of the girl in the glass case a statue that comes alive.

Five versions of Cinderella[1] (*ATU* 510A)

(a) Rhodopis: Strabo 17.1.33 and Herodotus 2.134f.[2]

The two notices on Rhodopis complement each other, and the slipper-test is not the only indicator of the story: the heroine's slave status and function as a courtesan supplies the 'persecuted heroine'; the name of her benefactor supplies the motif of supernatural help from a magic fish or tree (Charaxus' name means both 'sea-bream' and 'vine-pole'); the eagle supplies a third kind of supernatural helper. There are two hints of a connexion with the hearth: the unusual name Hephaestopolis, corresponding to references to the hearth in modern Balkan variants; and the votive offering of roasting-spits, which points in the same direction. There is no society ball, and no sibling rivals.

56 Cinderellas and Snow Whites

Rhodopis

(Rhodopis) came from Thrace, and she was a slave of Iadmon, son of Hephaestopolis, a man from Samos; she was a fellow-slave of Aesop the writer of fable…She arrived in Egypt, brought by Xanthus of Samos, and when she got there she was freed for a large sum by Charaxus of Mytilene, son of Scamandronymos, brother of Sappho the lyric poet. Having obtained her freedom, she actually stayed in Egypt and became so popular with lovers that she obtained a huge fortune for a person in her profession (Herodotus).

They tell the fabulous story (*mytheuousi*) that while she was bathing, an eagle seized one of her shoes from her maid and brought it to Memphis,[3] and while the king was dispensing justice in the open air, the eagle arrived over his head and threw the shoe into his lap. The king was aroused by the *rythmos* of the sandal and the strangeness of the event, and sent all around the country in search of the woman who wore it. When she was found in Naucratis she was brought up country to Memphis and became the king's wife (Strabo).

She wanted to leave a memorial of herself in Greece by doing something that no-one else would have thought of, and putting it in a temple, and laying it up at Delphi as her memorial. So having made a great many iron roasting-spits for oxen for a tenth part of her wealth, she sent them to Delphi[4] (Herodotus).

(b) Venus and Mercury/Anaplas[5]: Hyginus De Astronomia 2.16

An important variant, similar to Strabo as far as it goes, but showing that gods themselves can play the roles of human characters in fairy tales.

Venus

A good many have also said that Mercury, others again Anaplas, was induced by the beauty of Venus to fall in love with her; and since he was unsuccessful, he was downcast and felt insulted; but Jupiter took pity on him and when Venus was bathing in the river Achelous, he sent an eagle, which brought her sandal to Amythaonia[6] in Egypt and gave it to Mercury. Venus went in search of it and came to her admirer. And when he made love to her (*copia facta*), he set the eagle in the sky in gratitude for her favour.

(c) Aspasia of Phocaea[7]: Aelian, Varia Historia 12.1

Here poverty provides the persecution of the heroine, unable to afford a cure for disfigurement. Aphrodite serves as 'helpful animal' (the dove) before becoming 'fairy godmother'. The rose petal beauty treatment hints at Rhodopis' name in (a) above ('Rosy-cheek'). The revulsion at the satrap's procurement and Cyrus' unwelcome advances offer a grimly realistic 'flight from the ball', when she attempts to escape, while her shameless competitors correspond to the sibling rivals of the fairy tale. The necklace suggests a cultural adjustment to a ring-token: by giving it to the prince's mother she is enacting the bride's correct submission to the seniority of her mother-in-law, and so clearing the way for 'marriage to the prince'. If this seems over-ingenious, it is worth bearing in mind that a fair number of Cinderellas dispense with the token-test altogether. The coercion used in this version is a reminder of the not infrequent violence of the prince in oral versions of 'the ball'.

Aspasia

Aspasia, the daughter of Hermotimus, came from Phocaea[8] and was brought up as an orphan; her mother had died in childbirth. Afterwards Aspasia was brought up in poverty, but she was taught modesty and self-control. She used to have a recurrent dream that offered her the prophecy of good fortune, and gave a hint of good luck in the future, that she would live with a fine and noble partner. And while she was still a child, she had a growth below her face, just underneath her chin. It was unsightly to look at and distressed father and daughter alike. So her father showed her to a doctor, who undertook to cure her for a fee of three staters. Her father said he did not have the money, and the doctor said that he for his part did not have enough of the medicine. And Aspasia naturally was distressed at this and went out to cry. As she put a mirror on her lap and saw herself in it she was very distressed. She took nothing to eat in her misery, but at just the right moment she fell asleep and as she slept, she dreamt that a dove arrived, turned into a woman,[9] and said: 'Never fear, and have done with doctors and drugs alike. But take all Aphrodite's withered garlands of roses, grind them up and put the powder on the growth'. When she heard this, the girl did as she was told and the growth disappeared. And once more Aspasia was the most beautiful girl of her time, and had regained her beauty from the most beautiful goddess...

Once Aspasia visited Cyrus, son of Darius and Parysatis,[10] the brother of Artaxerxes. She had been reluctant to go and her father had been reluctant to send her, but she went of necessity, as often happens when cities are taken or tyrants or satraps have their way. At any rate it was one of Cyrus' satraps who had brought her to Cyrus together with other girls...When she first came to him, he just happened to have come from dinner, and was on the point of having drinks according to Persian custom: for the Persians after filling themselves with food spend a long time in their cups and toasts; they prepare for drinking as (Greeks) do for a wrestling bout.[11] While they were in the midst of the drinking, then, four young Greek girls were brought to Cyrus, including Aspasia, the girl from Phocaea. They were most beautifully turned out. The other three had been groomed by their serving women, who had come with them. Their hair had been done and their faces were made up with face-powders and cosmetics. And they had been schooled in how to win Cyrus' attention, and how to flatter him and not turn away if he approached them, and not to be annoyed if he touched them, and to let themselves be kissed – in fact the skills of courtesans and the techniques of women who traffic in their beauty. So each vied with the others to outdo the rest in beauty. But Aspasia did not want to put on an expensive dress, nor did she like the idea of an embroidered wrap; she could not even bring herself to take a bath…But she was beaten into submission, and obeyed her instruction, although it caused her distress to be forced to act the part of a courtesan[12] rather than a modest girl. Now the others arrived and looked directly at Cyrus and smiled and put on a façade of pleasantness. But Aspasia looked down; her face was covered in fiery blushes, her eyes were filled with tears, and she was obviously embarrassed at the whole performance. And when he told the girls to sit beside him, they complied in a docile manner, but she took no account of the order until the satrap took hold of her and forced her to.[13] And when Cyrus touched them and looked over their eyes and cheeks and fingers, the rest allowed him, but she would not; when he so much as touched her with the tip of his finger she gave a yell and told him that if he did so he would be sorry. Cyrus was delighted at this. And when she got up and tried to run off because he had touched her breasts, the son of Darius, contrary to Persian custom, was greatly impressed by her noble behaviour, and said to the trafficker, 'This is the only girl you have brought who is free and unspoilt. The others behave like courtesans, in their looks and even more in their manner'. From this moment Cyrus loved her more than any woman he ever had to do with. And later his love for her deepened, and she loved him in turn; the pair fell so much in love that they were close to equals and did not fall short of a Greek marriage[14] in their harmony and unselfish devotion…

Once a necklace was brought to Cyrus from Thessaly, sent by Scopas the younger; he had obtained the gift from Sicily. The necklace seemed to have been worked with amazing skill and ornament. So everyone Cyrus showed it to was amazed, and delighted beyond measure with his treasure, he at once went to Aspasia in the middle of the day. He found her asleep, and slipped under the bedcover and lay down quietly beside her and stayed still without a sound while she slept. When she had had her sleep and saw him, she embraced Cyrus in her usual way and kissed him. He took the necklace out of its box and showed it to her, making the remark that this necklace was worthy of a king's mother or daughter. She agreed and he said: 'So I am giving it to you as a present; put it on just as you are and show me how it looks on your neck'. But she was not overwhelmed by the gift but gave him a clever and civilised reply: 'And how can I presume to put on a gift worthy of your own mother? Rather send this to her, Cyrus; I will show you the beauty of my neck even without it'.[15]

(d) Joseph and Aseneth[16] *(Hellenistic version)*

This variant offers a pious heroine, reduced to despair by the sight of the Biblical Joseph as 'the prince'. Her rolling in ashes offers the most explicit treatment of association with the hearth; her handmaids born on the same day offer a very mild hint of the traditional sibling rivalry. We have a fairy godfather in the man from heaven who announces the impending marriage to Asenath and commands her to change from a black robe of mourning to a 'bride-show' outfit. As in the case of Aspasia, the token test is unusual, and again a cultural explanation is in order: as in the case of Christ washing the disciples' feet, it is a gesture of subservience. And again, as in the story of Aspasia, it is actually unnecessary to the conclusion of the plot.

Aseneth

(10.2) And Aseneth was left alone with her handmaids; she was in a listless state and wept till sunset. She neither ate bread nor drank water, and she alone stayed awake when everyone else was asleep.[17] And she opened the door, and went down to the gate and found the doorkeeper asleep with her children. And Aseneth quickly took the leather curtain down from the door and filled it with ashes. She brought it back up to her room and put it on the floor. And she closed the door firmly and put the iron latch across, and wept and wailed aloud…(10.9) And Aseneth got up and quietly opened the door and went into her second room, where she had the chests with her clothes, and opened her chest and brought out a black and mournful tunic (this was the one she wore when her firstborn brother died). And Aseneth took off her royal attire and put on the black tunic and undid the gold girdle and tied a rope round her waist and put off the headdress and diadem from her head and took the bracelets from her hands…(10.16) and she took sackcloth and put it round her waist and took the ribbon from her hair and sprinkled it with ashes…(10.18) And when she got up early in the morning she was amazed to see that her tears had turned the ashes underneath her to mud; And Aseneth fell once more on her face on the ashes till sunset. And she did this for seven days without food or drink. (11–13; in her anguish she prays to God.[18]) (14) And when Aseneth had finished her confession to God she was excited to see the morning star rise from the Eastern sky and when she saw it she rejoiced and said: 'The Lord God has heard my prayer, for this star is the herald and messenger of the great day'. And amazingly the heavens were rent near the morning star and an indescribable light appeared. And Aseneth fell on her face on the ashes and a man came out of heaven towards her.[19] And he stood over her head and called her: 'Asenath'. And she said, 'Here I am sir, tell me who you are'. And the man said: 'I am the commander of the Lord's House and the commander-in-chief of the whole host of the Most High. Stand up and I will talk to you'. And she raised her eyes and looked and there was a man who looked just like Joseph in his dress, his crown and royal sceptre, but his face was like lightning, and his eyes were like the light of the sun, and the hair of his head was like flames of fire, and his hands and feet were like molten iron. And Aseneth saw him and fell on her face at his feet in great fear and trembling. And the man said to her: 'Take courage, Aseneth, and do not be afraid, but stand up and I will speak to you'. And Aseneth stood and the man said to her:

> Take off the tunic you had put on, the black one, and the sackcloth from your waist, and shake the cinders from your hair and wash your face with

living water.[20] And put on a brand new robe and shining girdle, the double girdle of a virgin. And come again to me and I will tell you the words sent to you.

And Aseneth went into her chamber where the chests of clothing were and opened the chest and took off her black robe and took a new resplendent dress and put it on…(15) And she went to the man and when he saw her he said, 'Take the veil from your head, for today you are a holy virgin and your head is like that of a young man'. And she took it from her head, and the man said to her: 'Take courage, Aseneth: look, the Lord has given you Joseph for a husband and you will be his bride. And you will not be called Aseneth but City of Refuge'[21]… (15.9) And look: I am going to Joseph and I will talk to him about you, and he will come to you tomorrow, and will see you and be delighted with you and will be your husband. And listen to me, Aseneth, and put on your bridal dress, the ancient robe, the first robe stored in your chamber, and put on all your favourite jewellery, and adorn yourself as a bride and get ready to meet him. For he will come to you tomorrow and see you and be delighted with you.[22] And when the man had finished speaking to Aseneth, she was full of joy and fell at his feet…(19) And a little slave came and said to Aseneth: 'Joseph is at the gate of our house'. And Aseneth came down with her seven handmaidens to meet him. When he saw her Joseph said to her: 'Come to me, holy virgin, because I have received a message from heaven telling me all about you'. And Joseph stretched out his hands and they had a long embrace, and were revived by each other's breath. (20) And she said to him, 'Come into my house', and she took his right hand and brought him into the house. And Joseph sat down on her father Pentephres' seat, and she brought water to wash his feet, and he said to her 'Let one of your maidens come and wash my feet'. And Aseneth said to him: 'No, sir, for my hands are your hands, and my feet are your feet, and no-one else but me shall wash your feet'.[23] And she insisted on washing his feet, and Joseph took her by the right hand and kissed her, and Aseneth kissed Joseph's head. (They marry the next day.)

(e) An ancient romance version: Longus, **Daphnis and Chloe**[24] *(extracts)*

The short novel by Longus contains a number of motifs which can be joined up to form a Cinderella-like plot. Chloe ('Young Shoot') is nourished first by a sheep, then protected by a foster-father Dryas ('Oakman'). She scrupulously worships the local nymphs in their grotto, who collectively exercise a fairy godmother role. At a local festival she enacts the story of Pan and Syrinx, hiding in a wood from her friend Daphnis, a herd-boy soon to be revealed as 'the prince', and so offering a 'flight from the ball'. The nymphs reveal where he can find a purse, guarded by the corpse of a dolphin, to provide a dowry; his aristocratic birth is revealed, and a second time Chloe runs off; but her own aristocratic status is confirmed by birth-tokens including a pair of (miniature) golden slippers, identified by her real father. The couple are free to marry. Once again the token test is different, but its variations tend to be at the hands of literate authors, as in the case of Aspasia and Aseneth. The individual motifs (as of helpful animals and the like) are not of course peculiar to this tale; but their coalescence as a group points in the direction of *Cinderella*.

Chloe

(1.4) Already two years had gone by, when a shepherd grazing his flocks in the neighbouring pastures, Oakman (Dryas) by name, also came across a similar discovery and a similar sight. There was a cave of the nymphs, a big rock with a hollow inside and rounded on the outside. The statues of the nymphs themselves had been carved out of stone. They had bare feet, their arms were bare up to their shoulders, their hair came down to their necks; there was a belt round their waists, a smile on their faces[25]...

(1.5) When he came near, he saw nothing of what he expected, but the ewe was giving her teat like a human mother and offering a plentiful supply of milk[26]; the child was not crying but greedily moving between the nipples a mouth that was clean and shining, for the ewe licked its face clean once the child had taken enough milk...This child was a girl, and it too had identity tokens: a belt threaded with gold, golden sandals,[27] and golden anklets. (1.6) The shepherd thought his discovery was some gift of the gods, and taught by the sheep to feel pity and love the child, he took up the baby in his arms, put away the tokens in a bag and prayed the nymphs to look after the child that had taken sanctuary with them and bring it good luck.

(The dance)

(2.37) Daphnis and Chloe were quick to jump up and danced the story Lamon had told. Daphnis imitated Pan, Chloe Syrinx. He tried to persuade her with his advances, while she smiled and paid no attention. He chased after her and ran on tiptoe to imitate hooves, while she acted out being weary in flight. Then Chloe hid in the wood as if concealing herself in a marsh,[28] while Daphnis took the great pipes of Philetas and piped a plaint, like a lover, a wooing song, like a suitor, and a summoning, like someone in search of his love.[29]

(3.27) Daphnis, having got much less than he had asked for, did what poor lovers usually do: he wept, and once more called on the Nymphs to help him. And they stood before him as he slept at night, in the same form as previously, and the eldest of them spoke. 'Chloe's marriage is the business of another god, but we will give you gifts to charm Dryas. The ship belonging to the young men from Methymna, whose willow mooring-rope your goats ate a while ago, was that day carried far from the shore by the wind, and a sea-squall turned the water rough and it was shipwrecked on the headland rocks. The ship itself was destroyed and most of its contents, but a purse of 3,000 drachmae was washed up, and is lying covered in seaweed near the body of a dead dolphin, so that no-one passing has even gone near it, but takes a quick detour to avoid the smell of the rotting carcase. But you go to it, and when you've gone up to it pick it up, and having picked it up, give it as a gift.[30] It is enough for now for you to seem not to be poor, but later on you'll actually be rich'. (3.28) After that they disappeared along with the night, and when daylight came Daphnis leapt up and delightedly drove his goats to the pasture with plenty of whistling, and kissed Chloe and worshipped the nymphs and came down to the sea, as if he wanted to splash about and went along the shore next to the breakers in search of the 3,000 drachmae. And he was not likely to have much trouble, for the stench of the dolphin hit him: it had been washed up on the shore and was clammy with decay. Using the stench as a guide he went right up to it at once and removing the seaweed he found the purse, full of silver. This he picked up, put in his wallet and did not go far before blessing the Nymphs and the sea itself. Although he was a goatherd, he now considered that the sea was sweeter than the land, since it was helping him to win his marriage with Chloe. (3.29) Having taken possession of the 3,000, he no longer held back, but as if he were the wealthiest not only of the farmers there but of all mankind, he at once went to Chloe and told her the dream, showed her the purse, told her to guard the flocks till he came back, and rushing eagerly to Dryas and finding him with Nape threshing corn, he was utterly daring and launched into his proposal of marriage...

(4.31) Dionysophanes looked at Daphnis and seeing that he was pale and secretly crying soon guessed that he was in love, and showing concern for his own son rather than someone else's daughter, he carefully examined Dryas' words. And when he saw the birth-tokens as well, the golden slippers, the anklets and the belt, he called for Chloe and told her not to worry; she already had a husband,[31] and would soon find her parents. And Clearíste took her aside and dressed her as her son's future wife. And Dionysophanes took Daphnis up and asked him on his own if Chloe were a virgin, and when he swore that nothing more had happened than kisses and oaths, he was delighted and sat him down at the drinking-party. (4.32) So it was possible to find what beauty is like when it has the addition of order. For when Chloe was dressed and had her hair up and had washed her face, she seemed so much lovelier to everyone that even Daphnis could scarcely recognise her.

(4.34) And after a great deal of thought Dionysophanes fell into a deep sleep and had the following dream. He seemed to see the Nymphs asking Love now at last to give his consent to the marriage. And he unstrung his little bow and laid aside his quiver and instructed Dionysophanes to invite all the noblest among the Mytilinaeans to a drinking-party, and when he had filled up the last mixing-bowl, to show the recognition-token to each of them, and sing the wedding-song. When he saw and heard this he got up in the morning and after giving orders for a lavish feast, to invite the best of the Mytilinaeans as his fellow-drinkers. And when it was already night and the mixing-bowl had been filled for their libation to Hermes, a servant brought in the tokens on a silver tray, and taking them round from left to right, showed them to everyone. (4.35) Now none of the rest recognised them, but Megacles,[32] seated in the last and most honoured place because of his age, recognised them and gave a great shout like a youngster. 'What's this I see? What has become of you, my little daughter, so you are still alive, or has some shepherd come across you and only walked off with the tokens? Tell me, I beg, Dionysophanes, where did you find my child's tokens?' (At last the couple marry.)

Three versions of Snow White

Like *Cinderella*, *Snow White* presents a range of possibilities. Over three contrasting narratives we can find a number of features known to the modern tale: these include the idea that the heroine's rival has powers of divination: in Xenophon she is actually called Manto ('prophetess'), but she does not actually track her rival by such means. The red-and-white colour coding appears, but forms the names of her two servants ('Mr. White and Miss Rose'). The compassionate executioner is on call, but instead of dwarfs respecting the chastity of Snow White, we have a single herdsman with the same honourable intentions. We can follow the plot through to the motif of attempted poisoning – by *Snow White* herself, and her being laid on a bier. One of the two verse workings by Ovid has the advantage of her name Chione ('Snow Girl'), but shows up a touch of expurgation in modern versions, as there are rapes by Mercury and Apollo using the means of the first two murder attempts in the modern tale, before an actual murder attempt succeeds and the corpse is burned. A second version seems to offer the happy end of the story without any beginning: a King with a Dwarf name (Pygmalion, 'little fist') is able to bring the girl back not from a coma but from having been realised as a statue, and with the traditional kiss.

(a) Xenophon of Ephesus books 2–3 passim[33] *(ATU 709)*

Anthia

(2.9)…Anthia, Leucon ('White') and Rhode ('Rose') were taken to Syria. And when Manto[34] and her train reached Antioch (for that was where her husband Moeris came from), she bore a grudge against Rhode but hated Anthia. So she at once ordered Rhode to be put on a ship together with Leucon, to be sold as far away from Syria as possible, and planned that Anthia should live with a slave, one of the meanest at that, a goatherd in the country; that way she hoped to get her revenge on her. She sent for the goatherd, Lampon, gave him Anthia, and told him to make her his wife, and if she refused his instructions were to use force. And so she was taken to the country to live with the goatherd. And when she got to where Lampon pastured his goats, she went down on her knees and implored him to take pity on her and respect her chastity. She told him who she was, how she had once been a lady, had had a husband, and had been taken prisoner.

When Lampon heard her story, he took pity on her and swore that indeed he would not molest her, and tried to reassure her. (2.11) Anthia lived for some time with the goatherd, while Moeris, Manto's husband, made frequent visits and fell passionately in love with her. At first he tried to hide it, but finally he confided his love to the goatherd and promised him a great reward in return for his cooperation. The goatherd made an agreement with Moeris, but for fear of Manto he went to her and told her about Moeris's feelings. She flew into a rage. 'I am the most miserable woman on earth', she exclaimed.

> Will I be bringing my rival everywhere I go? Because of her I was first robbed of a lover in Phoenicia, and now I am in danger of losing my husband. But Anthia will not get away with attracting Moeris as well, for I will take my revenge on her for what happened in Tyre at the same time.

For the moment then she said nothing; but while Moeris was away she sent for the goatherd and ordered him to seize Anthia, take her into the thickest part of the wood, and kill her, and promised him a reward. The goatherd for his part was sorry for the girl, but for fear of Manto went to Anthia and told her her fate. … The goatherd was moved to pity by her plea, since he thought he would be committing an unholy act by killing so beautiful a girl who had done no wrong. He took hold of her, and yet he could not bring himself to kill her but said this to her:

> Anthia, you know that my mistress, Manto, has ordered me to take you and kill you. But I fear the gods and have pity on your beauty; I am willing instead to sell you far way from here, in case Manto finds out that you are not dead and takes her malice out on me…

(3.5) With this she grovelled at the feet of Eudoxus the Ephesian doctor and begged him not to refuse to give her the poison; and she brought out twenty minas of silver and her necklaces which she gave to Eudoxus…he promised to give her the poison and went away to get it…Meanwhile after a short delay Eudoxus arrived, not with a lethal drug but with a sleeping-potion so that nothing should happen to the girl… (3.6) She made an excuse that the tension had made her thirsty and ordered one of the servants to bring her water to drink, and when a cup was brought, she took it while no one was in the chamber with her, threw in the poison, and wept…With his she drank the drug and immediately fell into a deep sleep; she collapsed to the ground when the drug took its full effect. (3.7) When Perilaus (her rescuer from the robbers) came in and immediately saw Anthia lying there, he was dumbfounded…he laid her out in all her finery and surrounded her with a great quantity of gold. And no longer able to bear the sight, when day came he put Anthia on a bier (she was still lying insensible) and took her to the tombs near the city. And there he laid her in a vault, after slaughtering a great number of victims and burning a great deal of clothing and other finery. (She eventually is reunited with her husband Habrocomes.)

(b) Chione[35]: Ovid, Metamorphoses 11.293–334 (ATU 709)

Chione

(293) [Chione's father, Daedalion, son of Lucifer] subdued kings and their peoples by his prowess… (301) He had a daughter *Snow Girl* (Chione).[36] She had reached the age of 14 and was ready for marriage; and endowed as she was with exceptional beauty, she had a 1,000 suitors. It so happened that Phoebus and Maia's son Mercury were returning, the one from his favourite haunt of Delphi, and the other from the summit of Mount Cyllene. Both of them saw the girl at the same time and both, at the very same moment, fell in love with her. Apollo put off his hopes of making love to her till night, but Mercury did not put up with any delay: he touched the girl's cheek with his sleep-inducing wand. At that powerful touch, she lay there, and suffered the god's violent act.[37] When night had scattered the sky with its stars, Phoebus took the form of an old woman, and enjoyed the same pleasures that Mercury had stolen earlier. When her pregnancy had taken its full course, Snow White gave birth to twins: to Mercury with his winged feet a cunning child, Autolycus,[38] who would turn white to black and black to white; and to Phoebus, a son Philammon, famed for his singing and the music of the lyre.

(320) But glory is an obstacle to many, and certainly to her: she had the audacity to think herself more beautiful than Diana[39] and found fault with the goddess' appearance. This provoked the goddess to savage anger: 'You will not find fault with my actions!', she cried; and without delay she bent her bow, shot her arrow from the string, and sent her shaft through the tongue which had brought it on herself. Her tongue fell silent; and the words she was trying to voice failed; her life-blood left her as she was still trying to speak…But her father…bitterly lamented the loss of his daughter.[40] And when he saw her body burning, four times he tried to rush in to the heart of the funeral pyre; four times he was driven back. Then he abandoned his limbs to a frenzy of flight (and turned into a hawk).

(c) Ivory Snow-White and King Little-Fist (Pygmalion): Ovid, Metamorphoses 10.243–297 (ATU 709)

'Ivory Snow-White'

(243) Because King Little-fist (Pygmalion[41]) had seen these women leading a criminal life, he was outraged by all the vices with which nature had infected women's minds, and so he lived without a wife, and for a long time had had no consort to share his bedchamber.[42] But in the meantime he carved snow-white ivory (*niveum ebur*) by amazing art and gave it the form of a woman fairer than any ever born; and he fell in love with his own creation. She had the face of a real maiden – you would have thought she was alive, and she wanted to move, except that modesty held her back, so well did his art conceal its art. Little-dwarf

was amazed and his heart was inflamed with love for the image of a body. Often he set hands to the work, to test whether it was the original ivory, or a real body. No longer could he admit it was only ivory. He kissed it again and again and thought it kissed him in return, and spoke to it and held it and thought that his fingers sank into the lips he touched, and feared to redden the limbs he pressed. At one moment he would whisper loving words to her; at another he brought her the presents girls love: shells and polished stones and tiny birds and flowers of every colour: lilies, painted balls and the amber tears for the Heliads fallen from the trees; he decorated her limbs with clothes, put jewels on her fingers, and long necklaces on her neck; light pearls hung from her ears, and little chains over her breast. All the ornaments suited her; and yet she seemed no less beautiful wearing nothing. He placed her on bedclothes dyed with Sidonian shells, called her the companion who shared his bed, and placed her neck on soft feathers as if it could feel them.[43]

(270) The festival of Venus had arrived, when the whole of Cyprus celebrated the goddess, and heifers were cut down, their curved horns gilded, and the incense was burning: Little- dwarf performed the rite at the altar, and stood there and timidly whispered: 'If you gods are able to grant all things, I pray for a wife like the ivory image' (he did not dare to say 'the ivory maiden'). Golden Venus was at her own festival and understood the meaning of his prayers. And as an omen of the kindly goddess the flame burst forth and thrust its point through the air. When he came home, he made for the image of his girl, and lying on the bed he kissed her; she seemed hard. He applied his lips once more and felt her breast with his hands; as he felt it the ivory softened and lost its hardness and lay underneath his fingers and gave way, as the honey of Hymettus melts in the sun and bends into a thousand shapes when held in the fingers and becomes pliable by being applied. As he stood dumbfounded, he hesitated to rejoice and feared he was mistaken. Again he was in love and again he felt the object of his desire in his hands. She was flesh and blood; the veins surged when his finger touched them.

(290) Then indeed did the Paphian hero utter fulsome prayers of thanksgiving to Venus. And at last he pressed real lips with his own. The girl felt the kisses he offered her, and blushed; and she raised her hesitant eyes to the light and saw both the sky and her lover. The goddess was present at the marriage she herself brought about; and when the moon had driven her horns to fullness nine times over, she gave birth to a daughter Paphos, after whom the island is named.[44]

Notes

1 Opie and Opie (1980), 152–166; Wehse, *EM* 3 (1981), 39–57; Dundes (1982); Philip (1989); Anderson (2000), 24–42; Hansen (2002), 85–89.
2 The Matching information from Herodotus makes it clear that the same Rhodopis is in question. Hansen prefers to treat the Strabo material as simply the end of the tale. If the Rhodopis material in Herodotus is included, we have much more of it (cf. Hansen, 24).
3 Naucratis was a culturally Greek settlement, Memphis the old Egyptian capital.

4 The practice of offering the tools of one's trade as a thank-offering to a patron god was widespread in antiquity: a sailor might dedicate an oar to Poseidon, a soldier his weapons to Ares. Here a collection of roasting spits reinforces the connexion with the hearth.
5 The eccentric version known only to Hyginus necessarily ends in *katastērismos*, transformation into a star. The tale is a close mythological doublet of the previous version, with deities instead of humans. It is unusual in that the supernatural helper helps the hero rather than the heroine.
6 Amythaonia: a part of Elis named after the hero Amythaon, an ally of Jason.
7 An unusual and largely unnoticed version: the central incident is told as historical legend by both Xenophon (*Cyropaedia*, 1.10) and Plutarch (*Pericles*, 24.7; *Artaxerxes*, 26), but without the miraculous elements of the prophecy of good fortune, or the miracle of Aphrodite's intervention. This presentation underlines the moral subtext of the story more explicitly than most. The heroine is poor but virtuous, showing both obedience to Aphrodite and chastity in the face of threat or temptation.
8 On the Western Seaboard of Asia Minor, and so effectively under Persian control until Alexander the Great: a useful paradigm for the contrast between Greek and Persian/ barbarian.
9 By implication the goddess herself.
10 I.e. Cyrus the Younger.
11 Cyrus' after-dinner entertainment serves as 'the ball' of Perrault's canonic 17th-century version. Just as Rhodopis is actually a courtesan, this further adult version presents the girl in a clearly humiliating (and actually dangerous) position. The three 'rivals' put forward for the king's entertainment are unrelated to Aspasia, but have the same function as ugly sisters/sibling rivals.
12 Compare the role of Rhodopis, who is actually just that.
13 The heroine's modesty here corresponds in function to the 'running away from the ball'. 'The prince' has to have his honourable intentions put to the test.
14 A touch of the Greek bias against 'barbarian' mores.
15 We might otherwise explain the necklace as a 'bride-show' motif: in this case her bare neck is the ultimate bridal asset.
16 The love story of the Biblical Joseph and Asenath has come down to us in a short Hellenistic Jewish Romance, with close affinities to the more popular side of the Greek novel (ed. Philonenko, 1968; discussion, West, 1974, 70–81); there is also a fairly different Medieval version, discussed by Aptowitzer (1924); English version reconstructed by Schwartz (1988), 156–162. In the latter there are also clear affinities with the Cinderella story: persecution is provided by the rape of Dinah, Asenath's mother; the eagle takes both child and tokens to Egypt; some at least of the variation is accountable through the Jewish background (Asenath is presented as a non-Jew and a native Egyptian noblewoman, who has to convert); in the Medieval version she is already of Jewish heritage through her mother Dinah.
17 Thanks to her lovesickness for Joseph on the strength of a single sighting, Aseneth puts aside her rich attire and confines herself to her room, where she also rolls in ashes, in the only Graeco-Roman version to make direct use of them.
18 Piety and obedience are often emphasised in the character of Cinderella: here she has regarded her past pagan life as sinful.
19 There is no reason for the fairy god-person to be rigidly female: the well-known early Chinese version (Yeh-Hsien) from the 9th century CE likewise uses a male character for the role.
20 This is the critical transformation, and prepares for the essential 'bride show'.
21 Change of name corresponds to the change of identity in the clothes themselves. Again the oral tradition preserves changes from Ashiepattle or Katie Wooden-cloak or the like to some name that is felt to be less insulting.
22 The Medieval version described by Aptowitzer uses not the slipper but an amulet token, and the eagle as initial supernatural helper, to get Asenath's mother Dinah to Egypt in the first place.

23 A trace and no more of the 'sibling rivalry' element. Aseneth's seven handmaids were born on the same day as their mistress, and live with her in the manner of seven sisters, but only she is to have physical contact with her future husband. 'His feet are my feet' is as near as we shall get to 'It fits! It fits!'

24 *Daphnis and Chloe* is generally acknowledged as an ancient novel with strong links to classical and Hellenistic poetry and myth. But the plot mechanism also embodies a number of essentials of the Cinderella plots for Chloe (helpful animals, helpful fish (here represented by the dolphin, a marine mammal), supernatural helper, flight from the ball, recognition by slipper), and some elements of the male 'Cinderello' story for Daphnis.

25 The piety and obedience of both the lovers reinforces the role of the nymphs as supernatural helpers.

26 The nurturing of the heroine in the wild by an animal is often done in the fairy tale while she is a persecuted adult (or by means of a cow or an 'ear cornucopia'). Here the familiar (and socially authentic) device of infant exposure prompts the motif. Often too it is the magic animal which actually provides the wealth for dresses and jewellery for the ball; here these motifs only need to be associated.

27 The golden slippers set the plot up for a final slipper-test.

28 The 'flight from the ball' is enacted as the story of Pan, pursuing the nymph Syrinx till she finally disappears (there being no 'ball events' in timeless rural Lesbos).

29 The hero's taking of ancestral pipes resurfaces in a Scottish Cinderello tale; text in Philip (1989), 91–94 ('The finger lock'), where the supernaturally provided special bagpipes mark the hero's coming of age.

30 Frequently in folk versions the supernatural helper provides, often quite magically and abruptly, the wherewithal (gold, jewels, and the like) necessary to elevate the status of the hero/ine and so bring about the wedding. The at least semi-realistic novelist has to bring all this about naturally. The nymphs supplying information about the purse beside the stinking dolphin offer an ingenious way of embodying this motif, and so significantly advancing the plot. The dolphin adds another 'helpful animal' to the initial sheep.

31 Daphnis' parentage is revealed naturally by his peasant foster-father to save the hero from sexual exploitation. The tokens do not cause the recognition of Chloe as the runaway from the ball, but as the lost noblewoman exposed by a wealthy parent.

32 Megacles ('Bigshot') is now revealed as Chloe's father; despite the different motivation, the slipper test itself proceeds in a normal and recognisable way.

33 The basic outline of a *Snow White* story: the rival with 'prophetic' powers; a coded version of the heroine's name in her attendants 'white and rose-colour'; attempted murder in the woods; lethal sleep of the heroine.

34 The name of Anthia's jealous rival Manto actually *means* 'diviner', and so supplies the 'mirror on the wall' motif. Katoptromancy (divination by mirror) was known in Antiquity, but is not explicitly specified here.

35 Opie and Opie, 227–237; Jones (1983, 1990); Anderson (2000), 43–60; Kawan, *EM* 12 (2007), 129–140.

36 The name simply means 'Snow-girl', though translators do not hesitate to use 'Snow White', without intended reference to the modern tale. The heroine of the *Chione* romance is likewise fourteen and has multiple suitors.

37 For the rape of the heroine in a coma, cf. Basile's *Sun, Moon and Talia*, a *Sleeping Beauty* tale (Appendix 1). The modern tale expurgates the rapes but keeps the means (magical sleep, old woman disguise) to activate two further murder attempts instead.

38 With Sisyphus, an ancient master-thief, and so a suitable child of Mercury/Hermes.

39 She is finally killed by the jealous Diana/Artemis, not for her beauty but for her boasting: compare the murder of Niobe's children, Ovid *Metamorphoses*, 6.165–301, again because of their mother's boasting. Usually the last murder attempt is supplied by a pin driven into her head, an over-tight bodice, or the like.

40 The pyre eliminates any possibility of a happy ending or a glass case; though of course Semele survives death by conflagration (above c.2), so that a more optimistic ending is theoretically possible even when a pyre is used.
41 Literally 'little fist'. The Pygmalion tale is usually seen as a mythological tale in its own right, and Pygmalion is felt as uniquely associated with the love of a statue. In fact the motif has a wider frame of reference as a theme for ancient rhetoricians (pseudo-Lucian *Amores*, Philostratus *VS*, 598f., *VA*, 6.40). But the story in effect embodies the latter half of *Snow White*: the heroine in a coma, her worship by the dwarfs, and her revival by 'the prince'. A rare example of the folktale tradition has a dwarf marry the girl.
42 The living women of Cyprus whose behaviour is impure, in contrast to the unsullied purity of the statue itself.
43 For the worship of the statue of Aphrodite that a devotee intends to marry, cf. Philostratus *VA*, 6.40.
44 The Cnidians in the episode described by Philostratus are enthusiastic in support of the marriage, as potential propaganda for 'their' Aphrodite.

4

OTHERWORLDLY ENCOUNTERS

Ghost stories can show a good deal of diversity, as the two contrasting presentations of the haunted house serve to underline; returns from the dead to pick up property or visit a lover may differ still more widely. The animated servants in *The Sorcerer's Apprentice* underline the role of magic in creating little automata. Wrongful admission to the lower world takes us in yet another direction, closely followed by an ancient Rip van Winkle, and the mysterious Aristeas and Hermotimus whose souls take leave of their bodies. The curse of dying by day and reviving by night in a Greek wonder-romance adds a sinister side to Egyptian magic.

The Haunted House[1]: Lucian, *Philopseudeis* (*Lovers of Lies*) 29–32 (*ATU* 326A, Soul Released from Torment)

(29) At this point the Pythagorean[2] Arignotus[3] came in, the long-haired man with the impressive look, you know the one with a great reputation for wisdom, nicknamed 'the holy one'. And when I saw him I gave a sigh of relief: I thought to myself 'Good show!: a two-headed axe has arrived to oppose their falsehood. For the wise man will shut them up when they tell such marvellous tales'. And I thought that was the proverbial god from the machine who had been wheeled in by Fate. But when he had sat down – Cleodemus gave him his seat – he first asked about Eucrates' illness, and when he had heard from the patient that he was already feeling better, he asked 'What were you debating among yourselves? For I overhead it as I came in, and you seemed to be about to have a really good time'.

'What else', said Eucrates, 'but trying to persuade this man as hard as iron' – pointing at me[4] – 'to believe that there are such things as spirits and apparitions, and that dead men's souls walk about in the upper world and appear to anyone they want to?' For my part I turned red and looked down, out of respect for Arignotus, while he replied,

> Look, Eucrates, perhaps Tychiades is saying this, that only the souls of those who died a violent death go about, for example if a man hanged himself or had his head chopped off or was crucified or departed life in some such manner, but not those who died in the natural course of events; if that is what he is saying, it is not to be altogether written off.

'Certainly not', said Deinomachus, 'But he thinks that not even those ghosts exist, nor can they be seen in physical form'.

(30) 'What do you mean?', said Arignotus, giving me a nasty look: 'Do you think that none of these things occurs, even although practically everyone sees them?'. 'Cite in my defence', I replied, 'if I do not believe, that it is because I am the only person not to see them; if I did, I too of course would believe just like yourselves'. 'But', he said,

> if ever you go to Corinth, ask where the house of Eubatides[5] is, and when they point it out to you beside the Craneion, go in and say to the doorkeeper Tibeius[6] that you want to see the spot where the Pythagorean Arignotus raised the demon,[7] and drove it out and made the house habitable for the future.[8]

(31) 'What was that, Arignotus?', asked Eucrates. 'It was uninhabitable', was the reply,

> for a long period because people were afraid, and if anyone did try to live there he fled at once in terror, driven out by some fearful, frightful ghost. So it was already falling to bits and the roof was falling in, and absolutely no-one was brave enough to go in. When I heard this, I took my books – I have a great many Egyptian[9] ones on these kinds of subject – and I entered the house when people have their first sleep, although my host tried to get me to turn back, all but physically restraining me, when he heard where I was off to, into disaster with my eyes open, so he thought.[10] But I took a lamp and went in on my own, and putting down the lamp in the largest room I sat down on the floor and was busy reading; but the spirit confronted me,[11] thinking that he had come up against some layman and expecting to terrify me the way he had terrified the others – he was filthy and long-haired, and blacker than the darkness itself. And looking over me he tried to get the better of me, attacking from every side to try to overcome me, one moment as a dog, the next as a bull or a lion.[12] But I reached for my most blood-curdling curse, chanted it in Egyptian, and drove him into a corner of a dark room; after noting where he went down, I was able to rest for what remained of the night.

In the morning, when everyone was in despair for me and thought they would find me dead just like the others, I came out contrary to everyone's expectation, and went to Eubatides[13] with the welcome news that it was now possible for him to live there, since it was purified and free of its terrors. So I took him along, with many of the others – for they were following in amazement at the event, and leading him to the spot where I had seen the ghost go down, I gave orders to dig with picks and shovels. And when they did so they found a mouldering corpse buried some six feet down, with only the bones still in order. We took it up and buried it, and from that time the house has ceased to be troubled by ghosts.

(32) When Arignotus said this, a man of superhuman wisdom and respected by all, there was no-one else in the company who did not condemn me for my crass stupidity for not believing in such things, especially since it was Arignotus who had spoken. Nonetheless I did not flinch before his long hair or the reputation that surrounded him: 'What's this', I said, 'Arignotus? Even you have turned out just like the rest, you the only hope for truth, full of hot air and fantasies; for that proves the proverb: "Our treasure has turned to dross"'.

The Haunted House: Pliny the Younger, *Letters* 7.27.4–11 (*ATU* 326A)

(4) Now surely this account I shall give you, just as I heard it, is both more frightening[14] and no less amazing. (5) There was at Athens a spacious mansion house, but with a notorious and ominous reputation. The silence of the night was broken by the sound of iron, and if you listened more intently, the rattle of chains was heard, at first in the distance, then close at hand: soon an apparition appeared, an old man worn out with leanness and filth, with a long beard and hair standing on end; he had shackles on his legs, and chains on his hands that he kept shaking about. (6) So the inhabitants spent miserable and awful nights there as they stayed awake with fear. Illness would follow their sleepless nights, and as their fear increased, death would result. For from time to time too, even after the apparition had left, the recollection of it remained before their eyes, and fear was engendered that lasted longer than the reason for it. So the house was deserted and condemned to remain empty and was left exclusively to this awful figure; but it was on the market, either for sale or let, in the hope that someone unaware of such a dreadful thing might want it. (7) Now there arrived in Athens the philosopher Athenodorus,[15] who read the notice and heard the suspiciously cheap asking price, carefully found out all about it, and nonetheless or rather all the more (was eager to) rent it.[16] When it began to get dark, he gave instructions to be bedded down in the fore part of the house. He called for writing-tablets, pen and lamp; he sent all his servants to an inner quarter,[17] and turned his mind, eyes and hand to writing, to prevent a vacant mind from conjuring up imaginary

noises and empty fears. (8) First, as everywhere else, the still of night; then the clanking of iron and the moving of chains; he did not raise his eyes, nor did he stop writing, but strengthened his resolve and closed his ears. The hubbub became more intense and advanced, one moment audible at the door, the next in the room itself. He looked behind him, saw the ghost and recognised it from the description. (9) It stood and beckoned with its finger as if summoning him. But he gestured it to wait a little and returned to his writing, while the ghost rattled its chains about the writer's head; he looked round and saw it beckoning him as before. Without delay he took the lamp and followed. (10) It travelled slowly, as if weighted down with chains. After it turned into the courtyard of the house, it suddenly vanished. The moment he was alone Athenodorus gathered some grass and leaves and marked the spot. (11) Next day the authorities arrived[18] and gave orders for that specific place to be dug up. They found bones bound and held fast with chains; the bones were bare and corroded by the chains, now that the corpse had rotted away over time with exposure to the soil. They were taken up and given a public burial. Afterwards the house was duly free of the properly buried ghost.

Godfather Death[19]: Lucian, *Philopseudeis* 25 (ATU 332)[20]

And Cleodemus said,

> The things you saw are not new, nor has no-one else seen them, since I myself had a sight of something similar not long ago when I was ill, and Antigonus here was keeping an eye on me and looking after me. Now it was the seventh day of my fever, and the temperature was at its height. And everyone was outside, the doors were closed, and I was left alone. For you yourself, Antigonus, had given the order, in the hope that I should fall asleep. So then, as I was awake, there stood beside me a very handsome young man, wearing a white cloak, then he made me get up and led me through some chasm into Hades, as I immediately realised the moment I saw Tantalus and Tityus and Sisyphus. And to cut a long story short, when I arrived in court – Aeacus and Charon and the Fates and the Furies were there – someone like a king (Pluto, no doubt) was sitting reading off the names of the people about to die, as they had reached the end of their allotted lifespan.[21] The young man brought me in front of him. But he was annoyed and spoke to my guide: "His thread has not yet spun its full length", he said, "so let him be off. But see that you bring me the blacksmith Demylus, for he is living over the limit set for his spindle". And I ran back up full of glee, and that instant the fever left me. But I brought back the news to everyone that Demylus was about to die. He was our next-door neighbour, and people said that he too had some sort of illness. And it wasn't long before we heard the mourners wailing over him.

Godfather Death: Plutarch *Moralia* fr. 176 Sandbach (*ATU* 332)

We ourselves were there when Antyllus was recounting to Sositeles and Heracleon how he had not long before been ill, and the doctors did not expect him to survive. Now he came round a little from some shallow trance state, but did not do or say anything that suggested insanity, except that he maintained he had died and come back from death and would not die at all from that current illness, but the people who had brought him received a reprimand from their master.[22] They had been sent to fetch Nicandas, but had brought himself (Antyllus) instead. Now Nicandas was a shoe-smith, but someone educated in the palaestra and well known to many. Hence the young lads would go up and tease him as a runaway or someone who had bribed the messengers from the other world. But he himself clearly was uncomfortable and took it badly. At length he fell victim to a fever and suddenly died two days later; whereas Antyllus here recovered and is doing well, and is the most hospitable host.

The Ghost Reclaims Property[23]: Lucian, *Philopseudeis* 27f. (*ATU* 366, The Man from the Gallows)[24]

(27) As we were saying this the two sons of Eucrates came in from the palaestra, one already from the ephēboi,[25] the other about 15, and after greeting us they sat down on the couch beside their father; I had a chair brought in for me. As if reminded by the sight of his sons, Eucrates said: 'So may I have joy of these two sons', putting his hand on both of them,

> I am going to tell you the truth, Tychiades. Everybody knows how I loved my wife of blessed memory, the mother of these two sons. And I have shown it by what I did for her not only while she was alive, but when she died too, when I buried all her ornaments, and the clothes she liked when she was still alive. But a week after she died I was lying on the couch just as I am doing now, consoling myself in my grief; for I was quietly reading Plato's book on the soul.[26] And in the course of this Demainete herself in person paid me a visit and sat down beside me, just the way Eucratides here is doing now

(and he pointed to the younger of his sons: he immediately gave a shudder the way children do)[27]; in fact he had been pale for some time at the story. 'But when I saw her', Eucrates went on,

> I put my arms round her, gave a loud groan, and burst into tears. But she did not let me cry, but took me to task because I had not done everything for her[28]: I had not burned one of her gold sandals; she told me that it was underneath the chest where it had accidentally fallen. And because of that we had not found it and had only burned the one. We were still chatting when a confounded pet dog under the couch – it was a Maltese – gave a

bark,[29] and she disappeared at the sound of the barking. But the sandal was found underneath the chest and was burned afterwards.[30]

(28) 'Is it right to keep doubting these manifestations, Tychiades, when they are plainly visible and appear as everyday events?' 'Certainly not', said I. 'People who don't believe and are so insulting over the truth should get their bottoms spanked just like children – with a golden sandal!'

The Animated Avenger[31]: Lucian, *Philopseudeis* 18–20 (ATU 366)[32]

(18) 'At any rate the business about the statue', said Eucrates, 'you would hear not only from me but from all our household, as it was observed by everyone in the house, boys and men, young and old'. 'What statue was that?', I said.

'Did you not see as you came into the hall, an exquisite statue standing there, the work of the sculptor Demetrius?'. 'Not the discus-thrower, the figure crouching just at the moment of letting go, head bent back towards the hand holding the discus, with one leg slightly bent, looking as if he is about to spring up after his throw?'. 'Not that one', he said,

> since that too is one of Myron's works, the discus-thrower you mention. Nor do I mean the one next to it, the one tying a fillet round his head, for that is by Polyclitus. But leave aside the ones on the right as you come in, including the two tyrant-slayers, the works of Critias and Nesiotes. But if you see a figure beside the fountain – a pot-bellied man, receding, his body half exposed by the way his cloak is hanging, with some of the hairs of his beard blowing in the wind, and prominent veins, like a real man, that's the one I mean[33]. He is supposed to be Pellichus the Corinthian general.

(19) 'Why yes', I replied, 'I did see one on the right of the waterspout, with ribbons and withered garlands, and with his chest covered in gilt leaves'. 'I added those gilt leaves', said Eucrates, 'when he cured me when I was at death's door with the ague every other day'. 'So this fine Pellichus here is a doctor as well?', said I. 'Don't joke about it', said Eucrates,

> or the fellow will be after you in no time. For I am aware what great powers this statue has that you're laughing at.[34] Or do you not suppose that he can send fevers against anyone he pleases, if it is possible for him to send them away? 'May the statue be kind and gentle, since it is so manly! But what else do all of you in the household see him doing?'

'As soon as it's night', he said,

> he comes down from his pedestal and goes on his rounds about the house, and all of us meet him sometimes even singing, and he has never done

anyone any harm. For one has only to run out of the way and he passes on without troubling any of those who've seen him. And he actually takes baths often and has fun all night long, so that we can hear the water splashing.

'See then', said I,

if the statue isn't Pellichus, but Talus the Cretan, the offspring of Minos? For he too was a bronze man of some sort and went his rounds on Crete, and if he were not bronze, Eucrates, but wood, then there would be nothing to prevent his being not the work of Demetrius but of Daedalus. At any rate, from what you say, he too plays truant from his pedestal.

(20) 'Take care, Tychiades, or you'll be sorry for your joking later on. For I know what happened to the man who filched the obols we offer him at each new moon'.[35] 'It should have been something absolutely dreadful, for such an act of sacrilege', said Ion, 'How did Pellichus punish him, Eucrates? For I want to know, however much Tychiades here is going to disbelieve'.

There was a large quantity of obols lying at his feet, and some other silver coins had been fixed to his thigh with wax, and leaves of silver, discharging vows or payment for a cure from one of the clients he had cured of a fever. And we had a Libyan servant, a real villain,[36] who was a groom. This fellow planned to remove all those, and actually did so after waiting until after the statue had come down. And the moment Pellichus returned and found that he had been robbed, see how he punished the Libyan and exposed his crime. For the miserable wretch went round the hall in a circle all night, not able to get out, as if he had landed in a labyrinth,[37] until he was caught with what he had stolen at daybreak. And then when he was caught he had a bad thrashing, and did not long survive, but died a miserable death from being whipped, he said, each night, so that weals would appear on his body the next day.[38] In the light of this, Tychiades, make fun of Pellichus and me as if it seems I am a contemporary of Minos already in my dotage.[39]

'But Eucrates', I said,

while bronze is bronze and Demetrius of Alopeke produced it, not a maker of gods but a maker of statues, I shall not fear the statue of Pellichus, whom I should not have feared in the slightest if he had threatened me when alive.

The Sorcerer's Apprentice[40]: Lucian, *Philopseudeis* 33–37[41] (*ATU* 325*, cf. Christiansen *ML* 3020)

(33) For when I was still a young man living in Egypt (my father had sent me off in order to complete my education[42]), I wanted to sail up to Koptos and from there to visit (the statue of) Memnon and hear the famous

tones resounding in honour of the sunrise.⁴³ Actually I didn't hear what all the ordinary people hear, just a meaningless voice; but Memnon himself opened his mouth and gave me an oracle in seven verses,⁴⁴ and if it weren't off the point, I would quote the verses to you. (34) But it was on the voyage up-river that I happened to come across a fellow passenger, a man from Memphis, one of the temple scribes there, a man of amazing wisdom who knew everything about Egyptian culture. They said he had lived underground for twenty-three years in the sacred shrines, receiving instruction in magic from Isis.

'You're talking about Pancrates',⁴⁵ said (the Pythagorean) Arignotus, 'my own teacher, a holy man, with his head shaven, clad in linen, always thinking about something, not speaking good Greek, tall, snub-nosed, with his lips protruding, and thin in the legs'⁴⁶: 'the very man' he said.

And at the outset I didn't know who he was, but when I saw him every time we put the boat in doing all sorts of wonders, especially riding on crocodiles and swimming along with them, as they fawned and wagged their tails, I realised that he was a holy man, and little by little I insinuated myself into his friendship till I was his companion and associate, so that he made me a partner in all his secrets.

And in the end he persuaded me to leave all my servants behind in Memphis and share his company all by myself. He assured me that we would not be at a loss for domestic servants. And after that, that was our arrangement. (35) But whenever we arrived at a stop-over, the man would take either the bar for the door, or the broom or even the pestle, dress it up in clothes, pronounce some spell over it, and set it in motion, so that it looked to everyone just like a man. It would go off to draw water and buy boiled meat and get the meals ready, and acted as our servant and attendant. Then, whenever he was finished with its services, he would use another spell to make the broom a broom again or the pestle a pestle.

I was very keen to find out exactly how he did this, but there was no way I could. For he was very jealous over this, although he was very accommodating in every other way. But one day I hid in the shadows and overheard the spell without his knowledge – it was no more than three syllables. And off he went to the public square after giving the pestle its orders. (36) And the next day while he was doing some business there I took the pestle, dressed it up just as he had done, uttered the syllables, and told it to draw water. And when it had filled the jar and brought it back, I said: "Stop: and don't go on drawing water, but go back to being a pestle".⁴⁷ But it was no longer prepared to obey my instructions, but just kept on drawing water, until it filled the house with jar after jar full of water. I had no idea what to do, for I was scared that Pancrates would be furious when he got back, as indeed he was – so I took an axe and split the pestle into two pieces. But the two parts each took jars and instead of one servant I now had two. In the meantime Pancrates came on the scene and realising what had happened turned the things back into wood again, just as they were before my spell; but he slipped away and left me; he just disappeared and I don't know where he went.[48]

'So still', said Deinomachus', 'you'd know how to turn a pestle into a man?' 'Of course', said Eucrates, ' – at least half-way, that is: for it isn't possible for me to change it back the way it was, once it turns into a water-carrier, but there'll have to be a deluge when the house is flooded!'[49]

(37) Won't you old men stop talking all this nonsense about marvels? And if not, for the sake of these young boys put off till some other time these amazing and frightening tales, in case before we know it they're crammed full of frightful things and strange imaginings. So you should spare them and not get them used to hearing such things, which will disturb them all through life and make them scared of any sound by filling them with every kind of superstition.

The Tale of Philinnion[50]: Phlegon of Tralles, *Peri Thaumasiōn* 1(*ATU* 307?/425B?)

(1)…[the nurse] made her way to the door of the guest room, and by the light of the burning lamp she saw the girl sitting beside Machates. (2) The sight was so amazing that she could not wait any longer but ran to (the girl's) mother and shouted in a loud voice 'Charito!' 'Demostratus!' She thought they should get up and go with her to their daughter, for she appeared to be alive in the guest room with the guest, through some divine will.

(3) When Charito heard this amazing story, the news was too much for her and the nurse was overexcited, so that first she was apprehensive and fainted; after a little while she brought her daughter back to mind and wept. Finally she accused the old woman of being out of her mind and ordered her to leave her at once. (4) But the nurse protested and spoke out, insisting that she was in her right mind and well, while the mother was hesitating and unwilling to see her own daughter; with difficulty Charito in part was compelled by the nurse, in part eager to know what had actually happened, and went to the guest-room door. <And> as some time had elapsed, about a couple of hours since the nurse's announcement, Charito got there rather late, so that by now the pair were already asleep. (5) The mother peeped in and thought she recognised her daughter's clothes and appearance, but she had no way of finding out the truth, and thought she should let things be. For she expected to get up early and take on the girl, and if she should be too late, she would interrogate Machates about the whole business. For she thought he was unlikely to tell any lies about something so important. And so she went away without a word.

(6) But when dawn arrived it turned out that the girl had gone, either by divine will or slipping away of her own accord, while her mother was annoyed at her departure: she expected the guest to give an account from the beginning, and begged

Machates to tell the truth without concealing anything. (7) The young man was upset and at first didn't know what to say, but reluctantly he eventually admitted that her name was Philinnion. And he told her how she had come to him at first, and how much she had desired him, and that she had said she was with him without her parents' knowledge; and anxious to prove the truth of his story, he had opened the chest and taken out the gold ring he had received from her, and the breast-band she had left behind the previous night. (8) And when Charito saw such convincing evidence she cried out, and tore her clothes and cloak, and throwing off her head-dress she fell to the ground, and casting herself on the tokens she began grieving all over again. (9) When the stranger saw what was happening, with everyone hysterical and in mourning as if they were on the point of burying the girl, he became upset and begged them to stop: he said he would show them the girl if she returned. She was won over and told him to take care not to forget his promise to her. (10) When night fell and the time came when Philinnion usually arrived, they kept watch, anxious to know of her arrival, and she duly came. And when she came in at the usual time and sat on the bed, Machates pretended nothing was amiss, but wanted to get to the bottom of the whole business, in particular not believing that he was sleeping with a corpse who was so careful to come to him at the same time, and was still taking meals and drinking with him; he did not believe what the others had told him, and thought that grave-robbers had dug up the tomb and sold the clothes and the gold to the girl's father. So wanting to know the truth he secretly sent the slaves to call them. (11) And soon Demostratus and Charito arrived and saw her and at first were dumb and awestruck at the amazing sight, but then cried out loudly and fell on their daughter. But at that point Philinnion spoke to them:

> Mother and father, you were unfair to grudge me to spend three days with your guest in my paternal home, doing no-one any harm. So you will soon be sorry for your meddling, while I must go back to my appointed place. For I did not come here without divine approval.

(12) With this she immediately became a corpse, and was laid out on the bed, quite plainly such. Her mother fell on her and her father gathered round and there was terrific confusion and mourning all through the house because of their grief: this was an unbearable calamity and an unbelievable sight. And soon word spread through the city and reached me. (13) And so that night I held back the crowds gathering at the house, taking precautions that there should be no civil disturbance as a result of the spread of such a report. (14) At crack of dawn the theatre was full. After a full account had been received, it was resolved first of all that we should go to the tomb and open it, to see whether the body was on its resting place, or whether we should find the site empty. For it was not as long as six months since the girl's death. (15) And when we had opened the chamber to which all the family were transferred and laid to rest, all the bodies were seen to be lying on their biers, or their bones in the case of older burials, but at the spot where Philinnion had been laid and was known to have been buried we found only the iron ring that belonged to the stranger, and the gold cup, which she took

from Machates on the first night. (16) And at once we were amazed and dumbfounded; we went immediately to the guest room in Demostratus' house to see the corpse, to see if it was really visible. We saw it lying on the ground and we thronged to the assembly: what had happened was of great import, and incredible. (17) In the assembly there was vigorous uproar and scarcely anyone could make sense of the events, but first of all Hyllus stood up: he was reckoned to be not only the best seer among us, but also a skilful augur (on other occasions he had proved skilful in this craft). He ordered us to bury the girl outside the boundaries…

The Fairy Lover[51]: Eumelus fr. 8B Fowler

Arcas[52] the son of Zeus or Apollo and Callisto the daughter of Lycaon…was hunting with his hounds and came across one of the Hamadryad nymphs in danger of perishing when the oak-tree in which the nymph had been living was destroyed by a river in torrent. But Arcas turned back the river and secured the bank with an earthwork. And the nymph – her name was Chrysopeleia[53] ('golden dove') made love with him and gave birth to Elatus and Amphidamas, from whom the Arcadians came.

The Fairy Lover: Charon of Lampsacus *FGrH* 262 F12 (Schol. Apollonius Rhodius 2.476/83a)

For Charon of Lampsacus says that Rhoicus, seeing that an oak tree was about to topple as never before, told his slaves to prop it up. And the nymph about to die along with the tree appeared to him, thanked him for saving her life, and told him to ask her for whatever he wanted. And when he said that he wanted to sleep with her, she said that no harm would come of it, but he must have nothing to do with any other woman, and their messenger would be the bee.[54] And once the bee flew alongside while he was playing draughts. And having cried out too fiercely he had angered the nymph, so that she injured him.[55]

Alcestis[56]: Apollodorus 1.9.15[57] (*ATU* 899)

[Admetus wooed] Alcestis, the daughter of Pelias. But he had promised his daughter to the man who could yoke a lion and a boar to a chariot; Apollo performed the feat and gave them to Admetus, who brought them to Pelias and won Alcestis. And as he was sacrificing to celebrate the marriage, he forgot a sacrifice to Artemis; and so when he opened the bridal chamber he found it full of coiling snakes. Apollo told him to appease the goddess, and obtained the request from the Fates that whenever Admetus was due to die he should be freed from death if someone should volunteer to die in his place. And when the day came for him to die and neither his father nor his mother was willing to die for him, Alcestis died on his behalf. But Kore[58] (Persephone) sent her back up again, or as some say, Heracles fought with Hades <and brought Alcestis up to him>.

An Out-of-Body Adventure: Aristeas of Proconnesus[59] Herodotus 4.13–15 (cf. Stith Thompson Motif E721.1, Soul wanders from body in Sleep)

(4.13) Aristeas of Proconnesus,[60] the son of Caystrobios, says in his epic poem that possessed by Apollo he arrived among the Essedones, and that beyond them there live Arimaspi with one eye, and beyond them the griffins that guard the gold, and beyond these the Hyperboreans who stretch to the sea...[61]

(4.14) And I have said where Aristeas who has told us this came from, and I will give the account I heard about him in Proconnesus and Cyzicus. For they say that Aristeas, who was as nobly born as any of his fellow-citizens,[62] went into a fuller's shop in Proconnesus and died. And the fuller shut up his shop and went to tell the dead man's relatives. And when word had spread through the city that Aristeas had died, a man from Cyzicus arrived from the town of Artace (the port of Cyzicus) who disputed the report, declaring that he had met with Aristeas on the latter's way to Cyzicus and had been in conversation with him. And while he was insistently arguing, the dead man's relatives had arrived at the fuller's with the funeral preparations. But when the premises were opened up there was no trace of Aristeas, either dead or alive. And that after 6 years Aristeas appeared in Proconnessus and composed the verses which the Greeks now call the *Arimaspea*, and having done so disappeared a second time.

(4.15) That is the account given in these towns; but the people of Metapontum in Italy had this experience, 240 years after Aristeas' second disappearance, as I discovered by reckonings from Proconnesus and Metapontum. The Metapontines say Aristeas appeared to them and instructed them to dedicate an altar to Apollo, and set up a statue beside it of Aristeas of Proconnesus himself; he explained that Apollo had appeared in their territory alone among Italian peoples, and that now Aristeas followed him; when he had done so, he was a crow; and with that he disappeared. And the Metapontines say they sent to Delphi to ask the meaning of the vision of Aristeas. And the Pythia ordered them to obey the apparition, as it would be better for them. And after receiving this instruction they carried it out. And now there stands a statue of Aristeas beside that of Apollo, and round about it a bay-tree grove; the statue is in the market-place.

An Out-of-Body Misadventure: Hermotimus of Clazomenae Pliny the Elder *NH* 7.174, cf. Apollonius Paradoxographus *Mirabilia* 3 (Stith Thompson Motif E721.1.2.3, Soul of Sleeper prevented from returning by burning the Body)

We find among other examples that the soul of Hermotimus of Clazomenae used to leave his body and wander off, and would report from a distance many things that could not be perceived except by someone actually there,[63] while his body remained in a semi-conscious state, until enemies of his known as the Cantharidae[64] burned his body and removed as it were the sheath to which his soul was returning.[65]

The Long Sleep: Epimenides of Crete[66]: Diogenes Laertius 1.109, 115[67] (*ATU* 766, The Seven Sleepers)[68]

Epimenides,[69] according to Theopompus and many others, was the son of Phaestius, though others give him a father Dosiades, others again Agesarchas. He was a Cretan from Cnossus, though by letting his hair grow long[70] he belied his origins. This man was once sent by his father to search for a sheep in the wild; he turned off the way at midday and fell asleep in some cave[71] for 57 years.[72] Then he got up[73] and continued to look for the sheep, imagining that he had only slept for a short interval. But when he could not find the sheep, he returned to the farm, only to find everything changed[74] and another owner in possession, and he went back to the town in total confusion. And there, when he went into his own house, he came across people who wanted to find out who he was. At last he found his younger brother,[75] who was already an old man, and it was from him that he learned the truth. And so his reputation spread throughout Greece and people considered that he enjoyed divine favour.[76]

Paapis and the Magic Sleep: Antonius Diogenes, Photius *Codex* 166 (cf. Stith Thompson Motif E155.1, Slain Warriors Revived Nightly)

In this island of Thoule Deinias joins with a girl called Derkyllis and falls in love with her: she was from a noble family of Tyre, and was accompanied by her brother Mantinias. In keeping her company Deinias found out about the wanderings of the brother and sister, and all that an Egyptian priest Paapis did, who had moved to Tyre when his own land was being ravaged, and although he seemed in the first place kindly to his benefactors and their whole household, after that (he heard) all the mischief Paapis had done to the household and themselves and their parents. They arrived in Eryx, a town in Sicily, where she was arrested and taken to Aenesidemus, the ruler of Leontini. Here she fell in once more with the thrice-wicked Paapis, who was staying with the ruler...(later) Paapis, pursuing in the footsteps of Dercyllis and her companions caught up with them on the island (of Thoule) and imposed upon them by his magic art the pain of dying by day, and reviving at night.[77] And he put this on them by spitting directly into their faces. But one Throuskanos, fervently in love with Dercyllis, when he saw his love afflicted by the punishment inflicted by Paapis, and was madly distressed, made a sudden attack, hit Paapis with his sword suddenly and killed him, only thus finding a way to put an end to his countless mischief. And Throuskanos committed suicide when he saw Dercyllis lying apparently dead...Azoulis found the means of Paapis' magic, and how to rescue them from their suffering, having found the means of inflicting and curing it. From Paapis' magic bag he also found how Dercyllis and Mantinias could rescue their parents from their terrible affliction: Paapis had injured them by a ruse, under pretext of doing this for their own benefit, having made them lie for a long time as if dead. Then Dercyllis and Mantinias hurried to their home city to revive and rescue their parents.

Notes

1 Rölleke *EM* 5 (1987), 584–593; Stramaglia (1999), 144–162; Felton (1999); Anderson (2000), 112–114; Ogden (2007), 205–224.
2 Pythagorean: the sect did enjoy limited revival under the early Roman Empire, as evidenced by the prominence of the 1st-century sage Apollonius of Tyana, who likewise is credited with visiting Egypt and performing exorcisms. Pythagoreans early and late believed in transmigration of souls and had a reputation for mysticism, both traits put to malicious use here.
3 Arignotus: 'very well known' ('Professor Prestigio').
4 The speaker is the sceptical Lucian's port-parole Tychiades ('Son of Chance', 'Everyman').
5 Perhaps no more than a variation of Eucrates, the host and central character of the tales.
6 More corroborative detail, over which Lucian takes special care.
7 A supernatural being, covered by 'demon', 'ghost' or 'spirit' in English.
8 Arignotus acts throughout as his own self-publicist.
9 Many of the subjects of Lucian's ghost stories come from or draw upon the barbarian fringe of the Greek world. Magical papyri survive in Egyptian demotic as well as Greek: collection and translation in Betz (1986).
10 Arignotus emphasises the risks, in order of course to maximise his own superiority. The lamp for reading is a constant of the tale: the exorcist will be literate and needs to shut out distractions.
11 The vain Arignotus presents the ghost as haunting for haunting's sake, instead of pleading for a proper burial: the last thing the unburied dead wish to do is drive off the best chance of laying their own ghost.
12 The metamorphoses of the ghost seem to me (pace Ogden) out of place in the popular tale, and suggest rather that Arignotus is thickening the texture for effect; the absence of this detail from other versions also suggests as much. By contrast the curse to 'control' an unruly spirit has a more authentic feel.
13 As noted by Pliny commentators, the purely private action, to inform Eubatides, is not correct procedure, and the proper burial is a public matter, not least because the concealment of the improperly buried corpse is a criminal issue. In fact fuller versions of the tale can expect to include the corpse's explanation of how he came to be killed in the first place. Cf. Plautus, *Mostellaria*, 497–505, and Cicero, *de Divinatione*, 1.57; for the modern tale, e.g. Briggs (1970), 1.1.308.
14 More frightening than a rather tame story about a man dying in Africa after a prophetic dream in 7.27.2f. For the context of Pliny's trio of ghost stories, Baraz (2012), 116–130.
15 A likely candidate is the Stoic Athenodorus of Tarsus, an actual historical figure (PIR^2 A, 1288), friend of Augustus, though he has no other known connexion with Athens.
16 Less out of ambition, as in Arignotus's case, than out of curiosity.
17 As properly in the layout of a Greek house.
18 Once again supernatural appearances are a matter of civic concern and public safety: the authorities must be informed: compare most notably the case of Philinnion below. There is no speculation in either author as to the reason for the ghost to be buried where he was; nor is there any need. Burial could not have been allowed within city boundaries, and so any such would automatically point to a suspicious death. Pliny correctly has a representative of the community perform the burial of an unknown. Sherwin-White (1966) compares the *lex coloniae ursonensis*. See also Felton (1999), 62–76; Stramaglia (1999); Ogden (2007), 205–224.
19 Moser-Rath *EM* 5 (1987), 1224–1233; Anderson (2000), 115f.; Ogden (2007), 171–193.
20 A man is sent back from the dead because of a case of mistaken identity: the testimony is carefully co-ordinated with that of the doctor: it is important that the door is confirmed as shut. The story is carefully limited to the narrative viewpoint of the corpse, so that Hermes as *psychopompos*, escorter of souls, is not identified by name,

and Pluto's own identity is only inferred. The mistake seems to be a combination of 'the wrong house' (the intended victim lived next door) and the vague similarity between the names Demylus and Cleodemus. Examples from Augustine and Gregory the Great use the mistaken identity of two men of exactly the same name: texts in Ogden (2007), 173ff.
21 Lucian has a particular aversion to beliefs about the underworld, popular or otherwise, and this is an opportunity to score a point about disorganisation down below; but the tale itself is not his, as shown by the following example, which is chronologically earlier.
22 Once more Pluto and for example Hermes are not identified; nor in this case is any reason given for the confusion: the names are not similar, nor is there any indication that Antyllus had a similar occupation.
23 Drascek *EM* 9 (1999), 175–179; Anderson (2000), 114f.; Ogden (2007), 195–204.
24 A ghost comes back to reclaim lost property. This is generally told as a serious and cautionary tale, with horrific penalties for graveyard robberies, especially involving severed limbs or the plundering of gold body-parts.
25 A grouping for youth training, indicating an age in the late teens.
26 Plato's *Phaedo*, a favourite 'set text' for philosophical reflexion, combining discussion of the immortality of the soul with an account of the death of Socrates. It was favourite reading in exile for Dio of Prusa (Philostratus *VS*, 488).
27 A rare glimpse of child/adolescent reaction, indicating disapproval on Tychiades' part: Eucrates is already brain-washing the children with his own credulity.
28 There is just the faintest hint of a nagging wife about Demainete here, comically preoccupied with a trivial item: Lucian's implication is 'imagine the dead unable to rest just because of a forgotten shoe'.
29 Instead of a cock crowing, and again deliberately trivialising: Maltese dogs were 'toy' dogs and fashion accessories, to judge by Lucian, *de Mercede Conductis*, 34; he continues to trivialise in the banter following the tale.
30 Compare the case of Periander's wife (Herodotus, 5.92), which Lucian holds up to ridicule: Felton (1999), 78–81; Ogden (2007), 195–204.
31 Ogden (2007), 137–159.
32 An animated statue (of undistinguished nature) or manikin, to which people hung bizarre attachments, is responsible for the death of a thief.
33 Lucian takes care to emphasise that the animated statue is not a masterpiece of classical sculpture, but commemorates an ugly, droll, troll-like figure.
34 For the powers of healing statues, Ogden (2007), 145.
35 When bills were due to be paid: Aristophanes *Clouds*, 754ff.
36 And so a shifty barbarian.
37 Continuing the association of Pellichus with Talus the Cretan above.
38 Compare the fate of a servant beaten by witches in Petronius, *Satyrica*, 63.5–10.
39 Useful further parallels to the manikin in Lüthi (1976), 83–94.
40 Anderson (2000), 103–105; Hansen (2002), 35–38; Ogden, 231–270; de Blécourt, *EM*, 14 (2014), 1165–1168.
41 The celebrated *Sorcerer's Apprentice* tale is related to a genuine folktale: a novice gives orders to tiny servants from a magic book and has to find enough for them to do to break the spell. The master magician may be the devil himself.
42 Egypt is here seen as part of an ancient 'Grand Tour': see Casson (1974), 257–261, 271–286.
43 One of the two colossi was credited with emitting a sound as described; the effect was ended by reconstruction under Septimius Severus, some time after the current version.
44 Again, the teller is concerned to advertise his own credentials: even an Egyptian oracle honours him (cf. Heliodorus, 2.35f.: Calasiris claims a spontaneous oracle from Delphi).
45 Pancrates ('All-Powerful'), inviting confusion with one Pachrates, a genuine Egyptian name attached to a prophet from a temple in Heliopolis, who performed magical

demonstrations, including power over demons, in front of the Emperor Hadrian, and probably identical with the Pancrates of Athenaeus 15.677C, honoured with membership of the Museum at Alexandria.

46 The caricatural description represents a stereotypical view of the Egyptian seen through Greek eyes. A papyrus formula could be used for crossing the river on crocodiles' back: Harpocrates was depicted riding on crocodiles; the *historia monachorum* has anchorites doing so. See also 'Menas and the crocodile', c. 10 below. Lucian seems the likely perpetrator of the detail that the crocodiles fawn and wag their tales. Schwartz (1963) ad loc. comments on the absence of magical papyrus support for the precise feat described here.

47 The modern form of the tale usually deals with a magic book which produces little servants who cannot be kept busy enough; one has to invent a task beyond them to break the spell.

48 Sometimes the story ends in the turning to stone of the magician: perhaps the mention of the oracular statue of Memnon is a reflection of such a detail in the story.

49 The climax of the whole work as far as the sceptical Lucian is concerned: it is impossible for Eucrates to make good his boast, and so the audience has only to take his word for it.

50 Anderson (2000), 117–119; Hansen (1996), 79–85; (2002), 392–397. I have preferred *ATU* Type 307 to Hansen's allocation to Type 425J; but the tale is a curiosity by any reasonable criteria.

51 For an extended sequel to the story, below on Rhoicus.

52 For the case that this is an early King Arthur figure (as Arktouros), Anderson (2004; 2007).

53 For the case that this bird is the merlin, Anderson (2007), 231ff. There is circumstantial evidence to connect the story with the oracular activity at Dodona: Anderson (2007), 243f.

54 Jacoby notes instances where the bee-sting is a punishment for adultery.

55 For a resemblance to the medieval romance of Sir Launfal, Anderson (2007), 235. A third partial telling of the tale (Schol. Theocritus, 3.13c) has the unknown Rhoicus as a Cnidian, the tree located rather unexpectedly in Nineveh.

56 Megas *EM* 1 (1977), 315–319; Anderson (2000), 116f.

57 Apollodorus' version follows the latter of the two courses in order to involve Heracles. A second large-scale account exists in the late Latin verse tale *Alcestis Barcinonensis*. As a daughter of Pelias, Alcestis was one of her father's innocent murderesses at the instigation of Medea. Admetus ('undaunted') seems to specialise in the extant sources in getting other people to do unpalatable tasks for him. Artemis plays 'bad fairy' roles in which she takes offence and has to be placated by some kind of commuting of the sentence. Neither of Admetus' parents is willing to die on their son's behalf. In the Islamicised version in tale 5 of the Medieval Turkish *Book of Dede Korkut*, the angel Azrael takes the recalcitrant parents instead of the self-sacrificing wife. For Modern Greek versions, Kakridis (1949), Appendix 3.

58 Persephone having been the victim of premature abduction to Hades is not unmoved by such requests, most notably in such cases as Eurydice or Protesilaus.

59 This and the following notices on Hermotimus and Epimenides relate to a trio of wonder-workers who amaze by their bilocations, their capacity to disappear or their incredible feats of endurance; they are similar to the non-Greek figures who amaze in Lucian's *Lovers of Lies*.

60 For the background of Aristeas, Bolton (1962); Bremmer (1983), 25–53. Commentary: Asheri et al. (2007), ad loc.

61 The northern area of reference may be consistent with Aristeas' credentials as a shaman; but for scepticism about such a role, see now Bremmer (2002), 27–40: 'Travelling Souls? Greek Shamanism reconsidered'.

62 And so by implication a credible claimant.

63 Apollonius elaborates: he could foretell rainstorms, droughts, earthquakes and plagues, among other things.

64 'Sons of the Scarab-beetle'. An Egyptian association of this insect was with the sun and its powers of regeneration: presumably the cremators were professional rivals who wanted to test Hermotimus' own powers to destruction, and succeeded.
65 Apollonius *peri thaumasiōn* 3 adds a commemorative temple, from which women were excluded because of the wife's failure to protect the corpse.
66 Hansen, 392–397; Kandler *EM* 12 (2007), 662–666.
67 So Theopompus *Philippica FGrH* 115 F 67a; a similar account evidently based on the same source *FGrH* 115 F 67b in Apollonius *peri thaumasiōn* 1.
68 A 'Rip van Winkle' story, with some specific detail, as of a local legend. What is missing here is any account of what Epimenides thought he was doing in the interval, to correspond to Rip's encounter with the little man with a cask, and the mysterious lost valley with its ancient occupants. Hansen correctly compares the much later Christian Legend of *The Seven Sleepers of Ephesus*.
69 A real person, and so an appropriate hero of a tale of unexplained time-warp: he is credited elsewhere with out-of-body soul flights, and with purification of Athens after the Kylonian purge.
70 One marker of an impressive holy man, to judge from Lucian's description of Alexander of Abonouteichos, *Alexander* 11.
71 And so less likely to be found. According to Maximus of Tyre (16.1) the cave was that of Dictaean Zeus.
72 Sometimes, as in the case of the Seven Sleepers, the time is much longer.
73 He is however credited in Maximus of Tyre (16.1) with dreams of truth and justice in the interval.
74 More developed versions of the tale may signify change: the fall of Jerusalem to Nebuchadnezzar, in the story of Abimalech; the prevalence of Christianity, in the tale of *The Seven Sleepers*; the American Revolution, in the case of *Rip van Winkle*.
75 A family member is needed to vouch for the otherwise long-forgotten disappearance.
76 Compare the prestige of Lucian's figure Pancrates, who allegedly spent 23 years underground (but without timewarp), *Philopseudeis*, 34. Pliny (*NH* 7.134, 175) adds that Epimenides lived for only 57 days after the 57 years, but died at the age of 157. Hansen seems puzzled by the lack of motivation in the accounts; but Epimenides seems a prime candidate for just this kind of adventure.
77 This is highly unusual in classical practice: perhaps the nearest is the story of Castor and Pollux, who share their immortality by being alive on alternate days (Lucian, *Dialogi Deorum*, 25); or warriors slain by day and revived at night, Stith Thompson Motif E155.1.

5
SIREN WOMEN[1]

The fear of women as masters of magic is in evidence in a number of examples here, although Homer in particular is strangely reticent about the contents of the witch's brew, or for that matter its actual purpose, while St. Augustine saw it as to provide draft labour when required. I offer two presentations of an Empousa, among the nastiest of child-scarers; a revealing attempt by Dio of Prusa to make a blood-curling story of material he plainly does not take too seriously; and a view of Hylas that relates him to a fairy tale known to the Grimms.

CIRCE[2]: Homer, *Odyssey* 10.203–399 (cf. *ATU* 567; Stith Thompson Motif G263.1, witch transforms lovers into animals; cf. also Scobie, 1983, Type IIA)

(203) But I counted all my well-grieved comrades into two bands, and set a leader over each. I led the one, godlike Eurylochus the other. Speedily we shook lots in a bronze helmet, and out jumped the lot of courageous Eurylochus. And he set out, and with him 22 doleful companions; and they left us lamenting behind.[3] And among the glades they found the dwellings of Circe, built of polished stones in a wide clearing. And around about it were mountain wolves and lions, which she herself had enchanted when she gave them wicked drugs. But they did not rush at the men, but stood fawning with their long tails, and as when dogs fawn about their master as he returns from a feast, for he always brings titbits to delight their hearts – so did the wolves with their strong claws fawn on them. But they were afraid when they saw the dreadful monsters.[4] And they stood in the vestibule of the fair-tressed goddess, while they heard Circe[5] sweetly singing inside, as she moved back and forth before her divine loom, weaving the work that goddesses weave, fine, elegant and resplendent. And Polites, a leader of men, was the first to speak: he was my dearest and most

trustworthy companion: 'My friends, someone is moving back and forth before a great loom, sweetly singing,[6] and the whole floor resounds about her, either a goddess or a woman: but let us call her at once'. (229) And at this they raised a shout and called to her. She at once came out, opened the shining doors, and invited them in. And they all followed her unawares, but Eurylochus hung back, suspecting that this was a trap. And she brought them in and sat them down on couches and seats, and she mixed them a potion, cheese and barley meal, and yellow honey with Pramnian wine. But into the food she mixed wicked drugs, so that they should forget all about their native land.[7] But when she had given them it and they had drained their cups, then at once she struck them with her wand and shut them in the swine-pens. And they had the heads, the voice, the bristles and the shape of swine, but their minds remained unchanged, just as they were before.[8] And when they were penned up in tears, Circe tossed them mast and acorns and cornel-berries to eat, the kind of food that swine bedded on the ground are used to eating.

(244) But at once Eurylochus went off to the swift black ship to report on his comrades and their unseemly fate. Nor was he able to utter a word, for all his efforts, for he was distressed at heart with dreadful grief. And his eyes were filled with tears, and his spirit could only lament. But when all of us had cross-examined him in our bewilderment, he then told us the dreadful fate of the rest of his comrades:

> Illustrious Odysseus, we went through the woodlands as you ordered. Among the glades we found a fine palace built of polished stones in a wide clearing, and there someone moving back and forth at a great loom and singing in a shrill voice, either a goddess or a woman, and they raised a shout and called to her. She immediately came out and opened the shining doors and invited them in. And together they all followed, unaware. But I held back, suspecting a trap, and they all disappeared in a body, nor has any of them appeared again, although for a long time I sat and kept watch.

(261) At this I threw my silver-studded sword across my shoulders, a great sword of bronze, and put my bow about me, and ordered him to lead me back along the same road. But he took hold of me in both hands and entreated me by my knees and spoke winged words to me in his distress:

> Do not bring me there against my will, divinely nourished Odysseus, but leave me here. For I know that neither will you return, nor will you bring any other of your comrades back safely. But let us flee with these men all the quicker, for we may still escape an evil day.

At this I replied, 'Eurylochus, do indeed remain here in this place, eating and drinking beside our hollow black ship; but I will go; for me there is a compelling need'. With these words I went inland from the ship and the sea. But when as

I went through the sacred groves I was on the point of reaching the great house of Circe of the many potions, Hermes of the golden wand met me as I made my way there; he was in the guise of a young man, with the first down on his cheek, whose youthfulness is most appealing.[9] He clasped my hand and addressed me in these words:

> Where then, unfortunate man, are you wandering to alone on the slopes, with no knowledge of the place? These companions of yours are held like pigs in Circe's house, with stout-built sties as their quarters. Have you come here, then, to release them? I tell you that you will not return home either, and you will stay there with the rest. But come now, I will free you from your perils and save you. Take this powerful drug and go to the halls of Circe: it will protect your head from the evil day. And I will tell you all the dire ploys of Circe. She will make you a mixture, and throw drugs into the food. But even so she will be unable to charm you, for the powerful drug which I shall give you will not allow it; and I will tell you everything. Whenever Circe drives you with her long wand, then you must draw your sharp sword from your side, and rush at Circe, as if threatening to kill her. And she will be afraid and will tell you to go to bed with her. Then do not any longer refuse the goddess' bed, so that she may set your comrades free and look after you yourself. But order her to swear the great oath of the blessed gods, to prevent her from plotting any ill against your person, and so that having stripped you she may not do you mischief and unman you.[10]

(302) With this, the slayer of Argus[11] plucked a herb from the ground, and showed me its nature. It was black at the root, with a flower like milk. The gods call it moly. It is difficult for mortal men to dig it up,[12] but the gods can do all things.[13] Then Hermes made his way through the wooded island and went off to mighty Olympus, and I went on to the palace of Circe, and my heart was full of dark thoughts as I went. And I stood in the threshold of the fair-tressed goddess. There I stood and called, and the goddess heard my voice.

And at once she came out and opened the shining doors and called me in, while I followed with troubled heart. And she brought me in and sat me on a silver-studded chair, beautifully wrought. And underneath there was a footstool for my feet. And she made me a mixture in a golden cup, for me to drink, and in it she put a potion, with evil thoughts in her heart, but when she gave it to me and I drained it and it did not bewitch me, she struck me with her wand and spoke, addressing me: 'Go now to the swine-pen and lie with the rest of your companions'. At this I drew my sharp sword from my thigh and rushed on Circe as if threatening to kill her. But she gave a great cry, ran underneath and took hold of my knees, and spoke winged words to me in her laments.

> Who are you among men, and where do you come from? I am amazed that after drinking that potion you are not bewitched. For no other man

has endured this charm, when he has drunk it and it has first passed the barrier of his teeth. But you have a mind within you that is immune to the charm. You must be Odysseus, man of many wiles: the gold-wanded slayer of Argus always used to say you would come on your return from Troy in your swift black ship.[14] But come now, put your sword in its sheath, and then let the two of us go to my bed, so that after mingling in our bed of love we may trust each other.

(336) But to this I replied:

Circe, how can you ask me to show you mercy when you have turned my men into swine within your palace, and holding me here you ask me to go to your chamber with guile in your heart and go to your bed, so that once you have stripped me you can do me ill and unman me? And I should not be willing to enter your bed unless you would bring yourself, goddess, to swear a great oath not to devise any other wicked torture against me.

(345) At this she immediately swore the oath, as I instructed. But when she swore and made an end of her oath, then I mounted the beautiful bed of Circe. And meanwhile her handmaidens laboured in the halls, four girls who did her bidding in the palace. They are the offspring of springs and groves and sacred rivers, that flow forth towards the sea. One of them threw beautiful rugs on the chairs, and spread linen cloth below them. Another drew up silver tables, and set golden baskets on them. And the third mixed honey-hearted wine in a silver mixing-bowl, and put round golden cups. And the fourth brought water and kindled a great fire beneath a huge tripod, and heated the water.[15] But when it boiled in the shining bronze, she made me sit in the tub and washed me from the great tripod, mixing it delightfully over my head and shoulders, so that she took the soul-destroying weariness from my limbs; but then she washed me and anointed me with oil, and threw a beautiful robe and tunic round me and led me to sit down on a silver-studded chair, a beautiful work of art, with a stool under my feet. And a serving-maid brought water in a beautiful golden vessel, above a silver basin, for us to wash; and beside us she stretched out a polished table; and a respectable lady brought bread and put food generously before us, and told us to eat. But I was sad at heart and sat thinking of other things, with my mind full of ominous thoughts.

(375) When Circe noticed me sitting there and not putting my hands on the food, she stood near me and addressed me in winged words:

Why, Odysseus, do you sit like this, like someone who is dumb, eating your heart out, while you do not touch food and drink? Can it be that you suspect some other trick? But you have no need to fear, for already I have sworn you a binding oath.

But at these words he replied:

> Circe, what man in his right mind could venture to taste food and drink before freeing his comrades and seeing them face to face? But if indeed you sincerely bid me to eat and drink, free them, so that I may see my trusty companions with my own eyes.[16]

At this, Circe left the palace, wand in hand, opened the door of the swine-pen, and drove them out, looking like 9-year-old swine. They then stood facing her, and she went through them and anointed each with another potion. Then the bristles fell from their limbs, which the baleful drug that lady Circe had given them had previously caused to grow. And they became men again, younger than they were before, and much more handsome and taller to look at.[17] And each of them recognised me and clung to my hands, and each was possessed by passionate sobs, and there was a terrible hubbub all through the palace, and even the goddess felt pity for them.

The Innkeepers and the Ass[18]: Augustine, *City of God* 18.18 (cf. ATU 567)

For when I was in Italy I too used to hear such things from a certain region in these parts, when they used to say that women who ran inns and were skilled in these wicked arts would give to any wayfarers they wished <something> in cheese which at once transformed them into beasts of burden, and they would transport any sort of goods (*necessaria quaeque*), then return to their own shape[19]; but they did not acquire the mind of a beast, but retained their rational human faculty, just as Apuleius in the books which he entitled *The Golden Ass*, either reported or claimed that after the application of a drug he became an ass while retaining his human mind.[20]

Augustine *ibid.*: (Stith Thompson Motif E721.1 Soul wanders from body in sleep; dreams explained as experiences of the soul on these wanderings)

For a man by the name of Praestantius used to say that his father had happened to take that particular drug in cheese in his own home, and lay in his own bed apparently asleep, but no-one was able to waken him. Yet some days later, he maintained, his father seemed to have wakened and reported what happened in the form of dreams: to the effect that he had become a horse and along with other beasts of burden had carried their grain ration known as Rhaetic because it is sent to Rhaetia. It was found that it had happened just as he had reported, although it had seemed to the man himself that he was <only> dreaming.[21]

The Empousa at Corinth: Philostratus, *Life of Apollonius of Tyana* 4.25[22] (ATU 327A, Hansel and Gretel)

At that time there happened to be a philosopher in Corinth called Demetrius, who had adopted the full vigour of the Cynics…The effect of Apollonius on him was the same as that of Socrates' wisdom on Antisthenes: he followed him wishing to be his disciple, and applied himself to his teachings, and he directed the more reputable of his own students to Apollonius.[23] Among these was a Lycian called Menippus, a man of 25, of sound judgement and physically well endowed, so that he looked like a handsome, noble athlete.[24] Now Menippus, so most people supposed, was loved by a foreign woman: she had a beautiful appearance and a very refined look, and claimed to be rich, although she was really none of these things, but only appeared to be. For as he has walking all alone on the road to Cenchreae,[25] an apparition encountered him in the guise of a woman, who clasped his hand and claimed that she had long been in love with him. She claimed she was a Phoenician[26] woman, and that she lived in a suburb of Corinth, naming a particular one. 'Come there in the evening', she told him 'and you will hear me singing and drink wine such as you have never drunk before, and there will be no rival to bother you; and we shall live together as two beautiful people'.[27] The young man agreed to this, for strong as he was in everything else to do with philosophy, he was a victim when it came to passion, and he went to her in the evening and from then on paid her constant attention as his lover, not yet realising that she was only an apparition.

But Apollonius looked at Menippus with the eye of a sculptor,[28] and he formed a picture of the young man and looked intently at him, and after noting his weakness, he said 'You are a handsome young man hunted by beautiful women, but you are cherishing a serpent and she you'. And when Menippus was amazed at this, Apollonius added, 'because you cannot marry this woman. You ask the reason? Do you suppose she loves you?' 'Of course she does', Menippus replied, 'since she treats me as a lover does'. 'And would you marry her?', he asked, 'for it would be delightful to marry a woman who loves you'. So <the sage> asked: 'When will the wedding be?' 'In hot haste', replied Menippus. 'And perhaps tomorrow'. So Apollonius waited for the time of the meal and confronted the guests who had just arrived: 'Where', he said, 'is the lovely girl who invited you?' 'There', said Menippus, and with a blush he made to get up. 'And which of the two of you has provided the silver and gold and the rest of the adornments for the banqueting suite?' 'The lady', he replied, 'for I have nothing else but this', pointing to his philosopher's cloak.[29]

But Apollonius asked: 'Do you know of the gardens of Tantalus, that they exist and yet do not?'[30] 'In Homer', they said, 'for we have not of course been down to Hades'.

> This is how you must regard this adornment as well. For it has no substance, but only the appearance of such. And so that you might be aware of what I mean, this fine bride is an empousa,[31] whom most people think of as lamias and bugaboos.[32] These creatures fall in love, and they have sex, but most of all they desire human flesh and they entice with sexual enticement anyone they want to eat in their feasts.

But the apparition said, 'None of your sacrilegious talk! Get out!' And she pretended to be disgusted at what she heard, and no doubt she tried to make fun of philosophers and claimed that they always talked nonsense. But when the gold goblets and what appeared to be silver were proved to be light as air, and all leapt off out of their sight, the wine-pourers and the cooks and the whole staff of servants disappeared when confounded by Apollonius,[33] the phantom appeared to shed tears and begged him not to torture her or coerce her to confess her true nature,[34] but when he persisted and would not relax his efforts she confessed to being an empousa, and to be fattening Menippus with pleasures so that she could devour his body, for she was in the habit of devouring beautiful young bodies, since their blood is uncontaminated.[35]

Meeting an Empousa[36]: Aristophanes, *Frogs* 285–298[37]

(285) XANTHIAS: But I hear a noise.
DIONYSUS: Where is it? Where?
X.: Behind!
D.: You go behind!
X.: No, in front!
D.: You go in front this minute!
X.: Oh good heavens I see a huge beast –
D.: What sort of beast?
X.: Dreadful – at any rate it's like all sorts. (290) One minute a bull, one minute a mule, and then a very luscious young woman –
D.: Where is she? I'm off to meet her –
X.: It isn't a girl any more. Now it's a dog –
D.: Then it must be Empousa!
X.: Well, its whole face is alight with fire –
D.: And does it have a leg of copper?
X.: (295) Yes, by Poseidon, and the other one is cow-dung, I tell you –
D.: So where am I to turn?
X.: And me!
D.: Priest, protect me, so that we can have dinner together!
X.: King Heracles, we're finished!

Sirens/Snake-Women: Dio of Prusa, *Oration 5*

(5.1) To spend effort on a Libyan tale and waste time elaborating over such trifles is not an auspicious task; for these stories do not encourage the greatest of talents to imitation. And yet we must not dismiss it out of contempt for such idle chatter.[38] For perhaps (the tale) would offer us no small advantage if it led us to our moral duty and served as a comparison with things that are real and true.[39] And using one's powers in this way seems to me like the way farmers use plants, if it works, for sometimes they graft and implant domestic and fruit-bearing varieties on barren and wild stocks, and produce useful instead of useless and profitable instead of unprofitable plants.

Now in this way if a useful and profitable moral is injected into unprofitable tales these are not allowed to be mere idle tales. And perhaps those who first made them up did so for some reason of this kind, hinting and symbolising for those able to understand them correctly. 'So much by way of introduction to my ode',[40] as someone says. I have still to recite the ode itself or tell the tale, and sing to what we should best liken the human passions.

(5.5) It is said that at some time long ago there was some dreadful and savage species, mostly found in the uninhabited parts of Libya. For that country even today seems to produce all manner of creatures, reptiles and other beasts.[41] Among them was the species this tale is about, whose body was a sort of compound out of totally incongruous parts, an absolute monstrosity, and it roamed about as far as the Mediterranean at the Syrtes[42] in search of food. For it hunted both wild beasts – lions and panthers, as these beasts hunt deer and wild asses – and sheep, but took the greatest pleasure in hunting men. And for that reason it found its way to the settlements as far as the Syrtes. This region is a bay of the sea penetrating far inland, and so they say it is an uninterrupted three-day voyage. But those who sail in cannot sail out again: for there are shoals, cross-currents and long stretches of sandbar to make the sea totally impassable and difficult. For the sea bottom in that area is not clean, but is porous and lets the water in without a solid floor. And that I think is the reason for the huge sandbars and dunes: there is a similar effect on land caused by the winds, but in this case because of the surf. The surrounding land is much the same, desert and sand-dunes. But shipwrecked sailors travelling inland from the sea, or Libyans forced to cross the land or losing their way – these the beasts appeared to and dragged off.

(5.12) The nature and appearance of their bodies is like this: their faces are those of beautiful women, and their breasts and bosoms and neck are very beautiful, like those of no mortal girl or bride in her prime, nor could any sculptor or painter picture them.[43] The skin-colour was brilliant, and their glance inspired affection and desire in the hearts of any who looked at them. But the rest of the body was hard and armoured with scales, and their lower part was all snake. And their hindmost part was the snake's head, utterly horrific. Now we are not told that these creatures are winged, like the sphinxes, nor do they speak as sphinxes do, nor utter any other sound, except a very shrill hissing sound, as dragons do. But they are very swift overland, so that nobody could ever escape them. And other creatures they overcome by strength, but men by guile, affording a glimpse of their bosom and breasts and at the same time enthralling their onlooker and implanting a passionate lust for intercourse. And men would approach them as they would women, while they remained perfectly still and often looked down, like modest women; but when a man came close they would seize him, for they also had hands that were like claws, which they would conceal till that moment. And so the serpent would at once sting the victim and kill him with its poison. And the snake and the other part of the beast would devour the corpse.

(5.16) This tale, then, was not invented for a child, to make it less rash and unruly, but for those who suffer greater and more total madness; since we have brought it to this point we should perhaps be able to show the nature of the appetites, that they are irrational and bestial, since they offer us a glimpse of some sort of pleasure, enticing the foolish by trickery and bewitchment and destroying them in the most poignant and pitiful way. And we must put these examples before our eyes and be afraid of them just as those bogeymen scare children[44] whenever they are aroused out of turn with a desire for food or play or something else – so we ourselves, when we have a desire for luxury or money or sex or reputation or some other pleasure, should not approach these wicked desires and be seized by them to destroy us and annihilate us in the basest possible way. And of course it would not be difficult for a leisured talker with more time perhaps on his hands than he ought to have, to interpret the rest of the myth as well in this way.

(5.18) For they add that some king of Libya set out to destroy this species of creature, enraged as he was at the destruction of his people. And he found many of them settled there, having taken over a dense wild wooded region beyond the Syrtes. So raising a huge force he found their dens: for they were easily visible from the tail-tracks of the serpents, and the dreadful stench from their lairs. Having so surrounded them on all sides he hurled fire into <the dens>, and after being cut off they were destroyed with their cubs, and the Libyans quickly took flight, resting neither night nor day, until, reckoning that they had a long start, they came to a halt beside some river. But those of the creatures who had been away hunting, as soon as they realised their dens were destroyed, pursued the army to the river, and destroyed the whole army, taking some of them as they slept, the rest exhausted by their efforts. At that point, then, the work of destroying the species was not brought to an end by the king. But later on Heracles, purifying the whole earth of monsters and tyrants arrived there too, set fire to the area, and those that were escaping the flames he cut down, clubbing those that attacked him and shooting with his arrows those that tried to run off.[45]

(5.22) So the tale perhaps hints that when someone of the many tries to purify his soul as if it were an inaccesible region full of dreadful monsters, and taking out and destroying the species of desires, expecting to be free of them and make a complete escape, but not doing it thoroughly, a little later this is lost and totally destroyed by his remaining desires. And Heracles son of Zeus and Alcmene saw it through and proved his mind to be pure and gentle, and that this is what his taming of the earth sets out to indicate.[46]

(5.24) Would you like me, then, to delight the youngsters as well by adding a short tailpiece to the story? For they so totally believe it and are so convinced it is true that they say that at some later time one of this species appeared to a party of envoys from Greece to the shrine of Ammon, with a heavy escort of cavalry and archers. For they thought they saw lying on a sand-dune a woman with a sheepskin thrown over her head, as Libyan women do, but she was exposing her bosom and breasts and her neck was thrown back; and they took her to be one of the courtesans from one of the villages going there for the crowd, and two young men struck by her appearance went towards her, one outrunning the other. But the creature, when she caught him, swept him down into a hollow in the sand and ate him up. And the other lad running past saw what had happened and raised the alarm, so that the rest of the party ran to help. But the creature rushed at the lad snake part foremost, killed him and made off with a hiss. The body was found rotting and putrifying. And the Libyan guides would not allow anyone to touch the corpse, as this would have meant death for all.[47]

Hylas and the Nymphs: Antoninus Liberalis 26 (*ATU* 316)

(1) When the Argonauts had designated Heracles as their leader, he brought along with him the orphaned son of Ceyx, Hylas, a young good-looking boy. (2) When they arrived at the narrows of the Black Sea and were passing the headland of Arganthone, there was a storm, and a swell: they dropped anchor and rested from the voyage. And Heracles prepared the heroes' dinner. (3) But Hylas went with a pail to the river Ascanius to draw water for the heroes. The nymphs saw him, daughters of the river, and fell in love with him, and as he was drawing the water they drew him down into the spring. (4) And Hylas disappeared, but Heracles when he did not return left the heroes and looked everywhere in the woods and kept shouting his name. The nymphs were afraid that Heracles would find that they were hiding him, and they changed Hylas to an echo which often replied to Heracles' shout… (5)… The local population still sacrifice to Hylas beside the spring, and the priest hails him three times by name and three times the echo replies.[48]

Notes

1. On Circe Page (1973), 51–69; Schönbeck *EM* 3 (1981), 57–59; Heubeck-Hoekstra (1989), 50–74. Scobie (1983), 229 classifies Circe's transformative witchcraft as his type IIA. It contains the motif of the observer who does not eat the magic food and can accordingly outwit the witch.
2. The tradition of the beautiful but cruel otherworldly enchantress who enslaves men in animal form is much older than the *Odyssey*: Gilgamesh enumerates the metamorphosed victims of Inanna/Ishtar, (VI ii–iii, Dalley, 78f.); and the tradition in the Near East continues in the Arabian Nights' *Tale of Bedr Basim* and others (Page, 60ff.). Overall Homer seems to sacrifice the logic of the tale in favour of smooth integration into the *Odyssey*.
3. The first expedition is largely redundant: Odysseus himself could have hung back like Eurylochus and received Hermes' help at that point. Eurylochus and his men do not of course recognise the enchantment at the time. For a slightly different perspective, Page, 53ff.
4. But not, as later in Apollonius Rhodius, assemblages of the spare parts of animals to make horrid hybrids (*Argonautica*, 4.672–682).
5. Daughter of the Sun, according to *Odyssey*, 10.138.
6. The oral style of the Epic allows the fact of Circe's movements at the loom to be reported well-nigh verbatim, on the grounds that one action merits only one description and is perceived in the same way each time, largely regardless of the angle of vision of the reporter.

7 Circe's witches' brew is remarkably consistent, right up to the comparisons of St. Augustine, below.
8 The description of the metamorphosis is very cursory, as if Homer wants to maintain an atmosphere of domestic realism throughout: Ovid puts the report into the mouth of one of the crew, Macareus (*Metamorphoses*, 14.248–307), with rather more emphasis on how the changes affect the victim. The purpose of the metamorphosis is not made clear, and it may not have been clear to Homer: often, but not always, in mythological tradition metamorphosis serves as a punishment. There is not a preponderance of draft-animals here, nor a suggestion that the animals will be used for either food or bestial practices.
9 A 'normal' form of theophany throughout ancient literature.
10 It is odd that Circe should prefer to enchant and dehumanise Odysseus rather than seduce him, again a detail drawing attention to the lack of firm motivation in Homer's version.
11 Argeiphontes (Slayer of Argus): the exact nature of Argus is not clear: Gantz, 201f.
12 For speculation on the nature of *moly*, Page, 64–68.
13 Hermes as the god of tricksters, rogues and good luck tends to play 'magic helper' parts in ancient fairy tale. The role of Hermes in the *Arabian Nights*' version is played by a friendly sheikh who tips off Bedr Basim (Page, 61).
14 Something of a lame contrivance, as in the corresponding recognition-scene of the Cyclops story, below c.8.
15 Again touches of opulence and secrecy characteristic of fairy-tale fantasy ('in the palace in the wood…').
16 Something of an afterthought, and not for the first time for Odysseus…
17 A rather lame excuse: compare Odysseus' transformation at the hands of Athena for the Nausicaa episode, 6.227–237.
18 Scobie (1983) studies Apuleius' *Golden Ass* and the following two examples under *AT* Types, 567, 449A and *ML*3045; Marzolph *EM* 14 (2014), 292–295. Augustine for his part shares a common North African background with Apuleius, though the first episode is located in Italy.
19 Here, in contrast to the presentation of Circe, there seems to be genuine motivation for the transformation.
20 Cf. Yolen (1986), 308ff. ('The Blacksmith's wife of Yarrowfoot').
21 Some kind of hallucinogen seems to be implied. Cf. the description of a witch's flying ointment in Apuleius 3.21 and Harper (1977), 105.
22 Philostratus introduces a popular local tradition with a veneer of philosophy, as far removed as possible from the presentation in 'Hansel and Gretel': Scherf *EM* 6 (1990), 498–509. Demetrius the Cynic is a genuine historical figure, friend of the Younger Seneca and of Paetus Thrasea.
23 Apollonius enjoys a kind of unchallenged superiority throughout the *Vita Apollonii*.
24 Philostratus, or one of his family, is interested in physical description, especially in *Heroicus* and *Gymnasticus*.
25 One of the ports of Corinth.
26 And so an oriental voluptuary…
27 She is singularly direct: compare the overtures of Melite, the Ephesian widow, to Clitophon in Achilles Tatius, 5.11.5f.; but these are done, as traditionally, by a go-between.
28 Again, Philostratus has an interest in art work as part of his *paideia*, and may well be the author of the first set of *Imagines*.
29 Menippus has no resources of his own, so at least the foreign woman is not parasitic on his wealth.
30 Gardens of Tantalus: usually expressed as having receding and returning waters, hardly the same idea as here (cf. *Odyssey*, 11.582–592).
31 A 'nasty', notably described to Dionysus in Aristophanes *Frogs*, 288–294, below. See also below c. 11.

32 Lamias and bugaboos: traditional child-eating monsters used to scare children: e.g. Plutarch *Moralia*, 1040B; Strabo, 15.3.
33 Illusory banquets are an orientalising theme, expressed in a number of ways in vernacular texts. One thinks of the feeding of the 4/5,000 in the Christian gospels (Mark, 6.37–44, 8.1–9; Matthew, 15.32–39); but also of the tale of *Judar and his brothers* in the *Thousand and One Nights*, where a Moorish magician can produce a meal from a mysterious container, (Dawood, 341f.).
34 Evil spirits normally remonstrate against the interventions of the exorcist or holy man: cf. Mark, 5.6–10.
35 Compare Hansel and Gretel; empousas feed on human flesh. This might be true of innocent pre-pubertal children used in human sacrifice, but less likely for a 25-year-old fully-grown man.
36 K.J. Dover on *Frogs*, 286–298.
37 Dionysus the god is en route to the underworld, and being naturally cowardly in Comedy he tries to put his servant Xanthias between himself and a shapeshifting apparition. Empousa's shape as a beautiful woman suggests a siren quality; it may well be, as Dover suggests ad loc., that Xanthias is having fun at Dionysus' expense. Empousa could be identified with Hecate herself, as at Aristophanes fragment 515.
38 A good example of the condescension which attaches to popular storytelling, dismissed as trivial by a political idealist such as Dio, but lavishly indulged just the same.
39 Such nonsense has to have a didactic motive attached in order to legitimise it.
40 Cf. Plato, *Laws*, 722D.
41 On the *Libycus*, Anderson in Swain (1999), 154–156. Sophistic preambles (*prolaliae*) frequently draw their material from exotic locations in order to entertain the audience with diverting fare before settling into a more serious agenda.
42 A whirlpool region off the coast of Libya, proverbially inhospitable.
43 The overall function of the creatures appears to be similar to that of the Homeric Sirens (*Odyssey*, 12.158–200); but the latter are sometimes depicted in visual sources as winged, and not serpentine.
44 I.e. by terrifying fairy tales.
45 Philosophic tradition often idealises Heracles as a purifying crusader.
46 Compare the parable of the choice of Heracles (Virtue rather than Vice) in Dio's first Oration (1.58–84).
47 A reminder that Dio apparently considers a horrifying as well as obscene tailpiece as suitable for young ears.
48 Strabo (12.4.3) describes a re-enactment of the search for Hylas at a local Bithynian festival; and the local Mariandyni were noted for their style of ritual lament. The three times repeated cry and sacrifice corresponds to the threefold sacrifice described in Grimm tale 181, 'The Nixie in the Pond', where the objects offered are a comb, flute and spinning-wheel. The modern tale is more complex than the Hylas story, with a beginning in which the boy's father is tricked into promising his son to the supernatural agent:

> A poor miller is tricked into promising his new-born son to a water-sprite. When the boy grows up he is apprenticed to a hunter, becomes one himself, and acquires a wife. On a hunting-expedition he unknowingly washes beside the millpond and is taken by the water-sprite. The wife has it revealed to her that only if she offers first a comb, then a flute, then a spinning-wheel, will her husband be progressively revealed to her. They are united, but have to change to a frog and toad when the pond floods, before finally finding each other in human form.

6
REWARDS AND PUNISHMENTS I

The magical world is evident once more in Hephaestus' version of the 'himphamp' or magic trap as a punishment for adulterers. Likely to incur the severest divine displeasure are impiety to the gods, especially by murder, sacrilege or in the breaking of the laws of kinship or hospitality (*The Cranes of Ibycus*; *Erysichthon*; *The Log as Life-token*; *Philemon and Baucis*); so too is the reneging on bargains ('*The Pied Piper of Troy*'). The moral dimension of fairy-tale often asserts itself against foolish greed, as in several variants on *The Three Wishes*. Perhaps most characteristic among the repertoire of Fairy-tale punishments is Mercury's lengthening of an ungrateful woman's nose!

The Magic Trap[1]: Homer, *Odyssey* 8.266–366[2] (*ATU* 571B, Lover Exposed)

(266) But the lyre-player struck up a sweet song about the love of Ares and the lovely-garlanded Aphrodite: how first they slept together in secret in the house of Hephaestus, and how Ares gave her many presents, and shamed the marriage-bed of Lord Hephaestus. But at once Helios came with the news, since he saw them making love together. And when Hephaestus heard the painful tale, he went off to his forge, plotting malicious revenge from the bottom of his heart, and placed his great anvil on its block and cut out bonds that were unbreakable and inescapable, so that they should stay stoutly in place. But when at last in his anger against Ares he had forged his trap, he went to his bedchamber, where his own bed stood, and he draped the thongs around the bedposts and hung many down from the ceiling like fine spider-webs, so that no-one, even among the blessed gods, could see them, so cleverly were they forged.[3] But when he had hung all his trap about the bed, he made to go to Lemnos, the stoutly built citadel, by far the dearest land of all to him. Nor did Ares of the golden reins keep watch,

when he saw the famous smith Hephaestus going off, but he made for the house of far-famed Hephaestus, desiring the love of well-garlanded Cythera[4]. And she had just arrived from her father, the mighty son of Cronos, and had sat down. He came into the house, and clasped her and spoke to her in these words[5]: 'Come, my darling, let us go off to bed and lie down, for no longer is Hephaestus in the country, but already I suppose he is off to Lemnos, to the savage-tongued[6] Sintians'.[7] At this she thought it delightful to lie down. The pair went to the couch, and lay down to sleep. But round them fell the bonds forged by the cunning Hephaestus. They could not stir their limbs nor raise them up. And then at last they realised that no longer could they escape. And the illustrious god with the limp in both legs approached them, after turning back before reaching the land of Lemnos, for Helios had been on the lookout for him and had given him the word. And he made for his own home with a heavy heart, and stood in the vestibule as savage anger took hold of him. And he raised a terrible roar, and shouted to all the gods[8]:

> Father Zeus and other blessed and everlasting gods, come here so that you may see laughable and intolerable acts, how Aphrodite daughter of Zeus continually dishonours me as a cripple, and loves hateful Ares, because he is handsome and strong-limbed, but I am ill-shaped; yet no-one is to blame for that but my parents, who should never have conceived me. But you shall see how the pair went into my bed and are lying down together in the act, and I am stricken at the sight. Not that they will want to lie like this any longer, amorous as they are. Soon the pair of them will not feel like love-making, but my trap and bonds will hold them both until her father pays back all my wedding gifts[9] that I gave him in my wedding settlement for this shameless girl, because his daughter is good-looking but unfaithful.

(321) At this, the gods crowded towards his house with its bronze threshold.[10] Poseidon the earth-holder came and Hermes the helper, and the far-darting lord Apollo. But each of the lady goddesses stayed at home out of embarrassment. And the gods, givers of good things, stood in the vestibule, and unquenchable laughter arose among the blessed gods when they saw the clever devices of cunning Hephaestus. And one would say to the next:

> wicked deeds do not prosper: the slow catches the swift, just as now Hephaestus, slow as he is, has caught Ares, swiftest as he is of the gods who live on Olympus; and lame as Hephaestus is, he has done it by craft. And this calls for an adulterer's fine.

Such things they would say to one another. But Lord Apollo, son of Zeus, spoke to Hermes: 'Hermes, son of Zeus, guide and giver of good things, would you be willing to sleep in bed beside golden Aphrodite though pressed with strong bonds?'. Then the Argus-slaying guide answered him: 'Would that this might happen, far-shooting lord Apollo: would there were three times as many implacable bonds about us and you gods and all the goddesses looking on, if only I might sleep beside golden Aphrodite'.

(343) At this the immortal gods burst out laughing,[11] but Poseidon did not laugh, but kept praying Hephaestus, the renowned craftsman, to free Ares, and spoke to him in winged words:

'Free him, and I will pay you all your dues as you ask with the immortal gods as witnesses'. The far-famed doubly-lamed one answered him: 'Do not make me this request, Poseidon holder of the earth. Sureties are worth little for people worth little. How could I bind you among the immortal gods, if Ares should walk off, avoiding his debt and his bonds?'

(354) Then once more Poseidon the earthshaker replied: 'Hephaestus, should Ares escape the debt and run off, I myself shall pay you this'. Then the renowned doubly-lamed one answered: 'It is not possible, nor would it be right, to doubt your word'.[12]

(359) With this the mighty Hephaestus freed the bonds, and the pair, once set free from the strong fetters, at once leapt up: Ares went to Thrace, and laughter-loving Aphrodite went to Cyprus, to Paphos, where she has her precinct and her sweet-smelling altar. There the Graces washed her and anointed her with immortal oil, such as the immortal gods wear, and clothed her in lovely garments, wondrous to behold.[13]

The Life-Token Log: Ovid, *Metamorphoses* 8.425–525 (*ATU* 1187, Meleager; Stith Thompson Motif D2063.1.1, Tormenting by Sympathetic Magic)[14]

(425) Meleager pressed with his foot on the boar's deadly head,[15] and so announced: 'take my rightful share of the spoil, Nonacrian lady,[16] and may my glory be shared with you'. At once he gives her as spoils the boar's back, bristling with stiff spines, and the head, amazing for its great tusks. The author of the gift and the gift itself delighted her; but others were jealous, and there was a murmur across the whole band; from among them the sons of Thestius[17] held forth their arms with a great shout: 'Come, lay it down, girl, and do not usurp the honours due to us, nor let confidence in your beauty deceive you, or the lovesick giver of the gift will be not be able to help you!' And they took the gift from the girl and denied him the right to give it. The son of Mars Meleager could not bear this, and seething with swollen anger he exclaimed: 'You must learn, you who rob someone else's honour, how far deeds are different from threats', and with sacrilegious steel he drained the breast of Plexippus, who had not expected such an act. Toxius did not know what to do, and wanted at the same time to avenge his brother and feared his brother's fate. Meleager did not allow him to hesitate long, as he warmed with kindred blood once more the weapon still warm from the previous slaughter.

(445) Althaea was in the act of bearing thank-offerings for her victorious son into the temples of the gods when she saw the corpses of her brothers brought in. She filled the city with beating of breasts and pitiful wailings, and exchanged her gold-embroidered robes for black. But as soon as the murder was revealed, all her grief fell away and was turned from tears to a desire for vengeance.

(451) There was a log which the three sisters (the Fates) placed on the fire as Thestius' daughter was resting after her birth-pangs[18]; and as they firmly pressed the fatal threads with their thumbs, they chanted 'we give you, newly born baby, the same lifespan as the log'.[19] After they had made their prediction and left, Meleager's mother snatched the burning branch from the fire and sprinkled it with running water. For a long time it lay hidden away in the most secret of shrines,[20] and by its preservation it preserved your own life, young Meleager,[21] as well. His mother brought out this log and ordered torches and kindling to be put in place, and set the pyre alight with the hostile flame. Then four times she tried to set light to the brand, and four times she checked her impulse: the mother in her fought against the sister,[22] and her two opposing names (sister and mother) dragged her one heart back and forth. Often her face grew pale in fear of her future crime; often her seething anger gave a redness of its own to her eyes. And now her expression was like that of someone threatening some cruel deed, now her face you could suppose was capable of pity; and when the fierce ardour of her spirit had dried her tears, she nonetheless found still more tears, and as a ship, snatched by the wind and the tide running against it, feels the twin force and in its uncertainty tries to obey both, so did the daughter of Thestius wander between her confused feelings, in turn laying aside her anger and reviving it once laid aside. But the sister began to gain the upper hand over the parent, and to soothe her brothers' shades with blood she was pious in her impiety. For after the destructive flame grew strong, she exclaimed: 'May this dreadful pyre cremate my own flesh and blood', and as she held the fatal brand in her implacable hand, the wretch stood before the sepulchral altars and said: 'Triple goddesses of punishment, Eumenides,[23] turn your faces to your Furies' rites! I avenge one crime as I commit another; death must be assuaged by death; one crime must be added to another, one funeral to another; may an impious household perish in a heap of mournings. Should happy Oineus rejoice in his victorious son, should Thestius lose his offspring? Better for both to mourn. You now, my brothers' spirits, new ghosts, be aware of my duty and accept your funeral offerings shed at great price, the evil offspring of my own womb. Alas, in what directions am I being snatched? Brothers, pardon a mother, my hands are not equal to the task they have begun: I confess he has deserved to die; I cannot approve his executioner. So will he get off unpunished, and swelled by his own success hold the kingdom of Caledon, while you lie there, a tiny pile of ash and cold shades? I for one will not allow it; let the villain die and let him drag with him his father's hopes, his kingdom, and the ruin of his country! Where are my motherly feelings? Where are the pious duties of parents, and the pangs I bore for ten whole months? If only you had burned as a child with the first flames, and I should have suffered then.

You lived by my gift. Now you shall die by your own desert. Take the rewards of your deed, and give up the life twice given, first by birth, then by the removal of the brand, or add me to my brothers' burials. I want to act, yet cannot. What am I to do? Now my brothers' wounds are before my eyes, and the picture of that awful slaughter. Now duty and a mother's name break my resolve. Woe is me! You shall overcome in great misfortune, brothers, yet overcome nonetheless, provided that the solace I shall give to you, I myself shall follow as I follow you'.

(511) With this she turned her face away and, her right hand trembling, she threw the fatal firebrand into the midst of the flames. The brand itself either gave or seemed to give a groan, as it was caught by the unwilling flames and burned.[24]

(515) Unaware and far away, Meleager is burned by that very flame and feels his innards scorched by unseen fires, and overcomes his great pangs with courage. And yet he bewails the fact that he is dying a cowardly death in which no blood is shed, and declares Ancaeus happy for the wounds he sustained from the boar. Amid his groaning he calls on his aged father, his brothers, his dutiful sisters, his wife, with his dying breath; perhaps he even calls on his mother. The flames and the pain increase and then subside again: both are extinguished together and gradually his spirit departs into the insubstantial air, as white ash covers the glowing embers.[25]

'The Pied Piper of Troy':[26] Strabo 13.1.48; Apollodorus 2.5.9; 2.6.4; Servius on *Aeneid* 1.550 (*ATU* 570*, The Rat-Catcher; Stith Thompson Motif D1427.1, The Pied Piper of Hamelin)

There is no continuous 'Pied Piper' tale surviving in classical literature; but the three testimonia below show that the musician Apollo had an early reputation for dealing with a plague of rodents; and that he and Heracles in turn punished a city whose ruler refused to pay for services rendered by causing the removal of its children. The motif of the [lame] child that got away is also present.

(Strabo 13.1.48) In this place, Chrysa, there is also the temple of Sminthian Apollo; and the symbol which maintains the etymology of the title Sminthius, namely the mouse, lies under the foot of the god's image. These are the works of Scopas of Paros; and associated with the site is the history or the tale (*mythos*) about the mice. When the Teucri arrived from Crete (Callinus, the elegiac poet, first handed down an account of them, and many others have followed), they received an oracle to remain on whatever spot the earth-born should attack them. They say this happened to them round Haxitus. For at night a great multitude of field-mice swarmed out of the ground and chewed through the leather in their weapons and equipment. And there the Teucri stayed. And they named the site Ida after Mount Ida in Crete. Heraclides says that the mice swarming round the temple were regarded as sacred, and for this reason the statue is constructed with its foot resting on the mouse.

(Apollodorus 2.5.9) Apollo and Poseidon wanted to test the arrogance of Laomedon, and disguising as men they contracted to build the walls of <the

Trojan citadel>, the Pergamum, for pay. When they had done so Laomedon refused to pay. So Apollo sent a plague and Poseidon, a sea monster, carried up by a flood. (Servius on *Aeneid* 1.550) And so when Apollo was consulted…he said that maidens should be offered to the monster. When this had happened often and following an outcry Laomedon's daughter Hesione had been bound to a rock, a good many parents preferred to send their daughters abroad rather than lose them at home; for others handed them over to merchants to carry off.[27] (Apollodorus, 2.5.9, 2.6.4) Seeing Hesione exposed, Hercules promised to save her in return for the mares Zeus had paid as compensation for the seizure of Ganymede. Laomedon agreed to pay, and Hercules killed the monster and saved Hesione. But as Laomedon <again> refused to pay,[28] Hercules sailed off, threatening to make war on Troy… when he had captured the city he shot down Laomedon and his sons except Podarces[29] [Priam].

Moses and the Plague of the Firstborn: Exodus 8–12[30] (*RSV*)

(8) Then the Lord said to Moses:

> Go in to Pharaoh and say to him, Thus says the Lord: let my people go, that they may serve me. But if you refuse to let them go, behold, I will plague all your country with frogs; the Nile shall swarm with frogs which shall come up into your house, and into your bedchamber and on your bed, and into the houses of your servants and of your people, and into your ovens and your kneading bowls; and the frogs shall come up on you and on your people and on all your servants.

And the Lord said to Moses, 'say to Aaron, Stretch out your hand with your rod over the rivers, over the canals, and over the pools, and cause frogs to come upon the land of Egypt!'. So Aaron stretched out his hand over the waters of Egypt; and the frogs came up and covered the land of Egypt. But the magicians did the same by their secret art, and brought frogs upon the land of Egypt. Then Pharaoh called Moses and Aaron, and said, 'Entreat the Lord to take away the frogs from me and from my people; and I will let the people go to sacrifice to the Lord'. Moses said to Pharaoh, 'Be pleased to command me when I am to entreat, for you and for your servants and for your people, that the frogs be destroyed from you and your houses and be left only in the Nile'. And the Lord did according to the word of Moses; the frogs died out of the houses and courtyards. And they gathered them together in heaps, and the land stank. But when Pharaoh saw that there was a respite, he hardened his heart, and would not listen to them. (*Numerous plagues later, and as many broken promises*) (12.29) At midnight the Lord smote all the first-born in the land of Egypt, from the first-born of Pharaoh who sat on his throne to the first-born of the captive who was in the dungeon, and all the first-born of the cattle. And Pharaoh rose up in the night, he and all his servants, and all the Egyptians; and there was a great cry in Egypt, for there was not a house where one was not dead.

Snow White's Revenge: Servius Auctus on *Aeneid* 4.250

The Nile was the lover of Callirhoe, daughter of Ocean: from these parents was born a girl called Snow White; while she lived in the country <she was raped by a peasant>.[31] Jupiter ordered Mercury to raise her up and mingle her with the clouds. Hence it came about that the snows which the Greeks call *chiones*, symbolising the girl's pure life before her outrage, cling more to mountains; and so falling as snow they lay waste the crops, to show their revenge for the outrage she endured from the peasant.

The Spoilt Child: Cycnus Antoninus Liberalis, *Metamorphoses* 12[32] (Stith Thompson Motif H.1010, Impossible Tasks)

(1) Apollo and Thurie,[33] the daughter of Amphinomus, had a son called Cycnus. This boy had a handsome appearance, but his character was without charm and boorish. He was obsessively devoted to hunting, and lived in the country halfway between Pleuron and Calydon.[34] And he also had very many admirers because of his beauty. (2) But Cycnus in his arrogance[35] would have nothing to do with any of them. And soon he was loathed by his other admirers and abandoned, and only Phylius remained loyal to him. But Cycnus insulted even this admirer to excess. For at that time there appeared a huge lion in Aetolia,[36] which savaged men and flocks alike. (3) So Cycnus instructed Phylius to kill it without the use of a sword. He promised to do so and destroyed it by the following trick. Knowing what time the lion would be on the prowl he filled his stomach with a great deal of food and wine. And when the animal approached, Phylius vomited the food. (4) And the lion was so hungry that it took this food, and had its senses dulled by the wine, while Phylius covered his arm with clothing he was wearing and obstructed the lion's mouth. And taking up the corpse and laying it on his shoulders he brought it back to Cycnus and enjoyed widespread acclaim for his feat. (5) But Cycnus imposed another feat even more absurd: for in that region there were vultures, colossal creatures, who killed many men: these he commanded Phylius to take alive and bring back by any means whatever. (6) Now Phylius was at a loss at this command, but providentially an eagle that had snatched a hare let it fall half-dead before it could take it off home. And Phylius dismembered the hare and smeared its blood on himself and lay on the ground. So the birds set on him as if on a corpse, and Phylius, taking a grip of two and holding them fast, brought them home to Cycnus.[37] (7) But he imposed a third task, more difficult still. For he asked Phylius to bring a bull from the herd[38] with his bare hands and take it to the altar of Zeus. Phylius was at a loss as to how to respond to the order; he asked Heracles to come to his aid.[39] And in response to this prayer there appeared two bulls in heat over a single cow, and striking each other with their horns they fell to the ground. But Phylius, since they were exhausted, took one of the bulls by the legs and brought it to the altar, but at the wish of Heracles he

ignored the boy's further orders. (8) Cycnus was furious to be ignored, contrary to his expectation, and in despair he threw himself into the Conopic lake as it is called and disappeared.

And in addition to his own death, his mother Thurie threw herself into the same lake. And at the wish of Apollo both became birds on the lake. (9) And after they disappeared the lake too changed its name and became the Cycnaean lake, and at ploughing time many swans appeared there. And nearby stands the tomb of Phylius.[40]

The Cranes of Ibycus[41]: *Suda* s.v. Ibycus (*ATU* 960A)

Having been captured by robbers in a deserted place, [Ibycus] said that even the cranes which happened to be flying overhead would be his avengers. And he was in fact murdered, but after this one of the robbers seeing cranes in the city said: 'Look, the avengers of Ibycus!' But someone heard this and made enquiries about what had been said: the robbers confessed to the event, and were brought to justice: hence the proverb came about 'The cranes of Ibycus'.

Plutarch, *Moralia* 509E–510A (*ATU* 960A)

Were the murderers of Ibycus not captured by the same means? While they were sitting in the theatre and cranes came into view, they whispered laughingly to one another that the avengers of Ibycus had arrived. For those sitting beside them who overheard, as Ibycus had already disappeared for a long time and was being looked for, picked up on the remark and reported it to the authorities. And having been convicted in this way and led off for punishment, they were not punished by the cranes but by their own weakness of tongue, as if forced by a Fury or Avenging Spirit to confess to the murder.

The Grateful Dead: Cicero *de Divinatione* 1.27.56f. (*ATU* 505)

An instance concerning Simonides[42]: when he had seen some unknown person lying dead and had buried him, and intended to board a ship, he seemed to receive a warning from the man he had benefited by burial: if he sailed, he would die in a shipwreck. And so Simonides came home safe, but those who sailed on that ship were lost.

Foolish Wishes: *Appendix Perrotina* 4 (Stith Thompson Motif J2072.3)

Once two women had accorded Mercury[43] a mean reception, and entertained him on the cheap. One of them had a little boy still in the cradle, while the other had chosen to trade as a prostitute. (5) So in order to pay them back for their (miserable) services, Mercury had told each of them as he was about to leave and already going out the door: 'the person you see before you is a god[44]; I will grant you right away anything you ask'. The mother asked to see her son in a beard as soon as possible; (10) the prostitute asked that whatever she touched would follow her. Mercury flew off, and the women went back inside. Amazingly, the child began to bawl – in a beard; and when the prostitute was consumed with laughter at this, her nose filled up with mucus, as it does. (15) And so as she wished to blow her nose she took it with her hand and dragged it out till it touched the floor.[45] And as she laughed at someone else's misfortune, she too turned into an object of laughter.

Foolish Wishes:[46] Ovid, *Metamorphoses* 11.90–145 (*ATU 775*; Stith Thompson J2072.1 Short-sighted Wish)

(90) But Silenus was absent (from Dionysus' revels): the Phrygian peasants captured him tottering with old age and wine, and bound with garlands they led him to king Midas, to whom Orpheus and Eumolpus, from the city of Cecrops, had handed down orgiastic rites. The moment he recognised his associate and companion in the holy rites, he merrily celebrated the advent of his guest for ten successive days and nights. And already the eleventh dawn had driven off the lofty host of the stars when the joyful king went into the territory of Libya and restored Silenus to his pupil. To Midas the god gave the welcome but useless choice of whatever gift he pleased, delighting in the recovery of his teacher. Midas, destined to abuse his gift, said: 'bring it about that whatever I touch with my body should be turned into tawny gold'. Dionysus agreed to his wishes and paid him with a gift sure to harm him, saddened that he should not have chosen better.

(106) The Berecynthian[47] Midas went off delighted with his misfortune, and tested the truth of the promise by touching individual objects. And scarcely believing in his own powers, he pulled down a branch of a young holm-oak, a branch burgeoning with green; the branch turned to gold. He lifted a rock from the ground; the rock too turned pale with gold. He touched a clod of earth; at his powerful touch the turf became a lump of metal; he pulled off ears of dry corn; the harvest was golden; he held an apple taken from the tree; you would think he had received the apples of the Hesperides. If he put his fingers to the high gates, the gatepost seemed to shine. And even when Midas had washed his hands in liquid water, the flowing water would have served to deceive Danae. He could scarcely contain his hopes in his mind, as he imagined everything turned to gold. As he rejoiced his servants set before him tables laden with banquets, with an abundance of boiled fruit. Then at last if he had touched the fruits of Ceres with his hand, the fruits of Ceres would harden; or if he made to chew his meal with greedy teeth, he brought his teeth down hard on food that was tawny metal. If he had mixed the wine-god, giver of the gift, with pure water, you would see the wine flow solid through his open mouth. (127) Astonished at the strange misfortune, and both rich and wretched, he wished to escape his wealth and hated what he had only just prayed for. No amount of wealth could relieve his hunger. Arid thirst parched his throat, as he was deservedly tortured

by the hateful gold. He stretched his hands and resplendent arms to the sky, and exclaimed 'Pardon, father Lenaeus, god of the wine-presses, I have done wrong. But have mercy and wrench away my glittering curse'. The power of the god is kindly: Bacchus restored the man who confessed his wrongdoing and destroyed the gift he had given to honour his promise:

> You are not to remain surrounded by the gold you craved: go to the river that borders mighty Sardis, and make your way facing the river on its downward path; follow the high banks until you come to the source of the river. Bathe your head and body alike in the largest of its foaming springs, and as you do so wash away your ill-starred deed.

The king immersed himself in the stream as the god had ordered. The force of the gold touched the river and left the human body for the stream. Even to this day the pale fields are solid, their clods sodden with gold, having taken on already the seeds of the old vein.

The Foolish Wish: Aelian, *Varia Historia* 4.25[48]

Thrasyllus from the deme Aexone contracted an amazing and novel kind of madness. For he left the city and went down to the Piraeus, and lived there. He used to think that all the ships that docked there belonged to him, and wrote down their names and sent them off again, and was absolutely thrilled when they returned safely. For a long time he continued to suffer from this mental aberration. But his brother arrived from Sicily and handed him over for cure to a doctor, and through this he recovered his wits. But often he harked back to the time he spent in his delusions, and declared that he had never enjoyed himself as much as when in those days he was delighted at the safe return of ships which did not belong to him.[49]

Hospitality Rewarded: Philemon and Baucis[50] Ovid, *Metamorphoses* 8.618–724 (*ATU* 750B, Hospitality Rewarded)

(618) The power of heaven is immense and has no bounds, and whatever the gods have willed is accomplished. And to lessen your doubt, there stands an oak-tree next to a lime[51] on the Phrygian uplands, surrounded by a little wall. I myself have seen the place[52]; for Pittheus sent me to the fields of Pelops, once ruled over by his own father. Not far from this site is a marshland once capable of supporting life, but now a lake crowded with gulls and marsh-coots.

Jupiter once came there in mortal guise, and with his father came the grandson of Atlas,[53] the bearer of the caduceus, but with wings laid aside.[54] A thousand households they approached looking for a place to sleep; a thousand households barred their doors. But one household did receive them, tiny as it was, thatched with straw and marsh-reeds. But in that cottage the dutiful old Baucis and

Philemon her equal in years had been married in their youth, and in that cottage they had grown old together.

(633) They lightened their poverty by acknowledging it, and they bore it with resignation. It did not matter whether you looked there for masters or servants[55]: the pair were the whole household; the same pair both obeyed and gave the orders. So when the celestials reached their tiny household gods, and entered through their humble doorposts, bowing their heads, the old man laid out a couch, and invited them to rest their limbs; and busily Baucis threw over it a rough cloth and stirred the warm cinders, and brought yesterday's fire back to life and nourished it with leaves and dry bark, and with her ageing breath she brought it back to flames. And she brought down finely-split sticks and dry twigs. She broke them up and put them under the tiny copper kettle. And from the cabbage her husband had collected from their well-watered garden she removed the (outer) leaves; he took a two-pronged fork and lifted the smoked back of a pig hanging from a blackened beam, and cutting a tiny part of the back long preserved, he softened the cut portion in the boiling water; meanwhile they beguiled the passing time with their chat...

...A soft sedge-mattress was placed on a couch with willow frame and feet. This they covered with cloths, which they were accustomed to spread only at festival times, but even the drape was cheap and old, not unworthy of the willow couch. The gods reclined. The old woman tucked up her skirts and laid the table with trembling, but one of the three legs was shorter than the others. She used a tile to make it level. After this was put underneath and the slope was righted, she wiped her levelled table with green mint. Here were laid the two colours of olive, the berry of the guileless Minerva, and autumn's cornel-cherries pickled in vine-lees, and tiny onions and radishes and cream cheese, and eggs lightly cooked over the warm ashes, all on earthenware plates. After this a mixing bowl was set down, wrought of this same silverware, and beechwood cups, their hollow insides smeared with yellow wax. There was a short delay and the hearth sent forth its steaming feast, and wine of no great age was once again brought, then set aside to allow a small space for the second course. Here there were nuts, figs mixed with wrinkled dates, fragrant apples in wide baskets, and purple grapes picked from the vines; there was a white honeycomb in the middle,[56] and above all, friendly faces came to the table, and spontaneous and generous goodwill.

(679) Meanwhile they saw the mixing-bowl fill up again of its own accord as often as it was drained, and the wine too filling up by itself.[57] Astonished at the strange sight, the pair were terrified and made a prayer by turning their hands upwards, as Baucis and timid Philemon prayed for pardon for their food and their lack of preparation. There was a single goose, the guardian of their tiny estate, which the masters made ready to sacrifice to their divine guests. But the quick-winged goose tired out the pair slowed down by their age, and for a long time it escaped them and at last seemed to flee for refuge to the gods themselves, who told them not to kill it. 'We are gods, and your wicked neighbourhood will pay the punishment it deserves. But you will be granted immunity from this

punishment; only leave your home and follow our footsteps and go together to the mountain tops'.[58] Both obeyed, and leaning on their sticks, they struggled to plant their steps on the long slope. They were a single bowshot from the top when they turned their gaze and saw the other dwellings sunk in a marsh, and only their own home remaining.[59] And as they showed their amazement and bewailed the fate of their neighbours, that old house, tiny even for its two masters, changed into a temple.[60] The forked supports gave way to columns. The thatch turned yellow and assumed the appearance of a golden floor. The gates were highly wrought and the earthen floor was covered in marble. Then the son of Saturn spoke gently to them: 'Tell me, dutiful old man and wife worthy of a dutiful husband, what is your wish?' Philemon spoke a few words with Baucis; he revealed their common decision to the gods:

> We ask to be your priests and to guard your shrines, and since we have spent our years together in harmony, may the same hour take us both, nor may I ever see my wife's funeral pyre, nor should I be buried by her.[61]

Their prayers were granted. They served as the guardians of the temple, as long as life was granted to them; but worn out with the weight of years, as they chanced to be standing before the sacred steps relating the disasters that had befallen the place,[62] Baucis saw Philemon put forth leaves and Philemon, the older of the two, saw Baucis do the same. And already as the treetops were growing over their two faces, while they still could they exchanged their words: 'Farewell, husband', 'Farewell, wife,' they said together, as at the same time the bark covered over their lips and hid them.[63] Still on that spot the native Bithynians point out the neighbouring stocks from their twinned trunk. This was told me by old men who were not fools (nor had they any reason to deceive)[64]; I myself saw garlands hanging down over the branches,[65] and as I placed new ones there I said: 'Those the gods look after are themselves divine; those who worshipped are themselves to be worshipped'.[66]

Hospitality Denied: Ovid, *Metamorphoses* 6.317–381 (*ATU* 750E8, Flight to Egypt[67])

(317) One of them begins[68]: 'The farmers of old in the fertile Lycian fields did not spurn the goddess unpunished: the story is not well known because the men were humble,[69] yet it is amazing; I myself was there and saw the lake and the site famed for its miracle. For my father, already advanced in years and not able to travel a great distance, had told me to drive down from there choice oxen, and had given me a Lycian guide; and as I went the rounds of the pastures with him we actually saw in the middle of the lake the dark embers of an ancient altar standing surrounded by trembling reeds. The guide stood and with a fearful whisper exclaimed 'Have mercy on me', and in a like whisper I repeated 'Have mercy on me'. I was asking whether this was an altar of the Nymphs or Faunus or of a local deity, when my guide gave me this account: 'It is not a mountain spirit in this

shrine, young man. The goddess whom Jupiter's consort once banned from the earth claims it as hers…And now, when the hot sun scorched the fields in the land of Chimaera-bearing Lycia, the goddess (Latona), weary with her long labour, dried out with thirst from the heat of the sun, and drained of her breast milk by her greedy offspring, happened to see a little lake in the floor of a valley. There country folk were gathering osier bushes, and reeds and grasses from the marsh. Titania[70] approached and knelt on the ground to drink from the cool water. The peasant throng denied her, and the goddess replied as they barred her:

> Why do you prevent me from drinking? Water is for everyone.[71] Nature has not given anyone ownership of sunshine or air or gentle water; I have come to what is a service for all. But I beg and implore you to give it to me. I was not preparing to bathe my limbs and weary members, but only to relieve my thirst. Even as I speak my mouth is dry, my throat feels parched, and I am scarcely able to speak. A mouthful of water will be nectar to me, and I will acknowledge that it has saved my very life. By allowing me water you will have let me survive. Let these two children[72] persuade you, as they stretch out their tiny arms from my breast

(and by chance the children were indeed stretching out their hands). Who could have remained unmoved by the goddess' persuasive words? But these men persisted in barring her for all her pleas, threatened her if she did not keep her distance, and added insults besides. Nor was that enough: they also disturbed the very lake as well with their hands and feet, and moved the soft mud back and forth from the bottom of the lake with their malicious leaps. Latona's thirst gave way to anger, for now Coeus' daughter could no longer beg or bear to speak further to the unworthy in less than divine words, and lifting her palms to the heavens she said: 'May you live for ever in your precious swamp!'

(370) The goddess' wishes came to pass: it pleases them to live under water and now let all their limbs sink in the hollow marsh: one moment to lean their heads forward, one moment to swim in the whole lake, often to stand on the bank of the swamp, often to jump into the lake, but now too to indulge in their quarrels shamelessly. And though under water they still try to speak ill even there. Their voice too is now raucous, and their inflated necks are swollen. And their very din distends their spreading jaws. They stretch their unsightly heads, their necks seem to have gone. They have green backs; their stomachs, the greater part of their body, are white. They jump in the muddy water as new-formed frogs'.[73]

The Two Suitors: *Appendix Perrotina* 16 (Stith Thompson Motif K1371.1, Lover steals Bride from Wedding with Unwelcome Suitor; N721, Runaway Horse carries Bride to her Lover)

Two youths were wooing the same girl. The rich one won against the nobility and good looks of the poor one. But when the day fixed for the wedding arrived,

(5) the disappointed lover, as he could not bear his grief, made his way to the gardens next door; a little beyond them the rich man's country mansion was about to receive the girl from her mother's bosom, because his house in town had not seemed large enough. The procession sets forth, a huge crowd gathers (10) and Hymen carries the marriage-torch in front. But a little ass that used to make a little for the poor man was standing at the threshold of the gate. The bride's people happened to hire it to save the bride's feet from the hard plod of the road. (15) By the mercy of Venus there is a sudden wind storm, a thunderous crash in the sky, and at the same time a hard hail-storm scatters her fearful colleagues in all directions, (20) everyone forced to run for their own safely. The little ass comes into his familiar shelter nearby and announces his presence with a loud bray. The servants rush out, see the beautiful girl, and admire her; they announce the news to their master. (25) He is sitting amid a tiny group of companions consoling his lost love with drink after drink. When he hears the news, his joy is rekindled. And with wine and love cheering him on, he performs the sweet wedding rites amid the applause of his companions. (30) The bride's parents seek their daughter with a crier, the new 'husband' grieves for the loss of his wife. After the townspeople found out what had happened, they all approved the mark of divine favour.

The Fairy's Revenge[74]: Ovid, *Metamorphoses* 8.738–878 (cf. *ATU* 779E, The Dancers of Kolbeck)[75]

(738) Nor did the wife of Autolycus,[76] and daughter of Erysichthon, have lesser powers[77]: her father was the kind to scorn the divine power of the gods and offered no sacrifices on their altars. He is even said to have violated the grove of Ceres with his axe, and ravished the ancient groves with his steel.[78] There stood among them a huge oak strengthened by the years, one tree a grove in itself; fillets and mindful tablets and garlands wreathed its middle, proofs of the power of prayer.[79] Often beneath the tree nymphs led their festal dances; often with their hands linked together in line they encircled the measure of the trunk, and the measure of its wood was 15 ells; and it towered as high above the rest of the wood as the wood did above all the grass. And yet the son of Triopas[80] did not for that reason hold back his axe, and he ordered his servants to fell the sacred oak[81]; and when he saw them hesitate to obey the orders, the villain snatched the axe from one of them and uttered these words: 'Even if she were a goddess, let alone the favourite of one, now she shall touch the earth with her leafy top'. With this while he held his weapon poised for his slanting stroke, the Deoian[82] oak trembled and gave a groan,[83] and at the same time leaves and acorns alike began to pale, and the long branches too took on a pallor. And when his impious hand made its wound in the trunk, blood flowed from the severed bark, just as when a great bull falls victim before the altar, as the blood pours from the break in its neck. All were aghast, and one of the crowd dared to deter his sacrilege and stop the savage axe. The Thessalian

saw him and said 'receive the reward of a pious heart', and turning the steel from the tree to the man lopped off his head, and cut the oak with blow after blow. And from the heart of the oak a voice like this was heard: 'I am the nymph beneath this wood, dearest to Ceres, and as I die I prophesy that the punishment of your deeds is at hand, and this consoles me in my death'[84]. Erysichthon completed his crime, and the tree, tottering under innumerable blows and pulled down by ropes, fell down,[85] and with its weight laid low much of the wood.

(777) The wood-nymphs were amazed at their loss, and the loss sustained to the forest, and in their dark robes of mourning they approached Ceres and begged her to punish Erysichthon. The fairest of deities assented, and with a nod of her head waved the fields laden with heavy harvest. She strove hard to devise a pitiful kind of punishment, if anyone could have pity on him for his deeds: to rack him with ferocious hunger. Since the goddess herself could not approach (since the Fates do not allow Ceres and Famine to come together), she addressed one of the mountain nymphs, a rustic oread, with these words:

> there is a place on the furthest boundaries of icy Scythia, a gloomy soil, a sterile land without corn or tree. There dwell Cold and Pallor and Fear and gaunt Famine.[86] Order her to hide herself in the wicked innards of the sacrilegious wretch. Nor let abundance conquer her and let her overcome my power in the contest; and do not be afraid of the distance of your journey, but take my chariot and guide its dragons aloft with your reins.

And she gave her the reins; she was carried through the air in the chariot Ceres provided, and came down in Scythia. On the top of a hard mountain, which they call Caucasus,[87] she unyoked her serpents' necks and saw Famine in a stony field plucking the little grass with her teeth and nails. Her hair was matted, her eyes hollow, her face pale; her lips were white with decay, her throat rough with scurf; her skin was hard, and through it could be seen her innards; her bones stood out dry under her hollow loins; instead of a stomach there was only a place; you would have thought her chest hung loose and was held in place by the framework of her spine.

Her thinness made her joints look larger, the rounded knees were swelling, and her ankles came out as huge lumps.

(809) As soon as she saw her at a distance (for she did not dare to come near), she passed on the goddess' instructions. And although she stayed only a short time, and kept her distance, and although she had only just arrived, yet she seemed to have felt hunger,[88] and turned about and drove her dragons on their aerial reins back to Thessaly. Although always opposed to her task, Famine[89] carried out the instructions of Ceres, and carried through the air on the wind, arrived at the house as instructed. And immediately she entered the chambers of the sacrilegious king, held him relaxed in deep sleep (for it was night), in both her skinny arms, and breathed herself into him. She breathed on his throat and

chest and lips, and scattered hunger in his hollow veins. And when she had done so she deserted the fertile world and returned to the homes of want and her usual cavern.

(823) Still gentle sleep stroked Erysichthon with its gentle feathers. Under the guise of a dream[90] he sought banquets, moved his lips in vain and tired out tooth upon tooth, exercising his deluded gullet on empty food. And instead of banquets he devoured in vain the empty air. When his rest was at last at an end, the craving to eat burned within him, and reigned throughout his greedy throat and burning innards.[91] Without delay he demanded the produce of sea, earth and sky, and with the tables beside him complained of hunger, and amid feasts asked for still more feasts. What was enough for cities and peoples was not enough for one man; and the more he sent down to his belly, the more he desired. As the sea receives the rivers from a whole land and yet is not filled with the waters, but drinks up the rivers that have reached it from afar, and as the rapacious flame never refuses nourishment but burns innumerable brands, and the more it receives the more it seeks, made hungrier by the sheer bulk it receives, so the mouth of profane Erysichthon receives all his feasts and at the same time demands more. All food in him causes him to crave more, and always does his stomach become empty through eating.

(843) And already he had worn down his ancestral wealth through hunger and the deep abyss of his belly, but dreadful hunger still remained unabated, and the fire in his gullet raged unappeased.[92] At length, when he had used up his estate on his belly, there was still his daughter, too good for such a father.[93] In his poverty he sold her too: a high-spirited girl, she refused a master, and stretching her hands over the neighbouring waves, she said 'Snatch me from my master, since you have the trophy of my virginity that you yourself snatched'. Neptune indeed had it, and he did not spurn her prayer, but although her master following had only just seen her, Neptune changed her form and gave her a man's face and garments fitting for a fisherman. Seeing her, her master said:

> You who conceal the hook of dangling bronze in a little food, wielder of the rod of reed, may the sea be calm, may the fish in the sea be credulous and feel no hook till he is caught: the girl with dishevelled hair and poor attire who stood on this shore (for I saw her standing here) – tell me where she is, for her tracks go no further.

She realised that the god's gift was turning out well, and delighted that she was being sought from herself, she answered his question with these words:

> Pardon me, whoever you are, I have not turned my eyes from this pool in any direction; I have stuck to my concern for fishing. To assuage your doubts, so may the god of the sea assist my craft, (as it is true) that no-one for a long time on this shore, except for myself, nor any woman at all has stood here.

The master believed her, turned tail and walked the sand and went off deceived: her own form returned to her. But when her father realised that his daughter could change her shape, often he handed her over to masters, so that now a mare, now a bird, now an ox, now a deer, she went off and provided unjust sustenance to her greedy father. But when that evil force had consumed all his substance,[94] and had given new sustenance to his dreadful disease, he himself began to tear apart his own limbs with rending bite, and unhappily caused his body to grow by diminishing it.[95]

The Fairy's Revenge: Callimachus, *Hymn* 6.31–117[96] (ATU 779E)

(31) But when the favouring spirit was angry with the sons of Triopas,[97] then wicked counsel possessed Erysichthon. He rushed with twenty servants, all in their prime, all giant men each able to uproot a whole city[98]; he armed them both with two-headed axes and with hatchets, and there was a poplar, a huge tree reaching skywards, and at it by the middle of the day the nymphs used to disport themselves. This tree he struck first, and it let out a cry of woe to the rest. Demeter was aware that her sacred tree felt pain, and in anger she exclaimed: 'Who's been cutting my lovely tree?'[99] Immediately she took on the appearance of Nicippe, the girl the city had appointed as her public priest, with her garlands and a poppy in her hand, and the key hanging from her shoulder. And she spoke to calm the wicked and shameless man[100]: 'Child, who cut the trees sacred to the gods, child for whom your parents often prayed, stop and turn back your servants, in case mistress Demeter should be angry, the goddess whose shrine you are laying waste'. But he looked askance at her, more maliciously than a lioness eyes a hunter in the hills of Tmarus[101] – a lioness whose cubs are newly born, whose glance is most dreadful of all. 'Back', he said, 'or I shall fix my axe in your skin. These trees will make me a sturdy house in which I shall always have joyful banquets to satisfy my companions'.[102] So the young man spoke, but Nemesis set down on record his wicked utterance. (57) And Demeter was unspeakably furious, and wore her divine shape. Her footsteps touched the earth, her head reached Olympus. And the men were half-dead when they saw the great lady[103]; they bolted at once, leaving their bronze axes in the trees. She left the rest, for they only yielded to necessity under their master's hand; but she replied to the bad-tempered king, 'Yes, yes, build the house, you dog, in which to hold your feasts. For from now on you will have banquets galore'. And with as many words she wrought mischief for Erysichthon. At once she implanted in him a dreadful raging hunger, burning fiercely, as he was tortured by an awesome disease. The accursed wretch, as much as he ate, so much again he was seized with desire to eat. Twenty servants toiled to feed him, twelve drew off the wine. All that angers Demeter angers Dionysus as well, and Dionysus was furious with him too. His parents were ashamed, and would not send him to share a feast or dine with others, and found every kind of excuse. The sons of Ormenos arrived to invite him to the games in honour of Ithonian Athene. His mother refused them: 'He is not

here, for yesterday he went to Crannon to demand a hundred oxen owed him'. Polyxo, the mother of Actorion came – she was making ready for her child's marriage, and was inviting Triopas and his son. Tearfully she replied with a heavy heart: 'Triopas will come, but a boar drove at Erysichthon on fair-glenned Pindus, and he has been bound in bed for nine days'. Poor loving mother, what lying excuses did you not make! One man was giving a feast: 'Erysichthon is out of the country'. Another is having a wedding: 'Erysichthon was hit by a discus'; or 'He fell from his chariot', or 'He is counting his flocks on Orthrys'.

(87) Then within his house he feasted all day long, eating all manner of countless dishes. And his wicked belly would leap up always eating more, and all the food poured down, as if into the depths of the sea, in vain and with no thanks. And like the snow on Mimas,[104] like a wax doll in the sun, and even more than these he wasted away right to his sinews; only sinew and bone were left on the wretch. His mother wept, and again and again his two sisters gave a loud groan, and the breast that nourished him and his ten handmaidens. And even Triopas himself threw his hands on his grey hairs, beseeching the unheeding Poseidon with prayers like these:

> Look, false father, at this third generation of yours, if indeed I am the son of yourself and Canace daughter of Aeolus, but this miserable brat is my offspring: if only my hands had interred him, struck down by Apollo. But now he sits before my eyes, an ill-starred glutton. Either remove this tormenting disease from him, or take him and feed him yourself. For my tables are exhausted. My folds are bereft of livestock, my byres are already out of four-footed beasts, and already the cooks are saying there is nothing left.

But they unyoked the mules from the great wagons, he ate the heifer his mother was fattening up for Hestia, and the race-horse and war-horse, and the cat[105] that made the tiny vermin tremble. As long as there were provisions in the house of Triopas, only the rooms of his own house were aware of his affliction. But when his teeth had drained the great house, then did the king sit at the crossroads, begging for the crusts and the leavings thrown away from the feast.[106] Demeter, let it not be my friend who incurs your anger, nor the neighbour through the wall. Ill-starred neighbours are abhorrent to me!

Tricking the Enemy into the Oven[107]: The Bull of Phalaris[108]

Lucian, *Phalaris* A 11f. (ATU *327A, Hansel and Gretel*)

(11) There was a certain man in our city, a good metalworker but a wicked man. This fellow completely misunderstood my attitude and thought he would please me if he should devise some novel punishment, as if I wanted punishments of every conceivable kind. And assembling the bull he brought it to me: it was a

fine sight and a true likeness down to the very last detail, for it was only lacking movement and mooing short of the real thing. When I set eyes on it I at once exclaimed that this possession was worthy of Delphian Apollo, and that the bull should be sent to the god. But Perilaus stood beside me and said: 'but what if you were to find out the clever contrivance in it and the use it provides?' At that point he opened the bull's back and said:

> If you want to punish someone, put him into this contraption and shut him in, and attach these flutes to the bull's nostrils, and order a fire to be lit underneath, and the victim will moan and roar when he is seized by unremitting pain, and his shouting by means of the tones of the flute will generate the sweetest of sounds and will make mournful music and the most pitiful lowing, and afford you delight through the playing of the flutes.

(12) But when I heard that, I was disgusted at the man's perverted ingenuity and hated the very idea of his machine, and imposed a punishment on him to fit the crime. So I said 'Now then, Perilaus, if this is not a mere empty promise, get into it and show me yourself the true nature of your invention and imitate the victims' cries, to demonstrate the tunes voiced by the flutes'. Perilaus complied, but when he was inside I shut him in and ordered the fire to be lit below, and said 'Receive the just reward of your wonderful invention, so that you may be our first music-teacher as you play'. And so he suffered a just punishment, enjoying the fruits of his own inspired idea. But I ordered him to be taken out still alive and breathing so as not to pollute the work with a corpse, and had him thrown over the cliffs to remain unburied; purifying the bull I sent it to you the people of Delphi as an offering to the god. And I ordered the whole story to be engraved on it: the name of the donor, the name of the craftsman Perilaus, his invention, the just punishment, his fitting reward, the songs of the ingenious metal-worker and the first trying out of the music.

Hermes and the Golden Axe[109]: *Fabulae Aesopicae Collectae* Halm 308 (*ATU 729, The Merman's Golden Axe*)

A woodman beside a river lost his axe in the water. So at a loss he sat down beside the bank and wept. But Hermes, finding out the reason for his grief, was sorry for the man, and diving down into the river he brought up a golden axe and asked him if that was the one he had lost. When he said it was not, Hermes brought up a silver axe, but when he said this was not his either the god dived down a third time and brought up the woodman's own axe. When he said this was the one he had lost, Hermes recognised his honesty by giving him all three axes. The man joined his companions and told them what had happened. One of them decided to do the same. And going beside the river he deliberately threw his axe into the river and sat down and cried. Hermes appeared, and finding the cause of his weeping he went down as before and brought up a golden axe and asked if this was the one he had lost.[110] And when he was delighted and said 'Yes, that's the very one!' the god was disgusted at such shameless fraud and not only did not give him the golden one, but did not restore his own axe either.

Revenge on the Suitors: Ps.-Plutarch *Amatoriae Narrationes* 4 (*ATU* 780, The Singing Bone)

Phocus was a Boeotian from birth; for he came from Glisa, and was father of Callirhoe, a girl of surpassing beauty and modesty. The thirty noblest young men in Boeotia were her suitors. But Phocus caused one delay after another to the marriage: fearing violence at their hands, and to put an end to their wooing, he decided to leave the choice of husband to Delphi. But they were furious at his decision: they rushed on him and killed him; but the girl escaped in the commotion and fled through the countryside with the suitors in pursuit. But she came upon farmers making a threshing-floor, and they gave her shelter, for they hid her in the grain, and so her pursuers ran past. And she was rescued and observed the festival for all of Boeotia, and then going to Coronea as a suppliant she sat on the altar of Itonian Athena and related the lawless act of her suitors, revealing the name and origin of each. So the Boeotians took pity on her and were furious with the young men. They for their part saw this and fled to Orchomenos. The inhabitants refused them and they made for Hippotae, a village beside Helicon between Thisbe and Coronea, which accepted them. Then the Thebans sent men demanding the murderers of Phocus. But they refused to give them up. They sent a force with the other Boeotians under Phoedus, who was then in command of the Thebans. They invested the village, which was well defended, but with the inhabitants suffering from thirst they captured the murderers and stoned them. They enslaved the inhabitants and demolished the walls and divided the land between the people of Thisbe and Coronea. And they say that at night, before the capture of the Hippotai, a voice form Helicon was frequently heard saying 'I am here', and the suitors recognised this as the voice of Phocus.[111] And on the day they were stoned, the old man's memorial in Glisa was said to run with saffron…

Notes

1. Garvie (1994), 293–312; Wehse *EM* 8 (1996), 1056–1063; Hainsworth-Heubeck-West (1998), 363–372.
2. An adulterous pair are caught and exposed in a compromising position by means of a strange magical device which somehow locks them together. This may be a metal object forged by a smith, humorously called a 'Himphamp', or a magically 'adhesive' animal, such as a magical crocodile or a goose. Sometimes an agent reports to the husband, here a fellow god; in an ancient Egyptian example, the wronged husband Ubainer.
3. In the 'traditional' Himphamp version in Aarne-Thompson-Uther 571B the device is an iron chamber-pot, and the wronged husband, as here, a blacksmith. The precise mechanism in Homer is not clear: he is no less reticent than in the case of Circe and her shape-shifting potion.
4. I.e. Aphrodite, identified by a favourite shrine at Cythera.

5 Compare Ubainer's wife's speech, Parkinson (2007), 107f.
6 Lemnos and the Sintians carry a stigma, of base industrial work: it is aristocratic to wield weapons, not to make them.
7 In Afanas'ev's Russian version (13ff.) the merchant goes to his stall in the market (but does not actually devise the trap, which happens spontaneously).
8 Ubainer takes his case to the pharaoh, and the adulterers are killed; the merchant in Afanas'ev simply beats the lovers, not a practical punishment in the case of Hephaestus and Ares.
9 The merchant likewise refuses to release the lovers by calling off the magic goose, until his wife has made a full confession (Afanas'ev, 15), while Ubainer's wife's lover is trapped in the pool for a week till Ubainer himself is free to attend to the matter.
10 In Afanas'ev the crowd is in the market place, to which the errant pair have been dragged by the magic goose; others have stuck to it on the way.
11 Laughter is the emphasis of type *ATU* 571B: everyone sticks to the goose and makes the laughter-less princess laugh. There is no adultery in that instance.
12 The adulterer's game suggests a sophisticated and gentlemanly amusement, in contrast to the peasant slapstick of the Russian tale.
13 After the sexual humiliation she needs to purify herself: one does not actually beat even adulterous goddesses in Homer.
14 Commentary: Hollis (1970); Brednich *EM* 9 (1999), 547–551. A mother rescues her son from the Fates by preserving a log from the fire, when they had condemned him at birth to live no longer than the burning wood. She finally does burn the life-token log when he kills her brothers in a quarrel, and he dies accordingly. The tale illustrates several typically folkloric features:

1 The operation of the Fates at the birth of the child;
2 The preference of sibling kinship over offspring;
3 The operation of sympathetic magic.

The last of these entails the use of the life-token, similar to an external soul: destroy that and you destroy the object of vengeance. Ovid's version tends rather to emphasise the theatrical aspects of Althaea's inner torment, and the pathos of Meleager's ultimate fate. But the fairy-tale pattern is clear enough: the wise women have given Meleager a very specific lease of life, which his mother can control at will, punishing him for the murder of his two uncles as she pleases.

Kakridis (1949) offers no fewer than 13 modern analogues from Greece and Turkey. The motivations in the folktale versions vary considerably, such as a father's quarrel over property (3), a man's quarrel with his wife after his mother's death (4) or the wife burns it out of carelessness (9), ignorance (13) or adulterous passion for his brother (10). Kakridis (1949) lists thirteen variants of the story. The closest is the first, a Cypriot variant recorded in 1939 (Kakridis, 128), where the victim kills a single uncle, in this case because of a false rumour that the uncle had been planning to kill his mother; she then kills the son.
15 In Ovid's version the brothers are jealous of the honours given by Meleager to Atalanta for her prowess in the Caledonian Hunt; the Cypriot version motivates the jealousy through the hero's marriage to a princess.
16 I.e. Arcadian, after the local Mount Nonacris.
17 And so Meleager's uncles.
18 Seven days after the birth, as in Apollodorus 1.65, Cypriot; on the third day in a Turkish variant (Kakridis number 3, 129).
19 Meleager's mother Althaea kills him by means of a magic life-token in the form of the log: for the motif of fairies commuting a death sentence to one of a shorter life, cf. Perrault's version of *The Sleeping Beauty*, Opie and Opie (1980), 109. The Cypriot version gives the hero gifts (handsome appearance, a singing voice) from the first two fates, the life-sentence from the third (Turkish 3, riches instead of a singing voice).

20 Most modern versions have it in a chest; Apollodorus 1.8.2 and Bacchylides 5.141 have it in a *larnax*.
21 'Pathetic' second person by which the narrator affects to be a direct witness of the scene.
22 *Pugnat materque sororque*: Ovid rhetoricises the maternal conflict over a number of varied expressions.
23 The Eumenides' interest is as avengers of the murderer of kin, such as Orestes of his mother Clytemnestra, or the Theban brothers Eteocles and Polyneices of each other; on the theme of Intaphrenes' wife, Kakridis (1949) Appendix 3.
24 In the Cypriot version the victim falls down dead in the palace itself.
25 A note of genuine pathos after the contrivances of Althaea's speech.
26 Anderson (2000), 133–135. A king promises to pay an oddly-dressed musical rodent-catcher for services rendered. When he twice refuses to pay, first the girls, then the young men, are deported/destroyed; one boy lives to tell the tale. There is no continuous 'Pied Piper' tale surviving in classical literature; but the three testimonia above show that the musician Apollo had an early reputation for dealing with a plague of rodents; and that he and Heracles in turn punished a city whose ruler refused to pay for services rendered. This is a more complex Pied Piper story than the modern local legend centred on Hamelyn: three creditors are not paid (two gods and one hero) and so it is more difficult to produce a recognisable narrative. Apollo's credentials as a rodent catcher are well documented, but are not actually used in the story as transmitted. He does seem to have an odd costume, though it is difficult to work out what the oddity actually is.
27 I.e. only the girls are lost at first.
28 Yet a third supernatural helper is left unpaid. In effect we have three Pied-Pipers of Troy.
29 The purpose of the sole survivor in the Hamelyn version is to witness how the children actually disappear. In this instance it may be rather to witness the justice of Priam (whom Diodorus reports as the only son to advocate honouring the original agreement, 4.32.1–5). Normally the child is lame and cannot keep up. In the present instance he may simply be too young to fight.
30 The version in Exodus repeats the motif of the plague a number of times with different animals: but the ultimate effect is the same: the loss of the young male population, and then of the workforce, the children of Israel themselves. The rod of Aaron functions clearly enough as a magic wand. It demonstrates that the operations of the plague-god involve animals and the revenge of someone who can control them.
31 The phrase is supported by only one MS (F), but is clearly inferred from the rest of the narrative. If the missing portion had been longer, it might have supplied a death or suicide for Chione herself.
32 As told by Nicander, *Metamorphoses* 3 and the Laconian Areus in an Ode to Cycnus, both known only from Antoninus Liberalis, 12, whose commentator Celoria hails it rather contemptuously as 'showing the marks of being cobbled together by a village storyteller rather than an editor'. Hansen, 338.
33 Ovid gives her name as Hyrie.
34 As chief towns of Aetolia.
35 Mythographers are characteristically hard on arrogant lovers.
36 Compare the remark of Agathion, below c.12.
37 The method is familiar from the Second Voyage of Sindbad in the *Thousand and One Nights* (Dawood, 125f.), prior to the example cited by Celoria.
38 Again, compare the feats claimed by the Agathion known to Herodes Atticus, Philostratus *VS*, 554 (c.12 below).
39 Who had wrestled with the Cretan bull, the seventh labour.
40 A modern folktale parallel occurs in the north European story of Aioga, Anderson (2000), 22.

41 Hansen (2002), 89–92; Schmitt *EM* 8 (1996), 331–334. In addition to the idea that the robbers convict themselves there is also an element of the sanctity of artists, as shown also in the story of Arion of Lesbos, c. 10 below. This factor is not in evidence in the version known to Iamblichus (*Life of Pythagoras*, 27.126), where the victims are simply boys.
42 Röhrich *EM* 3 (1981a), 306–322.
43 Mercury/Hermes is an ambiguous figure, both patron of thieves and tricksters, and yet ensuring just deserts.
44 And so capable of being later transformed into a fairy or a local saint.
45 The extended nose is comparable to the sausage stuck to the end of the wife's nose in English versions of *The Foolish Wishes* (Middle Eastern versions have the husband's wish for an extended penis, expurgated in the West).
46 One foolish wish rather than three; or rather two, with the second cancelling the first, rather than as usually the third cancelling the second. Chessnut *EM* 14 (2014), 1076–1083.
47 i.e. Phrygian, after the local Mount Berecyntus.
48 As noted by G. Husson (1970) on Lucian's *Navigium*; also Hansen (2002), 476f.
49 This instance is presented as a genuine historical report of delusive behaviour; it has none of the secondary features of the tale type, and may be no more than an amusing anecdote, as Aelian himself probably intended.
50 Hansen (2002), 220–222; Hollis (1970), 108–128 (unmentioned by Hansen); Chessnut *EM* 14 (2014), 1076–1083.
51 The first metamorphosed from Philemon, the second from Baucis. These rustic cults are both Middle Eastern and Graeco-Roman.
52 Theseus and his old retainer Lelex, the present speaker, are guests of the river Achelous in his underground cave, waiting for his own floodwaters to subside after the Caledonian hunt. The story is told, like that of Erysichthon shortly afterwards, as an exemplum or cautionary tale against impiety and abuse of the laws of hospitality. The theophany of Jupiter and Mercury is well compared to the reception of Paul and Barnabas at Lystra in Phrygian Galatia (Acts 14); epigraphic evidence supports local joint worship of Zeus and Hermes.
53 Atlantiades: 'descendant of Atlas', the latter his maternal grandfather.
54 Hollis notes the general similarity with Odysseus' visit to the humble swineherd Eumaeus in *Odyssey*, 14, and the scenario where Theseus visits the equally humble Hecale in Callimachus' *Hecale*: but neither embodies the actual tale here, unless we see the wicked suitors as turning down the disguised Odysseus and paying with their lives.
55 An Ovidian humorous touch, comparable to the treatment of Deucalion and Pyrrha in *Met*. 1.355 (*Nos duo turba sumus* – 'we two are a crowd').
56 The rustic humble board and lifestyle are Italian rather than Middle Eastern, as Hollis points out (111f., 119).
57 For the self-replenishing bowl, cf. the widow's cruse made self-replenishing when the prophet Elijah visits, (1 Kings, 17.8–16).
58 Deucalion and Pyrrha in *Metamorphoses* 1 survive similarly while the wicked around them are drowned, but without the improvised theoxeny depicted here.
59 There was strong local tradition of flooding round Apamea and Iconium, both with reference to a local Deucalion legend and the early 3rd century tradition of an ark. William Calder saw what he interpreted as continuous flood tradition at Iconium until the 20th century. Hollis seems unduly cautious about how Ovid could know such information; but a broader knowledge of the nature and diffusion of flood tradition and its moral connotation (the wicked perish, the good are saved) explains the correspondence adequately; and Middle Eastern flood tradition goes back to Atrahasis and Gilgamesh.
60 A rare instance of a house rather than people or animals metamorphosed.

61 With ordinary disposal of the dead ruled out, the way is open for metamorphosis of the pair.
62 Either by reminiscing or recounting what is now the temple legend of the locality to others.
63 Synchronised metamorphosis, and a faintly ludicrous nuance. The site is Bithynian only in the loosest sense, and the reading must remain suspect.
64 Lelex here bears witness to local oral tradition, and the local hero-cult of the pair.
65 Hollis (109) noted a tree at the Cilician Gates 'covered with pious rags and surrounded by a rampart of small stones placed there one by one by modern travellers'.
66 Compare a Yorkshire local legend, (Briggs *DBF*, 2.2.349): A long time ago there was a village in the North Riding of Yorkshire called Simmerdale, at one end of which stood a church, and the house of a Quaker woman at the other end. It happened one day that a witch came into the village, and beginning at the house next to the church asked for food and drink, but her request was refused. And so she went on from house to house, without getting any food or drink, until at last she came to the Quaker woman's house. There, sitting in the porch, she was regaled with bread, meat and beer. Having finished her repast, she rose and waved an ash twig over the village, saying:

> 'Simmerdale, Simmerdale, Simmerdale, sink,
> Save the house of the woman who gave me to drink'.

When the witch had said these words the water rose in the valley and covered the village, except the old woman's house. Simmer water is now a peaceful lake, and on fine clear days people in the neighbourhood can see down in its placid depths the ruins of the village and the church.
67 *ATU* uses a Christian example: Gypsies refuse to give the Holy Family refuge, and in return they are condemned to wander ever after.
68 The narrator is among those who have just heard how Latona's grown-up offspring Apollo and Diana have murdered Niobe's children because of their mother's irreverent boasting.
69 *Res obscura quidem est ignobilitate virorum* ('The matter is unfamiliar because of the men's lowly status'). Ovid undervalues and underestimates the strength of local and oral tradition, in contrast to educated, literary transmission of material.
70 The goddess Latona (Leto), as daughter of the Titan Coeus.
71 Despite her extreme condition, an Ovidian heroine can always summon the energy for a smart rhetorical display!
72 The newly born Apollo and Diana, persecuted by Latona's rival Juno.
73 The Latin text postpones the nature of their transformation to the very last word: *ranae*.
74 A nature spirit (nymph, fairy) requests a king not to cut down her tree; her mistress inflicts him with the punishment of uncontrollable hunger. Two versions are given: Ovid's in *Metamorphoses* 8 and the earlier Hellenistic telling in Callimachus *Hymn* 6. A third elaborate version of the story survives as a Modern Greek folktale, reported by Jacob Zarraftis from an old woman from Asphendiou on Cos towards the end of the 19th century, and translated by R.M. Dawkins in his *Forty-five Stories from the Dodekanese* (Cambridge 1951), 134ff. under the title *Mygdonia and Pharaonia*. The scale is similar and some of the resemblances close enough to raise the suspicion (but not the proof) of a literary intermediary. The narrator expands on the cutting down of the trees, plural in this case, with the grotesque image of the bloodied tree-fairy. The king's sword is wedged in the tree he struck, and is used by a horrid nightmare image of Hunger who plunges it into the perpetrator's throat, where it implants hunger itself. The insatiable appetite is then duly narrated; the king sells his son but is about to eat his own daughter, before turning cannibal on himself and dying with his nails in his mouth. The appropriate use of the sword as the avenger is unique to this version; the description of the burning and cold sensations is reminiscent of the term Aithōn ('burner') for Erysichthon himself. Both touches hint at the possibility

of an independent version, close to the Ovidian horrors, especially in the description of Hunger, and far removed from Callimachus' light touch.
75 *ATU* offers a Christian example to typify the tale: the dancers of the fictitious Kolbeck profane a Mass in the church by holding a dance outside. The priest curses the dancers who are condemned to dancing perpetually till they dance themselves into the ground making a hole and they finally die. As the impious Erysichthon's hunger is cursed into becoming perpetual, so the impious dancers are forced to perpetuate their own form of impiety.
76 A son of Hermes, and likewise a trickster.
77 The tale of Erysichthon is told as a run-up to the metamorphoses of his daughter (Hyper)mestra, here unnamed.
78 A perilous impiety even in historical times: see Dio, 51.8 on P. Turullius, executed under Augustus for downing a grove of Asclepius to build boats; cf. Philostatus *VS*, 614 on Heraclides of Lycia.
79 Leaving Erysichthon in no doubt about its sacred character.
80 An alternative reading is *Dryopeius*, connecting him with the barbarous Dryopes; he himself was a king of Thessaly.
81 Oak as in the modern *Mygdonia and Pharaonia*, poplar in Callimachus.
82 As the oak of Deo, Ceres/Demeter.
83 Ovid emphasises the animate qualities of even the tree-form of the nymph; compare *Aeneid*, 3.22–46, the attempted uprooting of the bush that contains the corpse of Elpenor.
84 The Modern Greek version also includes a curse of the *sacrilegus* at this point.
85 It is Callimachus (*Hymn*, 6.63–65) who reflects the 'correct' explanation for Hunger as the punishment: the wood was intended for a banqueting hall.
86 Ovid uses the tale as a peg for a highly literary *ecphrasis* of Hunger herself, like his treatment of the Cave of Sleep or the dwelling of Envy, with their parades of appropriate allegorical figures.
87 Sometimes identified with the Rhipaean mountains, set vaguely in the north, and appropriate for the fantasy-landscape here.
88 As Iris in *Metamorphoses*, 9.630f. feels the effect of sleep.
89 The description of Famine offers a celebrated rhetorical *ecphrasis* in its own right; the Modern Greek version is quite close, perhaps even suspiciously so.
90 He dreams also in *Pharaonia*, but a more ominous dream: it is his sword still sticking in the oak that implants the hunger.
91 He was early named *Aithōn* ('burner') in respect of this torment.
92 The feeding of Erysichthon is described in much more detail in the other versions: Ovid has 'shot his bolt' with the horrific description of Hunger herself.
93 Ovid now moves to what is really a subsidiary tale: Hansen (2002), 189f. ('Hatchpenny'). Hypermestra uses her powers of metamorphosis to feed her father. In the folktale he has only a daughter and a son to sell. Ovid reserves his comic touches for the trickery of Hypermestra, pretending not to have seen herself... In Pseudo-Hesiod Erysichthon even tries to swindle Sisyphus by selling Mestra as a bride for Glaucus; Athena arbitrates and Erysichthon seems the loser.
94 It is not explained why the income from the daughter's metamorphoses can no longer support her father's cravings.
95 The tale ends not in tragedy but in a typically Ovidian grotesque: for a similar extreme of sick humour, cf. the picture of Marsyas' asking 'why are you wrenching me from myself?' when he is being flayed alive (6.385).
96 McKay (1962).
97 King of Thessaly.
98 Callimachus allows fairy-tale giants here: Erysichthon has twenty 'heavies', but Demeter reaches the sky in due course...The general mood is fantastic and light-hearted.
99 The form of question is not confined to the Seven Dwarfs and Three Bears.

100 The black-and-white moral indignation of the modern tale-teller, once more.
101 Tmarus: a mountain in north-western Greece south of Dodona.
102 And so the punishment of hunger fits the crime.
103 Giants though they be.
104 Proverbially inhospitable: the shoals and shallows extend from Tunisia to Cyrenaica. See Pliny *NH*, 5.26–41: the lotus-eaters were also localised here.
105 By a deliberate anti-climax.
106 His ultimate fate is not described: social humiliation rather than cannibalism is in question.
107 Scherf, *EM*, 6.498–509.
108 The context is a fictitious declamation in which Phalaris, an actual tyrant of Agrigentum, (6th century BC) justifies his gift of a dedicatory offering to Delphian Apollo. I can find no precise equivalent of the Hansel and Gretel story in a fairy tale context in Antiquity.
109 Hansen (2002), 42–44, noting the theme of 'unsuccessful repetition', and comparing a modern French Canadian version with a mermaid as the supernatural helper, appropriate to the context of the river. Uther, *EM*, 14 (2014), 132–135. Hermes here is an upholder of honesty, though he can just as readily be a patron of rogues.
110 In the minimalist telling of the story the bringing up of the silver axe is unsurprisingly dropped: the rogue has already established his mendacity.
111 Cf. the reaction to the death of the Biblical Abel (Genesis, 4.10: 'The voice of thy brother's blood crieth unto me from the ground').

7

REWARDS AND PUNISHMENTS II

Three innocent slandered maidens

Three romantic tales underline the themes of surpassing beauty, extreme jealousy and their un-looked for consequences against very well contrasted contexts. The first is told by one of the Minyads to her fellow tale-tellers to relieve the boredom of repetitive work: its consequences are equally tragic for the innocent victim of slander and its ungracious perpetrator, as they account for the aetiology of plants; the second is presented as historical legend leading to the foundation of Cyrene, thanks to a clever trick to preserve the life of another victim of slander; the third shows the incorporation of a traditional tale-type to form much of the material of a Greek novel, once again with a homage to historical fantasy, this time halfway towards the realism of New Comedy.

Leucothoe and Clytie: Ovid *Metamorphoses* 4.167–271 (cf. *ATU* 480, The Kind and the Unkind Girls)

(167) After a short interval Leuconoe began,[1] and her sisters were silent[2]...(195) 'You,[3] the sun who ought to look on all things, look only at Leucothoe and fix your gaze on one maiden when you owe it to the whole world...(204) you love her alone, ...<and not> Clytie, whom you scorn, however much she has sought your embraces and even now has the grave wound in her heart...(218) The god entered his beloved's chambers, taking on the appearance of her mother Eurynome. He sees Leucothoe amid her twelve handmaids, drawing the light threads on her whirling spindle. Then he kissed her as her mother would have kissed her beloved daughter, and said 'this is an intimate matter, servants take your leave, and do not deny a mother her private words'. The handmaidens obeyed; and when there was no witness left in the room he said 'I am the one who measures the long year, I am the one who see everything, by whom the earth sees everything; I am the eye of the world. Believe me, you are pleasing to

me'. The girl was afraid, as the distaff and spindle fell as her fingers lost their grip. Fear itself became her. Nor did he delay a moment longer, but returned to his true shape and accustomed brightness. But the girl, terrified at the unexpected sight, was overcome by the brilliance; she did not protest but suffered his force.

(234) Now Clytie was jealous, for the love of the sun still burned unmoderated within her. Goaded by anger at her rival she blazed the girl's shame abroad and spread the news to Leucothoe's father.[4] He was fierce and unmerciful as she stretched her hands out to the light of the sun and declared 'He forced me against my will'. Her savage father buried her deep in the ground and heaped up the heavy sand in a mound. Hyperion's son broke the mound with his rays and made a way for you to be able to bring forth your buried face; nor were you able, nymph, to raise your head, crushed by the weight of earth, and you lay there a lifeless corpse. Nor is the driver of the winged steeds said to have seen anything more pitiful since the flames that burned Phaethon. He for his part tried with the force of his rays to recall her cold limbs to the warmth of life, but since fate prevented his mighty efforts, he sprinkled the body and the ground with fragrant odour and with many words of grief he said 'And yet you will reach the air'. At once the body, imbued with divine nectar, melted away through the ground and dampened the earth with its fragrance; and a bush of frankincense arose slowly from its deep roots and broke through the mound with its top.

(256) As for Clytie, although love could excuse her grief and although grief could excuse her gossip, no longer did the source of light approach her, nor did he find anything attractive about her. For this reason she faded away, and her love became madness. She could not endure her fellow nymphs, but beneath the sky night and day she sat on the ground naked, with her hair uncovered and unkempt. And for nine days on end without food or water she fed her hunger only from dew and tears, and did not move from the ground. She only gazed at the face of the god as he went on his way and turned her face towards him. They say her limbs stuck to the earth, and her lurid paleness changed to a bloodless plant.[5] And she was in part red, and a flower covered her very like a violet. And she turns her head, though held fast by the root, and in her changed form preserves her love'.

Leuconoe spoke, and the wonderful event held their attention.

Phronime[6]: Herodotus 4.154f. (*ATU* 883A The Innocent Slandered Maiden)

(154) For the Cyrenians give a totally different account of Battus from the Theraeans: this is their version. There is a city in Crete called Oaxus, in which Etearchus became king. He had a daughter called Phronime, and when her mother died he married again. When the second wife entered the household she thought it her right to behave as a real stepmother to the girl, giving her a hard time, and contriving all manner of mischief against her; and finally she accused her of leading a loose life, and persuaded her husband that this was the case. The

king believed his wife and planned a wicked deed against his daughter. Now there was a merchant from Thera in Oaxus called Themison. Etearchus struck up a guest-friend relationship with this man, and made him swear to do whatever favour he should ask. And once he had sworn, Etearchus handed over his daughter and told the merchant to take her off and throw her into the sea. But Themison was furious at the deceit of the oath: he broke off the relationship and took the following action. He took the girl and sailed off; but when they were on the open sea he duly discharged the oath sworn to Etearchus by binding her with ropes, letting her down into the water, and drawing her up again, after which he reached Thera. (155) And there one of the prominent citizens, Polymnestus, took her as a concubine, and in time she gave birth to a son, with a weak voice and a stammer, called Battus.[7]

Callirhoe: Chariton, *Chaereas and Callirhoe*, 1.2–3.4 (extracts)[8] (*ATU* 882/883A The Wager on the Wife's Chastity/The Innocent Slandered Maiden)

(1.2) Callirhoe's unsuccessful suitors[9] were angry as well as disappointed. After previously fighting among themselves, they were now of one mind; because of this, as they felt insulted, they came together to plot. Envy led them in their war against Chaereas. And first a young man from Italy, son of the tyrant of Rhegium, got up and had this to say:

> If one of you had married Callirhoe, I should not have been angry: just as in gymnastic contests, only one of the competitors can win. But since a man who put out no effort into achieving the marriage has passed us by, I cannot endure the insult. We have exhausted ourselves with our sleepless nights at her house door, and flattering her nurses and maidservants and sending gifts to her attendants. How much time have we spent as slaves? And, worst of all, we have hated one another as rivals in love. But this man without means, poor, and no better than the next man has carried off the prize (without grovelling in the dust) in competition with kings. But let him have no joy in his prize and let us make the marriage fatal for the groom.

All of them approved, except the tyrant of Agrigentum, who spoke out against the murder.

> I do not object to the plan out of goodwill to Chaereas, but from prudent calculation. Remember that Hermocrates is not to be underestimated,[10] nor that it is impossible to fight him in the open; a cunning approach is better: for we take possession of our tyrannies by craft rather than brute force. Elect me general for our campaign against Chaereas[11]: I promise you the dissolution of the marriage. For I will arm Jealousy against him,

and taking Love as her ally she will bring about real damage. Callirhoe it is true is level-headed, and has no experience of malice and suspicion, but Chaereas, brought up of course in the gymnasium and not inexperienced in the follies of youth, is easily able to form suspicions and fall into youthful jealousy. And he is also easier to approach and talk to.

Even before he had finished speaking everyone voted their approval of his plan, and they entrusted him with carrying it out as a man equal to any unscrupulous ploy. So he embarked on the following stratagem. (1.3) It was evening when a messenger came with word that Ariston, the father of Chaereas, had fallen off a ladder on his estate and there was little hope that he would live. When Chaereas heard, although he was devoted to his father, he was distressed at having to go alone, for he was not yet able to take his bride. That night although no-one dared to offer her a lover's serenade, they secretly and without being seen left the signs of a wild party: the vestibule was hung with garlands, and sprinkled with perfumes; the ground was drenched with wine, and half-burned torches were thrown to the ground.

When day dawned, every passer-by stopped out of common curiosity, while Chaereas for his part, as his father was keeping better, hurried back to his wife. And seeing all the people in front of the door he was at first surprised. But when he found out the reason, he rushed in in a frenzy. And finding the bridal chamber still shut off, he nearly banged the door down. And when the maid opened it he burst in on Callirhoe, his anger changed to grief, and he tore his clothes and burst into tears. When she asked what had happened he was speechless: he could not disbelieve his eyes, nor could he bring himself to believe what he did not want to. And while he trembled in his confusion, Callirhoe, with no suspicion of what had happened, asked him to explain why he was angry. And with his eyes bloodshot and a hoarse voice, he said 'I am weeping over my misfortune, that you have forgotten me so quickly'. And he reproached her over the party. But she, as the daughter of a general, full of spirit, was revolted by the unjust accusation, and said 'No reveller has come to my father's house: perhaps your portals are used to parties, and your marriage is upsetting your boyfriends'. With this she turned away, hid her head, and went into floods of tears. But lovers' quarrels are easily quelled, and they were glad to accept each other's apologies. So Chaereas changed his tone and began sweet talk, and his wife was quick to welcome his change of heart. This made their love more ardent, and the parents of both considered themselves fortunate to see their children so devoted to each other.

(1.4) The man from Agrigentum, now that his first plan had been foiled, next took more drastic action with a plan that went like this: he had a parasite who was talkative and full of every sort of smooth talk and social charm. This man he persuaded to play the part of a lover: the close and highly-valued servant-woman of Callirhoe he was to fall in love with, and make her love him; so with some effort this fellow enticed her with expensive presents, and saying that he would hang himself if he failed to win her love. And a woman is easily convinced when she thinks she is loved. With this preparation then the producer of the drama found another actor,[12] not so attractive, but a resourceful and convincing talker. This man he instructed what he had to do and say, and he sent him to Chaereas, who did not know him. The man came to him as he was wandering around the wrestling-ground and said:

> I had a son, Chaereas, who was your age, and who admired and respected you when he was alive. And now that he is dead I think of you as my son, for indeed your wellbeing is to the good of the whole of Sicily. So give me a moment of your time and you will hear a serious matter that affects your whole life.

With such a speech the wicked rogue unsettled the lad's heart and made him full of hope and fear and suspicion. But when Chaereas asked him to speak he hesitated and made excuses that the present occasion was not suitable: it was necessary to put it off as they needed more time. Chaereas pressed him all the more, already expecting something very serious. So the man took him by his right hand and led him off to a quiet spot, then knitting his eyebrows and looking grief-stricken, and even shedding the odd tear. 'Chaereas', he said,

> I am telling you about a very regrettable matter, after wanting to tell you but hesitating a long while. But since you are already being openly insulted and the dreadful business is being gossiped about everywhere, I cannot bear to keep silent. For I am by nature opposed to wrongdoing and particularly devoted to you. You must know then that your wife is being unfaithful, and so that you can believe this, I am ready to point to the adulterer in the very act.
> Thus he spoke, but a black cloud of grief covered him,
> And he took sooty dust in both hands
> And poured it over his head and disfigured his lovely features.[13]

For a long time then he stood aghast, not able to open his mouth or lift his eyes. And when he pulled himself together, he said in a thin voice not like his own:

> I am asking an unhappy favour from you, to see with my own eyes my own miseries. But you must show me, so that I may have the more reason to do away with myself. For even if Callirhoe is doing me wrong, I shall spare her.

'Pretend', said the villain, 'that you are going off to the country, but keep watch on the house late in the evening, for you will see the adulterer go in'.

They agreed, and Chaereas sent word (for he could not even bear to go into the house). 'I am off to the country'. But that wicked villain and slanderer set up the scene. So when evening came Chaereas came to his vantage-point, but the man who had seduced Callirhoe's maid darted into the lane, playing the part of someone choosing to act in secret, but making every effort to be noticed. He had glistening hair and locks reeking of myrrh, eye-shadow on his eyes, a fine cloak and elegant slippers. His fingers sparkled with fine rings. Then, with much looking round, he went to the door, and knocking lightly he gave the usual sign. The maid was very anxious for her part, quietly opened the door, and taking him by the hand brought him in. When he saw this Chaereas no longer held back but ran in in order to take the adulterer in the act.

He for his part concealed himself beside the door of the courtyard, and at once went back out, but Callirhoe was reclining on her couch longing for Chaereas, and had not even lit the lamp, she was so downcast: but when there was a noise of footsteps she was the first to recognise her husband by his breathing and in her delight she ran toward him. But he could not find the words to abuse her, but overwhelmed by anger he kicked her as she came toward him. The blow hit her right in the diaphragm and took the girl's breath away. She fell and the maidservants carried her up and laid her on the bed.

(1.5) So Callirhoe lay there unable to speak and out of breath, looking to everyone like a corpse. Rumour acted as a herald of her misfortune, running right through the city and raising lamentation through the alleyways right down to the sea. Lamentation was heard from every quarter, and the business was like the sack of a city. And Chaereas, still seething within, shut himself in the whole night and tortured the maids, first and foremost Callirhoe's favourite, and found out the truth as he applied the fire and the knife. Then he was sorry for the dead girl and wanted to kill himself. But his closest friend, Polycharmus, prevented him, the kind of friend Patroclus was to Achilles according to Homer.[14] And when it was day, the authorities empanelled a jury to try the murder, expediting the trial out of respect for Hermocrates. But the populace too ran to the agora, all of them shouting their various opinions. And the unsuccessful suitors egged them on, especially the tyrant of Acragas: he was very pleased with himself and swaggering as if he had brought off a totally unexpected stroke. But there was a novel outcome, altogether unprecedented in court: once the charge was read out and his share of the water-clock was fixed, he accused himself still more harshly, instead of making his defence, and was the first to vote for his own conviction. He said nothing of what could have been justly brought in his defence, neither the slander, nor his own jealously, nor the lack of intent, but disregarded them all.

> Stone me to death in public: I have deprived the people of their crown. It would be a kindness to hand me over to the public executioner. This I should have deserved to suffer even if I had only killed the maidservant of Hermocrates. Find some unspeakable method of punishment. I have committed a worse crime than temple-robbery or patricide. Do not bury me, do not pollute the earth, but sink this body of mine in the depths of the sea!

At this there was an outburst of grief, and all of them abandoned the dead woman and mourned the living man.[15] Hermocrates was the first to speak in defence of Chaereas. 'I know', he said,

> that what happened was not intentional. I see the people who plotted against us. They shall not take a delight in two corpses, nor shall I cause pain to my dead daughter. I have often heard her say that she would prefer Chaereas to live rather than herself. So let us make an end of this unnecessary trial and go off to the necessary funeral. Let us not let her corpse be ravaged by time, nor disfigure her body with decay. Let us bury Callirhoe while she is still beautiful.

(1.6) The jury, then, voted to acquit Chaereas. But he would not acquit himself, but wished for death and devised every means to bring it about. And Polycharmus, seeing that there was no other way to save him, accused him:

> Traitor to your wife's corpse, will you not survive even to bury Callirhoe? Are you entrusting her corpse to the hands of others? It is now time for you to bury her with rich funerary offerings and arrange a funeral fit for a princess.

These counsels won him over, for they gave him a sense of honouring and caring for Callirhoe.

Who then could have done justice to describing that funeral?[16] Callirhoe lay decked in her bridal gown and on a gold-studded bier, more magnificent and striking than ever, so that everyone compared her to Ariadne asleep. And before the bier came first the Thessalian cavalry and their horses in ceremonial dress; after these the hoplites, bearing the insignia of Hermocrates' triumphs; then the council and all the magistrates, acting as Hermocrates' bodyguards and surrounded by the citizen body. And Ariston was carried along, still ill, calling Callirhoe 'daughter and lady'. Next followed the citizens' wives decked in black; then a royal treasure of funeral offerings: first the gold and silver of Callirhoe's dowry, beautifully ornamented clothing (Hermocrates had provided a great deal from the spoils of war), and the presents from relatives and friends. Last came the wealth of Chaereas: for he wanted, if possible, to burn all his possessions along with his wife. The young men of Syracuse carried the bier, and the mass of the people followed. Chaereas was heard lamenting louder than all the rest. Now Hermocrates had a magnificent tomb near the sea,[17] so as to be visible to sailors far out across the water. The sumptuous funeral offerings filled it like a treasure house. But what was meant to honour the girl's corpse gave rise to even greater events.

(1.7) For there was a man called Theron, a villainous fellow,[18] who sailed the sea for criminal ends, with pirates lying at anchor in the harbours on the pretext of being ferrymen; but Theron knocked them together as a pirate crew.[19]

This man chanced to run into the funeral and got his eyes on the gold; he could not sleep that night in his bed for saying to himself:

> Am I to risk my life fighting the sea and killing the living for the sake of tiny rewards, when it is possible to make a fortune from a single dead girl? Let the die be cast. I shall not give up on this profit. And yet who shall I recruit for the enterprise? Look carefully, Theron: which of your associates is right for the job? Zenophanes of Thurii? He is cunning, but cowardly. Meno of Messene? Bold, but treacherous.

He went through them one by one in his calculations, like a money-changer, rejecting many, but approving some as suitable. And so he found some of them in brothels, others in taverns, a suitable army for such a general. So saying that he had something important to say to them, he led them off behind the harbour and began with this:

> I have found a treasure-trove and have chosen you out of all <the band> to share it: there is too much for one, and yet it does not call for a great deal of effort; a single night can make us all rich. We are not inexperienced in this line of work, which is condemned by fools but affords profit to thinking men.

At once they realised that he was giving notice of some pirate raid or tomb-breaking or temple-robbery, and said 'Stop preaching to the converted, and just tell us the job, and don't let's let the opportunity go by'. Theron resumed from this point:

> You have seen the gold and silver that belongs to the dead girl. It would be fairer for it to belong to us who are still alive. So I have decided to open the tomb, then putting the treasure in the cutter, to sail to wherever the wind carries us, and sell the cargo abroad.

They approved the plan. 'For the moment, then', he said, 'back to your normal occupations. But when darkness falls each of you is to come down to the cutter with a builder's tool'.

(1.8) These men, then, went about their business, but as for Callirhoe, she had a second return to life; through lack of food she experienced an easing of her blocked breathing, and gradually and with difficulty she found her pulse. Then she began to move, one limb at a time, and opening her eyes fully she had the experience of awakening from sleep, and called Chaereas as if he were asleep beside her. And when neither her husband nor the servants replied, but everything was darkness and desolation, she felt a fearful shiver, and could not work out what had really happened. As she slowly came to, she touched the wreaths and ribbons, and made the gold and silver clink. And there was a heavy odour of spice. So then she remembered the kick and the fall resulting from it. Gradually she realised that loss of consciousness had caused her to be buried. So she screamed as loudly as she could, shouting 'I'm alive!' and 'Help!'. And when despite her frequent cries nothing further happened, she gave up hope of still being rescued, and laying her head on her knees she kept sobbing:

> what a dreadful business! I have been buried alive after doing nothing wrong, and I am dying a lingering death. They are mourning me as dead, while I am <alive and> well. Who will send word? It is unfair of you, Chaereas: I blame you not for killing me, but because you were so quick to throw me out of the house. It was not right for you to bury Callirhoe <so> quickly, not even if she were really dead. But perhaps you are already planning some other marriage!.

(1.9) Callirhoe, then, was absorbed in all her sorrows, but Theron waited for midnight and silently approached the tomb, touching the water gently with the oars. And when he was the first to disembark he organised his oarsmen as follows. He put four on watch, for anyone approaching, whom they were to kill if they could. If not, to give an agreed signal for their approach. He himself went to the tomb with four others. The remaining seven (for there were sixteen in all) he ordered to remain on the cutter, with the oars at the ready, so that if some sudden emergency should occur, they could quickly snatch the shore-party and make off.[20]

And when they put their crowbars in place and their strokes grew louder as they broke open the tomb, Callirhoe was seized by all her emotions together: fear, joy, anxiety, bewilderment, hope, disbelief:

> Where is the noise coming from? Has some spirit arrived for my poor corpse, as happens to all the dying? Or is it not a noise, but the voice of the powers below summoning me to them? More probably it is tomb-robbers. And so I have more tribulations to face! Wealth is no use to a corpse!.[21]

She was still working it out when the robber put his head forward and slipped a little way into the tomb. Callirhoe fell down in front of him, starting to plead with him. But he was terrified and leapt out. And with a shiver he yelled to his comrades, 'Let's get out of here! For there's a ghost guarding what's inside and won't allow us to come in!'. Theron laughed, calling him a coward, and deader than the corpse. Then he ordered someone else to go in. But when no-one would dare, he himself went in, with his sword at the ready. At the glint of steel Callirhoe was terrified of being killed; she drew herself back into the corner and begged him from there in a thin voice: 'Whoever you are, show pity on a woman who has had no pity from husband or parents. Do not kill the girl you have saved'.

Theron took courage, and as a quick-witted fellow, he gathered the truth. He stood thinking, and his first plan was to kill the girl, thinking that she would be an obstacle to the whole undertaking. But he quickly changed his mind at the prospect of profit, and said to himself: 'She too must be part of the tomb-treasure. There is plenty of silver and gold here, but the girl's beauty is worth more than all that'. So taking her hand he brought her out, then he called his companions and said, 'look, the spirit you were afraid of. Some pirates you are, terrified of a woman! Now guard her, for I want to restore her to her parents. And let us remove the hoard inside, since no longer is there even the corpse to guard it'.

(1.10) And when they had filled their cutter with the loot, Theron ordered the guard to stand aside a little way with the girl. Then he laid before them the question of what to do about her. Opinions were divided and rather contradictory. For the first speaker argued,

> We came for one purpose, comrades in arms, but Fortune, as it turns out, has given us something better. Let us make use of it. For we can do our business without risk. Now it seems to me that we should leave the tomb-offerings where they were, but restore Callirhoe to her husband and father, claiming that we were anchored near the tomb in the course of our usual fishing, but that we heard her voice and opened the tomb out of pity, so as to rescue the girl trapped inside. Let us bind the woman with an oath to back up all our claims. She will gladly do this in her gratitude to the benefactors who saved her. Think of all the joy we will bring to the whole of Sicily, and all the rewards we shall have! And at the same time when we do this we shall be acting righteously in the eyes of men, and piously in the eyes of the gods!

As he was still speaking another speaker opposed him:

> You have no sense of timing, you fool! Are you telling us to behave like philosophers? So robbing a tomb has turned us into reformed characters, has it?[22] Shall we take pity on her, when her own husband showed her none, but killed her instead? For she has done us no harm; but she will do us the greatest possible harm in future. For first of all, if we give her back to her family, it is not clear how they will judge what has happened, and impossible not to be suspicious of the reason we came to the tomb. And even if the girl's family thank us by dropping the charge, nonetheless the magistrates and the people themselves will not let off tomb-robbers carrying the cargo to condemn themselves. And perhaps someone will say it is more profitable to steal the girl, for she will fetch a high price because of her beauty. But even this has its dangers: for gold does not have a voice, and silver will not tell people where we got it. It is possible to make up some story about these commodities. But a cargo with eyes and ears and a tongue, who would be able to hide? Besides, her beauty is no ordinary human variety, so that we could escape notice. Will we say she is a slave?

> Who will believe that to look at her? So let us kill her here, and not carry round with us our own accuser.

Although many agreed with these suggestions, Theron did not support either of them.

> You are asking for danger, while you are knocking out our profit. I will sell the girl rather than kill her. For while she is being sold she will hold her tongue through fear, and once she has been sold let her accuse us once we are no longer there. But let's get aboard and set sail. For already it's almost day.

(1.11) When they weighed anchor the ship made excellent progress, for they were under no pressure from wind and wave, as they had planned no special route, but every wind seemed to favour them and stood on their stern. And Theron tried to console Callirhoe, attempting to deceive her with various notions. But she was aware of her position and that she had not been rescued for her own good. And she pretended not to be aware, but to believe him, fearing that if she showed her indignation they might do away with her. And saying that she was unable to bear the sea, she covered her face and wept: 'You, father', she said,

> defeated three hundred Athenian ships on this sea, and yet a tiny cutter has carried off your daughter and you are not coming to my aid. I am being taken off to a foreign land, and noble girl as I am, I have to be a slave. Perhaps some Athenian master will buy the daughter of Hermocrates. How much better it was for me to lie dead in the tomb. At least Chaereas would have been laid to rest with me. But now both in life and death we have been driven apart.

And so she was engaged in this sort of lamentation, but the pirates sailed past small islands and towns, for theirs was not a poor man's cargo, but they were looking for wealthy buyers. And they dropped anchor under a headland facing Attica. And there there was a spring with plenty of pure water and a lovely meadow. Then bringing Callirhoe they expected her to wash and rest for a little time from the sea, as they wished to preserve her beauty. And once on their own they discussed where to make for. And someone said:

> Athens is nearby, a great and prosperous city. There we shall find a horde of traders and a horde of rich buyers. For it is possible in Athens to see as many cities as you see men in a market-place.

All of them were for sailing to Athens, but Theron did not like Athenian curiosity.

> Are you the only ones who have not heard of Athenian love of meddling? The citizen body is talkative and fond of lawsuits. And in the harbour there are any number of informers who will find out who we are and where

we got that cargo of ours. Nasty suspicion will take hold of these wicked men. The Areopagus is right there, and the officials are more oppressive than tyrants.[23] We ought to be more afraid of the Athenians than the Syracusans.[24] The place we need is Ionia, for there there are royal riches flowing in from the whole of Asia, and people who practise luxury without asking questions. And I expect to find there some of my cronies.

So they took on fresh water and fresh supplies from merchantmen moored alongside. They made for Miletus, and after two days dropped anchor at a mooring 80 stades from the city, well suited to offer them shelter.

(1.12) Then Theron gave orders to ship the oars and make a shelter for Callirhoe and do everything to make her comfortable. This he did not do out of human kindness but out of greed, as a salesman rather than a pirate. He himself went off quickly to the city with two companions. Then he had no wish to look in public for a buyer or to make a talking-point of the business, but tried for a quick sale secretly and without a middleman. But this turned out difficult to carry through. For the property was not for ordinary buyers, or for some chance buyer, but for someone of means and princely standing, and yet he was afraid to go near such clients. So after too much time-wasting he could no longer bear further delay. And when night came he was unable to sleep, but said to himself,

> You are a fool, Theron, for already you have left gold and silver in a deserted spot for so many days, as if you were the only pirate. Do you not know that other pirates too sail the seas? And I am even afraid of my own men in case they desert me and sail off. For of course you did not recruit the most upright of men so as to stay loyal to you, but the most unscrupulous men you knew. Now, then, he said: you need to get some sleep, but at daybreak make off to the cutter and throw into the sea this woman who is superfluous at this point, and do not again bring aboard a cargo so difficult to get rid of. Meanwhile:

★ ★ ★

He fell asleep and saw in his dream doors closed. So he decided to hold off for that day. And wandering about he sat down in some shop with his thoughts in confusion.

Meanwhile a crowd of people went by, slave and free, and among them a man in the prime of life, with a black cloak and a doleful look. So Theron got up (for people are naturally curious), and asked one of the man's companions, 'Who's this?'. The reply was, 'I think you must be a stranger or have come from afar, since you do not recognise Dionysius, the richest, noblest and most cultured man in Ionia, a friend of the Great King[25]'. 'So why is he wearing black?'. 'He has (just) lost his beloved wife'. Theron sought to keep up his conversation still further, now that he had found a man who was rich and in need of a woman to love. So he no longer held out on the way back but asked 'What position do you have in his household?' And the man replied, 'I am the steward of his whole estate, and I look after his daughter, who is only an infant, orphaned of her poor mother before her time'; 'What is your name?' 'Leonas'.

> I met you at the right moment, Leonas; I am a merchant sailing at this moment from Italy, hence I know nothing of affairs in Ionia. A lady of Sybaris, the wealthiest woman in the city, had a very beautiful maid whom she sold out of jealousy, and I have bought her. So you stand to do well out of this, whether you wish to acquire a nurse for the child (for she is well enough trained), or whether you think it worthwhile to do your master a favour. It is more advantageous to you for him to have a slave bought, so that he does not bring in a stepmother for your young charge.

Leonas was delighted at this suggestion [which he acts upon, so that Callirhoe is sold to Dionysius].

(3.3) After the tomb-robbers had sold their cargo, too hot to handle, they left Miletus and set sail for Crete, hearing that it was a large and prosperous island, in which they expected it would be easy to sell their wares. But a strong wind caught them and thrust them into the Ionian Sea, and there they drifted indefinitely over empty waters. Thunder and lightning and a great pall of night took hold of the impious crew, and Providence demonstrated that they had previously enjoyed good weather only because of Callirhoe. And as they came close to death each time, God would not allow them to be released from their fear of it, but only prolonged their shipwreck. And so land would not accept these villains, and as they spent their long spell at sea they were reduced to a dearth of provisions, especially water, and their ill-gotten gains did not avail them, but they were dying of thirst amid their gold. And so slowly they repented of their evil deeds, accusing one another that <their wickedness had been> pointless. All the rest, then, were dying of thirst, but Theron even in those circumstances practised his villainy. For by stealthily stealing water he even robbed his fellow robbers. Now he considered that he had carried out a sort of professional task, but this was the work of Providence, saving him for torture and the cross.[26]

The trireme carrying Chaereas[27] ran across the cutter as it drifted, and at first they gave it a wide berth as a likely pirate-ship. But when it appeared to have no helmsman, and was drifting under the impact of the waves, someone from the trireme shouted: 'The ship has no crew! Let's not be afraid, but heave to and investigate the unexpected'. The helmsman agreed; Chaereas for his part was weeping below deck with his head completely covered. And when they came alongside, at first they called on the crew. And when no-one answered, someone from the trireme went aboard. He saw nothing other than gold and corpses. He passed the word to the crew, who were delighted and thought themselves in luck to have found treasure on the high seas. And with all the noise and excitement

Chaereas asked the reason. When he found out he too wanted to see the strange sight. But once he recognised the funeral offerings he tore his clothes to shreds and exclaimed as he gave a loud piercing cry:

> Alas, Callirhoe! These are your things! This is the wreath I laid about you! Here is the one your father gave you, this one is your mother's; and this robe is your bridal gown. This ship is now your tomb. But I see your things, and yet where are you? Among all we buried with you, only your corpse is missing!

When he heard this Theron lay like one of the corpses, and in fact he actually was half-dead. Now he had stiffly resolved not to let out a sound or make any movement. For he was not unaware of what awaited him. Men love life by nature and even in the utmost adversity they hope for a change for the better, as their creator implanted this erroneous idea in all of them, so that they should not shy away from life's miseries. So in the grip of thirst the first word he let out was 'water!'. And when it was brought to him, and he had received every attention, Chaereas sat down beside him and asked: 'Who are you, and where are you sailing to? Where did these come from, and what have you done to the girl who owned them?' The villain Theron remembered his old self and said:

> I come from Crete, and I am sailing to Ionia to look for my brother who is serving in the army. I was left behind by my ship's crew when they embarked quickly in Cephallenia. From there I took a passage on this cutter which was sailing past, as luck would have it. And we were driven into these waters by gale force winds. Then we were becalmed for a long stretch; all the crew died of thirst, while I alone was saved because of my piety.

So when he heard this, Chaereas gave orders for the trireme to take the cutter in tow, and at dawn he sailed home to the harbours of Syracuse.

(3.4) But Rumour, swift by nature, spread there first. She made still greater haste to give word of so much surprising news. So all ran down to the sea at this time, and there was a variety of emotions at once: people cried, were amazed, or curious, or incredulous. For the strange tale had them dumbfounded. When Callirhoe's mother saw her daughter's funeral offerings she let out a wail. 'I recognise everything: only you, daughter, are not here. A new kind of tomb robber: they have kept the clothing and the gold safe, and have stolen only my daughter!'. The shore and harbours resounded with women beating their breasts, and they filled earth and sea alike with their mourning. And Hermocrates, who was a natural leader and a man of affairs, said, 'We cannot conduct an enquiry here, but must examine matters in a more legal framework. Let us adjourn to the assembly. Who knows whether we shall need a jury?'

Not yet had the last word been said when already the theatre was full. That assembly women too attended. The citizen body then sat all agog. Chaereas came in first, dressed in black, pale and dishevelled, just as when he followed his wife to her tomb, and he refused to mount the platform, but stood below and at first wept at length; and although he wished to speak he was unable to. The crowd kept shouting, 'Come on, speak up'. With difficulty then he looked up and said:

> This occasion was not intended for speechmaking, but for mourning. But I am forced to speak for the same reason I am forced to live, until I can get to the bottom of Callirhoe's disappearance; for that reason I sailed from there, and I do not know whether my voyage has been favourable or not. For we saw a ship drifting in fair weather, oppressed by a storm of its own and foundering in a calm sea. In our amazement we came in close. I thought I was looking at my poor wife's tomb: all her possessions were there, except for herself. There was a mass of corpses, all of them strangers. And this fellow was found among them, half dead. I made every effort to bring him back to life, and I have guarded him on your account.

Meanwhile the public slaves brought Theron in chains into the theatre, with a suitable escort. For he was followed by the wheel, the rack, the fire and the whips, as Providence was paying him back the rewards for his efforts. But when he stood in their midst, one of the magistrates cross-examined him: 'Who are you?'. 'Demetrius'. 'From where?'. 'From Crete'. 'What do you know? Tell us!'

> I was sailing to Ionia to meet my brother, but I missed my sailing, then I took a cutter passing by. At that time I took them for merchants, though now I realise they were tomb-robbers. We were at sea for a long time, and all the others have died for lack of drinking-water, but I alone have been saved because I have never done anything wrong in my life. And so, Men of Syracuse, a body renowned for its humanity, do not be more savage to me than thirst and sea!.

When he said this the crowd felt pity towards him, and perhaps he would have won them over, and even gained his passage home, had not some spirit of vengeance for Callirhoe taken exception to his wicked lies. For it would have been the direst possible calamity for the Syracusans to have been persuaded that he alone was saved because of his piety when he was only saved by his impiety, so as to receive a still harsher punishment.

And so a fisherman sitting in the crowd recognised him and whispered to his neighbours, 'I've seen this man before, hanging about round our harbour'. So quickly the word spread, and someone shouted, 'He's lying!'. So the people turned about, and the magistrates told the man who had spoken first to step down. And although Theron denied the accusation, it was the fisherman they preferred to believe. And at once they called the torturers and put the villain under the lash. Even when they burned and cut him he held out a long time and almost got the better of the torturers. But conscience is a strong force in everyone, and truth is all-powerful. For slowly and with great difficulty Theron confessed, and so he began his account:

> Seeing the wealth that was being buried, I got a pirate band together and we opened the tomb. We found the corpse alive; we plundered everything and put it in the cutter. After sailing to Miletus all we sold was the girl; the rest we were transporting to Crete. And thrust out into the Ionian Sea by the winds, you yourselves have seen what we suffered.

And in making his confession he failed to mention only the name of the man who had bought Callirhoe.

When he had said this everyone was seized by joy and grief: joy that Callirhoe was alive, and grief that she had been sold. And so the death penalty was passed on Theron. But Chaereas begged for the man not to die yet: 'So that he can come and show me who bought her. Just think what I am forced to do – I am pleading on behalf of the man who sold my own wife!' This Hermocrates forbade: 'It is better', he said,

> to undertake a more laborious search than to relax the laws. I beg you, Men of Syracuse, to remember my feats as a general and my triumphs, and repay me by finding my daughter. Send an expedition for her, so that we can recover a freeborn girl from slavery.

While he was still speaking the citizen body shouted: 'Let us all sail', and of the council the great majority were willing to go. But Hermocrates said[28] 'I thank you all for this honourable gesture, but two envoys from the citizen body and two from the council will suffice, with Chaereas sailing as the fifth'.

This was decided and ratified, and Hermocrates dismissed the assembly on these conditions. And a great part of the population followed Theron as he was led away. And he was crucified[29] in front of Callirhoe's tomb, and he looked out from his cross over the sea over which he had carried the daughter of Hermocrates, whom not even the Athenians had been able to capture.[30]

Notes

1 The tale is the middle tale of three told for mutual entertainment by spinning women of Thebes, and illustrates a characteristic setting for oral tales.
2 The story seems best to belong with *ATU* 480, *The Kind and Unkind Girls* (*EM* 8, 1366–1375). Normally the good girl accomplishes tasks and is rewarded, the bad girl does not do them and is punished. The contrast is provided in this version by the plants they become: frankincense in the case of the virtuous girl, heliotrope in the case of the spiteful slanderer. Here there are two traces of a common context: the theme of the good girl at her spinning, and going down a well, here undergoing burial in the sand. Sometimes there is a role for a malevolent demon, who would correspond to the role of the rapist Helios.

3 Latin idiom allows intrusions in the narrative of direct address to the subject, either for variety or heightened emotional nuance.
4 Orchamus, an ancient king of Persia.
5 The heliotrope, supposed to turn toward the sun.
6 For the Innocent Slandered Maiden, Kawan, *EM* 8 (1996), 1402–1407. The jealous stepmother lends a folktale/fairy tale feel to the tale, as does the cunning way of circumventing the rash promise.
7 The future founder of the Greek colony of Cyrene.
8 Kawan *EM* 8 (1996), 1402–1407. The ancient version here appears as part of a lengthy romance. A good example of fairy tale treatment in Afanas'ev 415–418. There as here it is a general who despises not the hero this time, but the heroine, as the mere daughter of a merchant, and persuades an old woman to elicit the girl's secret mark (a golden hair under her arm) and steal her ring. This Russian version introduces actual magic: the slandered girl weeps diamonds into a glove, which she claims the false accuser stole from her house when he slept with her as he claims. To deny the theft he now has to deny ever having known her.
9 The unsuccessful suitors cut a faintly ludicrous spectacle, both in their degree of co-operation and in the image of tyrants or their sons behaving in the role of stereotypical lovers.
10 Hermocrates radiates enormous prestige as the architect of the victory over the ill-fated Athenian expedition to Syracuse, and his status is maintained throughout the plot.
11 The paradoxical spectacle of a democratic assembly of tyrants is typical of Chariton's light touch.
12 Theatrical metaphor is typical of the texture of the novelists, culminating in its florid use in late antiquity by Heliodorus.
13 A deliberately incongruous importation from Homeric scenes of physical combat and mourning: *Iliad*, 18.22–24.
14 Polycharmus' main function in the plot is to talk Chaereas out of suicide bids each time the plot lurches from crisis to crisis.
15 One of many contrived paradoxes on the fortunes of the lovers: cf. 4.1.1
16 The novels frequently arrange sumptuous spectacle appropriate to the tastes of a local urban aristocracy: cf. Xenophon of Ephesus 1.2.
17 This will serve as a significant marker at the end of the tomb-robbery plot, below 3.4.18.
18 Theron: 'wild', lawless'. Theron's lively and ironic style lends distinctive colour to his villainous role: he is throughout a pragmatic searcher after profit.
19 Pirates are among the most stable and characteristic personnel of the Greek novel, serving as the transport system in melodramatic and geographically wide-ranging plots.
20 The details of organisation contribute to precision in mundane details at variance with the fantasy of the plot.
21 Heroines' expostulations are particularly prominent in the texture of the novels in general: cf. 3.7.5.
22 The pirates invert normal human values in favour of stereotyped villainy.
23 The court of the Areopagus was used to try homicide cases, and the pirates have every reason to fear it.
24 Reardon (1982), 25 dismisses Theron's attitude as mere provincialism; but it is not mere fun at the expense of the Athenians, who in general are not the epicentre of romantic prose literature in later antiquity.
25 The Ionian cities in the era of Hermocrates still needed to maintain a cautious diplomatic relationship with the Persian Empire, of which they were in effect a part.
26 Theron maintains his professional villainy to the last.
27 Meanwhile following the discovery of the emptied tomb, Chaereas has gone off in search of his kidnapped wife.

28 Hermocrates is wryly used to curb the wilder excesses of the Syracusan citizen body, as previously, 1.5.6.
29 Scarcely less savage than the punishments produced by more obviously fairy tale plots.
30 Strictly speaking in this plot the tyrants who devised the intrigue should be subject to punishment: other versions of the tale in popular transmission tend to favour a scenario where the female victim is in male disguise, and finds herself passing judgement on her initial plotter.

8
TRICKSTERS

Cunning rather than heroism provides the impetus for trickster tales, even if the protagonist shows a great deal of heroism elsewhere. The cannibal giant seems close to the central stock of fairy-tale motifs: but Odysseus' negotiations with him suggest a veneer of politesse and sophistication lacking in most workings of the theme. The three workings of the robbers of the king's treasury advance cunning to a new level, with the grim beheading of one of the thieves to avoid detection. The offering of the king's daughter as a reward for the thief's cunning again seems consistent with fairy-tale values and expectations.

Blinding the Stupid Ogre[1]: Homer, *Odyssey* 9.177–566 (*ATU* 1137 The Ogre Blinded/Polyphemus)

(177) With these words I went aboard and ordered my comrades to embark as well and cast off the stern cables. And at once they embarked and sat on the rowers' benches, and sitting in order they beat the hoary sea with their oars. But when we arrived at the nearby land, there we saw at its edge near the shore a lofty cave, with a screen of laurel. And there many flocks, both sheep and goats, were quartered at night. And round about there was a high courtyard built with stones laid deep in the ground, and huge pine-trees and lofty-crested oaks. And there lived a great monster of a man,[2] who grazed his flocks on his own, and did not mix with others, but dwelt apart, a law unto himself. For he was an amazing creature. He did not look like a man who lives by bread; he was like a wooded peak among lofty mountains, which appears alone apart from the rest.

(193) So then I gave orders to the others to stay there beside the ship and guard it, but I chose 12 comrades, the best, and moved off. But I took a goatskin of dark sweet wine, a gift from Maron, son of Euanthes[3]: he was the priest of Apollo, the patron god of Ismarus, and we had protected him with his wife and child:

we respected him since he dwelt in the wooded grove of Phoebus Apollo, and so he gave me shining gifts: seven talents' worth of well-worked gold, a solid silver mixing bowl and in addition 12 wine-jars full of wine, sweet and undiluted, a drink fit for the gods. Nor did any of his slaves or housemaids know about it, only himself, his wife, and a single steward. And whenever they drank the honey-sweet red wine, he filled a single cup and poured it into twenty measures of water,[4] and a sweet divine bouquet rose from the mixing bowl. The effect was unrestrained. I took this and filled a great skin, and I put provisions in a bag. And in no time we arrived at the cave, but we did not find him inside; he was grazing his fat flocks on their pasture. And coming into the cave we were impressed at all we saw: the crates were filled with cheese, and the pens were crammed with lambs and kids. Each sort was in separate pens: firstlings, later lambs, and kids. And all the vessels were swimming with whey – milk-pails and bowls – well-wrought they were – into which he did the milking.[5] Then my companions begged me first of all to return with some of the cheeses, but then to drive off quickly to the swift ship the kids and lambs from the pens, and to sail off on the briny sea. But I did not pay heed to them[6] – it would certainly have been much better if I had – so that I might see him, and in the hope that he would give me gifts of hospitality. But when he appeared, he was not likely to be a kindly host to my companions.

(231) But then we started a fire, offered sacrifice, and ourselves took some of the cheeses and ate them, and sat inside the cave waiting for him until he returned driving his herd. And he carried a frightful weight of dry wood, to use at his supper, and threw it down inside the cave with a crash. But in terror we retreated to a recess within the cave. But he drove his rich flocks into the wide cave – all the ones he had milked, but left the rams and he-goats outside, within the ample courtyard. But then he heaved up and set in place the awesome rock that served as his doorway: two and twenty sturdy four-wheeled carts would not have been able to lift if from the threshold, such a huge mass of rock did he place in the doorway.[7] And he sat down and milked his ewes and bleating goats, every one in turn, and put each of the young under its dam. Then having curdled half the white milk, he collected it in wicker baskets and put it into store, while the rest he put in vessels to take to drink for his supper. But when he had quickly done his chores, he then kindled the fire, spotted us, and asked[8]:

> Stranger, who are you? Where are you sailing from over the ways of the water? Are you on business, or are you wandering at random the way pirates do over the sea, men who wander risking their lives and bringing ill on strangers from other lands?

(256) At this our hearts were dismayed, afraid at his deep voice and his monstrous nature; but still I gave him this for an answer:

> We are Achaeans, driven from Troy by all manner of winds over the huge gulf of the sea, making for home one way or another. So no doubt did Zeus

see fit to contrive. And we are proud to be called the host of Agamemnon son of Atreus, whose fame is now indeed the greatest under the heavens, for so great a city he sacked, and he slew many hosts. But we for our part coming upon you grasp your knees in supplication, hoping that you will provide us with some hospitality, or be generous to us in some other way, as is the law for guests. You must respect the gods, noble sir, we are your suppliants; and Zeus avenges suppliants and strangers: he it is who accompanies strangers to be respected.

(272) This was my case, but he at once replied with a cruel heart:

> You are a fool, stranger, or you have come from far away, that you tell me to fear or avoid the gods. For the Cyclopes have no regard for aegis-bearing Zeus, nor for the blessed gods, since in fact we are far superior to them. Neither would I spare either you or your companions to escape the hatred of Zeus, unless I were minded to do so.[9] But tell me where you moored your sturdy ship on your voyage here. Was it far away or near at hand? I should like to know.

(281) He said this to test me, but with all my experience I saw through it, as I replied in turn in cunning words.

> Poseidon the earth-shaker dashed my ship in pieces on the rocks on the edge of your country, by bringing her onto a cliff as the wind blew her in from the sea. But with these men here I escaped downright destruction.

That was my answer, but with his cruel intent he made no reply, but up he darted and got his hands on my comrades. He took two of them together and dashed them to the ground like puppies.[10] Their brains rushed out on the ground and stained the earth. He tore them limb from limb and prepared his upper. He ate them like a lion reared in the mountains, and left nothing: he devoured the entrails, flesh, marrow and bone. We for our part wailed and held out our hands to Zeus, at the sight of these wicked deeds, and our hearts were at a loss. But when the Cyclops had filled his great belly with human flesh, and then drank pure milk, he lay stretched out among the sheep within the cave. And I planned in my courageous heart to approach him and draw the sharp sword from my side and stab him in the chest where the midriff holds the liver, after feeling the spot with my hand. But another thought held me back. For there we too would have met certain death; for with our bare hands we could not thrust away from the lofty doorway the dreadful stone he had set in place. So then we wailed and waited for the shining dawn.

(307) And when the rosy fingers of early dawn appeared, then too he rekindled the fire and milked his splendid sheep, each in turn, and put the lamb to each mother, but when he had quickly performed his tasks, once more he seized

another pair and prepared his meal. After this he drove his rich flocks from the cave, after easily removing the great stone door. But then he replaced it, like a man putting the lid on his quiver. And the Cyclops whistled loudly as he turned his rich flocks to the mountain, leaving me however plotting mischief in the depths of my heart, hoping for revenge, and for Athene to grant me glory.[11]

(318) And in my heart this seemed the best plan. For there lay beside a pen a great club of green olive. This he had cut to carry with him once it had dried out: it looked to our gaze as big as the mast of a black twenty-oared ship, a broad-beamed cargo ship which crosses the wide sea – that was how big and thick it looked. I stood beside it and cut off as much as a fathom and handed it to my crew and told them to smooth it down, and they levelled it and I stood aside and sharpened the point, and at once took it and hardened it in the blaze of the fire.

(329) And I concealed it carefully away under the dung, which lay about the cave in huge heaps. But I ordered the others to cast lots for who should be bold enough to help me raise the stake and run it into his eye whenever sweet sleep might overtake him. And the very men drew the lots that I myself would have chosen. There were four of them, and I counted as fifth in the team.

(336) In the evening he came back, herding his lovely-fleeced sheep. And at once he drove all the fat flocks into the breadth of the cave, and did not leave any outside in the deep-fenced yard, whether out of suspicion, or because of divine prompting. But when he had raised up the huge stone door, he sat and milked the sheep and bleating goats, every one in turn, and put the young under each of the dams. But when he had quickly done all his tasks, once again he snatched a pair of my men and prepared his supper. And then I stood close to the Cyclops, holding an ivy-wood bowl of the dark wine. 'Cyclops', I said,

> here you are, drink wine, since you have been eating human flesh, so that you may know what sort of drink our ship held in its hold. I was bringing it as a libation for you, in the hope that you would take pity and send me home. But your mad behaviour we cannot bear: cruel creature, how would anyone of all mortal men ever visit you in the future, since you have not treated us with justice?

(353) At this he took the cup and drained it; he was overjoyed as he drank the sweet drink and asked me for it once again[12]:

> Be generous and give me another, and now tell me your name, so that I can give you a gift to gladden your heart. For the bountiful earth yields wine from its rich clusters to the Cyclopes as well, and the rain from Zeus increases it for them[13]; but this wine flows from a river of ambrosia and nectar.

At this time I gave him the sparkling wine once more. Three times I brought it and gave it to him, and three times the fool drained it. But when the wine had gone to the Cyclops' head, then too I spoke my honeyed words to him: 'Cyclops, you ask my famous name, and I will tell you it: and you give me the present you promised. My name is "Nobody".[14] Nobody is the name my mother and father and all my companions too call me'. That was what I told him, but he immediately replied from his cruel heart: 'Nobody, I shall eat last of all his comrades, after all the rest: that will be the gift I will give you'.

(371) He spoke, and rolled onto his back, and lay with his massive neck to one side. And sleep that subdues all men took hold of him. And his throat spewed out wine and chunks of human flesh, as he threw it up in his drunken stupor. And then I drove the stake beneath the deep ash until it grew hot, and encouraged all my companions so that no-one should take fright and falter. But as soon as the olive stake was on the point of bursting into flame, green as it was,[15] and took on a fiery glow, at that moment I pulled it close to me from the fire, and my comrades stood round me: and a god inspired us with great courage. They took the olive stake, sharp at the tip, and thrust it into his eye.[16] And I pressed it down from above and spun it round, as when a man drills a ship's plank with a drill, and the men below twirl it round with a thong, holding it from either side, as the drill keeps always running. Thus did we take hold of the bar with its fiery point and spun it round in his eye, and the hot blood flowed round about it. And all his eyelids and eyebrows round about the flame singed as the eyeball burned, and the roots of the eye crackled in the fire. And as when a bronze-worker dips a great axe or an adze in cold water to temper it and it makes a loud hissing sound – for from it comes the iron's strength, so did his eye hiss around the trunk of olive. And he gave a terrible cry, and the rock echoed round about, while we shrank back with fright. But he tore the stake from his eye, foul with all the blood. Then he threw it away from him with his hands in a mad fit; but he shouted loudly to the Cyclopes who lived on the windy crags in their caves round about.[17] And they approached, hearing the cry from their various quarters, and stood around the cave and asked what was troubling him. 'Why are you so upset, Polyphemus, that you cried out through the divine night and robbed us of our sleep? Surely no mortal is driving off your flocks against your will, or killing you with cunning or brute force?' Then mighty Polyphemus answered from inside the cave. 'My friends, Nobody is killing me with cunning or brute force'. They responded with winged words: 'If you are alone and no-one is offering you violence, you cannot escape illness from mighty Zeus, but you should pray to your father Poseidon'.

(413) With these words they went off, and I laughed in my heart that my name and my superb cunning had tricked them. But the Cyclops, howling and struggling in pain, groped with his hand and moved the stone from the door, and sat himself in the doorway with both his hands outstretched, hoping to catch anyone going towards the exit along with the sheep. For that no doubt was the sort of fool he took me for. But I plotted to find the best way of escaping death for both my comrades and myself. And I spun all manner of devices and plots; for I wanted us to survive, and there was a dreadful evil upon us. And this seemed to me the best plan: there were well-fed, thick-fleeced rams, handsome

huge beasts, with violet-dark wool. I silently bound these together with twisted withies, on which the Cyclops used to sleep, lawless monster that he was. I took three together: the middle one held a man, with the two others flanking it and protecting my comrades. And so three sheep carried each man. But as for myself, there was a ram that was by far the best in the flock. I took hold of him by the back and curled up under his shaggy belly. But as I clung with my hand to his amazing fleece, I held on upside down with daring heart. And so we groaned as we awaited the shining day. (437) And when early dawn appeared with her rosy fingers, at that moment the rams rushed out to their pasture, and the ewes bleated around their pens not yet milked, with their udders full to bursting. And their ruler, tormented by his dreadful sufferings, groped over the backs of all the sheep as they stood straight up. But the fool did not realise the men were bound beneath the udders of the woolly sheep. Last in line of his flock, the ram went out of the cave, sagging with the weight of his fleece and with me full of schemes. And mighty Polyphemus, feeling along his back, spoke to him:

> Dear ram,[18] why do you rush out like this through the cave, last of all? Never in the past have you been left behind by the sheep, but you were by far the first to graze the tenderly blooming grass, with your great stride, and first to arrive at the streams of the river, and first in the evening to want to return to the fold. But now you are the very last. You must be sorry for your master's eye, which a wicked man blinded with his sorry companions, dulling my senses with wine. Nobody — I tell you — has not yet escaped his destruction. If only you were to have my sense and powers of speech to tell me where he is skulking off from my wrath, his brains would be scattered all over the cave after I had dashed him against the ground, and my heart would be relieved of the troubles which the good-for-nothing Nobody has brought me.

(461) With this he sent the ram from him towards the entrance. And when we had gone a little way from the cave and the courtyard, I was the first to free myself from below the ram, and then I freed my comrades. And swiftly we drove off the long-shanked sheep, rich in fat, with many a backward glance, until we reached the ship. Our dear companions were overjoyed at the sight of us who had escaped death, while they wailed and groaned over the others. But I would not allow them to weep; yet by nodding to each with my eyebrows I forbade them, but ordered them to throw the fine-fleeced sheep quickly aboard and sail across the salt sea. And at once they embarked and sat down on their benches. And sat in formation they struck the hoary sea with their oars. But when I was as far away as a man can be heard when he shouts, at that moment I taunted the Cyclops[19]:

> Cyclops, it could not have been a weakling whose comrades you were minded to eat with your brute force in your cave. All too well were you destined to come to grief, you wretch, who did not flinch from eating

guests in your own home. And so Zeus and the other gods have paid you back.

(480) At this he grew still angrier in his heart, and broke off the cap of a great mountain and launched it at us. And it landed a little behind the dark-prowed ship, and almost hit the tip of the steering-oar. And the sea was churned up beneath the rock as it landed. And the wave surged back, driving the ship rapidly back to the shore, like a great wave, and pushed it back towards the land.

(486) But I took a long pole in my hands and pushed the ship away and along, and encouraged my crew by a nod of the head to fall to their oars, so as to escape our dire straits, and they threw themselves to the oars and rowed. But when at last our efforts had taken us twice as far from the shore, then I hailed the Cyclops and round about my companions tried from one quarter or another to dissuade me gently:

> You stubborn fool! Why do you wish to provoke a wild man, who even now has brought the ship back to dry land by throwing his missile into the sea, and we actually said we would perish in this very spot. And if he had heard any of us uttering a sound or speaking, he would have thrown a rugged rock and crushed together our heads and the boards of our ship, so strong is his throw.

In spite of these words, they could not persuade my courageous heart, but I addressed him once more with anger inside me: 'Cyclops, if any mortal man should ask who shamefully blinded your eye, tell them it was Odysseus who sacks cities, the son of Laertes, who lives on Ithaca'.[20]

(506) At this he answered with a groan:

> Alas, now indeed an ancient prophecy comes upon me. Here there was a prophet, a great and good man, Telemus son of Eurymus, who was by far the best of soothsayers, and he grew to old age as a prophet among the Cyclopes: he it was who said all this should happen in the future, that I should lose my sight at the hands of Odysseus.[21] But I was always expecting some huge handsome man to come here, girt with great might; but now a little man, worthless and a weakling, has robbed me of my eye after subduing me with wine. But come here, Odysseus, so that I may lay beside you gifts of friendship and urge the renowned Earth-shaker to give you a send-off. For I am his son, and he claims to be my father, and he himself, if he wishes, will heal me, but none other of the blessed gods or mortal men.

(522) To this I replied: 'If only I could deprive you of soul and life and send you into the House of Hades, as <surely as> not even the Earth-shaker shall heal your eye!'.[22] In response to these words he then stretched out his hands to the starry heavens and prayed the lord Poseidon:

Listen, Poseidon the Earth-shaker with the dark locks, if I am really your son, and you claim to be my father: grant me that Odysseus sacker of cities son of Laertes dweller in Ithaca may not return home, but if he is fated to arrive at his well-built house and see his friends and reach his native land, may he arrive late in misery, after destroying all his crew, on someone else's ship, and may be find sorrows in his household.[23]

Master-Thief: Herodotus 2.121 (*ATU* 950 Rhampsinitus)

They said that Rhampsinitus[24] succeeded Proteus… (a) This king had great wealth in silver, which none of his successors could exceed or approach. And as he wished to keep his treasure safe he built a stone treasury, which had one wall shared with the outer wall of his palace. And the builder planned this device: he prepared one of the stones to be easily removable by two men or even one. And when the building was finished, the king stored his treasure there. And as time went on the builder, at the end of his life, called together his sons (there were two of them) and explained to them that he had seen to it that they should enjoy a prosperous lifestyle, by the way he had contrived the building of the treasury. He explained clearly all about the removal of the stone, and gave the measurements to find it, telling them that if they preserved the secret they would be the stewards of the king's wealth. And he died, but the sons lost no time in setting to work: they went at night to the palace, easily found and handled the stone in the treasury, and removed a large quantity of treasure. (b) But when the king chanced to open the treasury, he was amazed to see the treasury vessels depleted, and did not know whom to accuse, as the seals were intact and the building securely shut. And when he opened the chamber a second and a third time and the treasure always seemed less (for the thieves did not stop their plundering), he took the following action: he ordered traps[25] to be constructed and laid round the vessels containing the treasure. And when the thieves came as before and one of them slipped in, when he approached a particular vessel he was instantly held in the trap. And when he realised the danger he was in, he immediately called his brother and showed him the way things were, and ordered his brother to slip in as quickly as he could and cut off his own head, so that he himself should not be seen and recognised, and bring about the death of his brother as well. The latter approved of the plan, and once convinced carried it out, and putting the stone back in place he left for home, carrying his brother's head. (c) And when day came, the king came into the treasury and was aghast to see the body of the thief in the trap without his head, and the treasury intact without any way in or out. And at a loss he took the following action: he hung the thief's body down from the outer wall, and set guards over it, with orders to arrest and bring before him anyone they saw weeping or lamenting over it.

But when the body was hung up, the thief's mother was greatly distressed; she spoke to the surviving son and told him to find a way of freeing his brother's body and bringing it home.[26] And if he neglected to do this, she threatened that she herself would go to the king and tell him that her son had the treasure. (d) And when she took the surviving brother to task and he could not win her round after a great deal of argument, he devised the following trick: he got ready asses and after filling skins full of wine he put them on the asses and then drove them off. And when he was at the spot where the guards were minding the hanging body, he tugged at the feet of two or three of the skins and loosened their fastenings, and when the wine ran out he beat his head and bawled loudly, as if he did not know which of the asses to attend to first. And when the guards saw a great quantity of wine running, they ran into the road with vessels as though they had made a great windfall by carrying off the spilt wine. The thief put on a show of anger and gave them all a rollicking[27]; the guards consoled him and in time he pretended to calm down and abandon his anger, and at last he drove his asses off the road and put his things in order. And when he and the guards fell into conversation and one of them joked with him and they started laughing, he gave them one of the skins; and they sat down there just as they were and were minded to drink, and brought him into their company and told him to stay and share the wine with them; and he let himself be persuaded and stayed. And when they grew merry towards him with the drink, he gave them yet another of the skins. As the wine flowed the guards became hopelessly drunk, and overcome by sleep they lay down where they were drinking. And as the night was far gone he cut down his brother's body, and to insult the guards shaved each one's right cheek, placed the body on the asses, and drove off home, having fulfilled his mother's instructions.[28]

(e) When the king was told that the thief's corpse had been stolen, he was outraged, and wished to find whoever contrived the trick at all costs, and took the following action, although I find it incredible.[29] He installed his own daughter in a chamber with instructions to receive all comers, but before sleeping with them, to force each man to confess to her the cleverest and the wickedest thing he had done in his life. And whoever told her the thief's story, to seize him and not allow him to escape. And when the girl carried out her father's instructions, the thief realised why she was doing this and wishing to outwit the king's cunning took the following action. He cut off the arm of a newly dead corpse at the shoulder, and went with the arm under his cloak to the king's daughter; when asked the same question as the others, he told her that his most impious act was to cut off his brother's head when he was trapped in the king's treasury, and the cleverest when he freed his brother's hanging body by inebriating the guards. And when she heard this she took hold of him, and in the darkness the thief stretched out to her the arm of the corpse and she took hold of that, thinking that she was taking hold of the thief's arm; while he, having given it to her, made off and escaped through the door.

(f) When word was brought of this to the king he was at his wits' end over the resourcefulness and audacity of the fellow, and at last he sent word to every city, granting immunity and offering a great reward if he would appear in the king's presence. The thief trusted the king and appeared before him; Rhampsinitus was greatly impressed, and gave him the daughter as his wife, because he was the cleverest of men. For insofar as the Egyptians were superior to all others in cunning, so he was superior to the Egyptians.[30]

Agamedes and Trophonius: Pausanias 9.37.3 (*ATU* 950)

Erginus took a young wife in response to the oracle, and had sons Trophonius and Agamedes. And Trophonius was said to be the son of Apollo and not of Erginus. And I believe this, as does anyone who has gone to consult Trophonius' oracle. They say that when they grew up they became skilled at building shrines for the gods and palaces for men. For they built Apollo's temple in Delphi and the Treasury for Hyrieus. And there they constructed one of the stones so that they could remove it from the outside. And they kept on taking something from the store. Hyrieus was speechless when he noticed that keys and seals were otherwise intact, while the supply of money continued to diminish. So among the vessels containing his silver and gold he placed traps or some other device to catch the thief who came in to steal the money. And when Agamedes came in he was caught in the trap: but Trophonius cut his head off, so that when day came Agamedes should not be put to the torture and he himself should not be informed on as a partner in crime. And the earth split open and received Trophonius at the grove at Lebadeia where the so-called pit of Agamedes is situated, with the monument beside it.

Agamedes and Trophonius: Charax of Pergamum (*FGrH* 103 F5 = schol. V Aristophanes *Clouds* 508) (*ATU* 950)

Agamedes, the ruler of Stymphalus in Arcadia, married Epicaste, who gave birth to the illegitimate Trophonius. These men were the greatest of their time in technical skills, and built the temple of Apollo in Delphi. In Elis they built the treasury for the gold of Augeas. In this they left a stone loose, and going in at night they stole money with Kerkyon as an accomplice, the legitimate child of Agamedes and Epicaste. And when Augeas was at a loss, he begged Daedalus, who was living as an exile from Minos, to seek out the thief. He set traps, and Agamedes fell victim and was caught. Trophonius cut his head off to avoid his being recognised, and fled, while Kerkyon fled to Orchomenos. When Augeas at the instruction of Daedalus set off in pursuit following the trail of blood, they fled, Kerkyon taking refuge in Athens; Trophonius went to Lebadeia in Boiotia, and making a trench he lived there. And on his death an accurate oracle appeared to him, and they sacrifice to him as to a god.

Notes

1 On Polyphemus: Hackman (1904); Frazer (1921), 404–455; Page (1955), 1–20; Heubeck and Hoekstra (1989), 19–42; Anderson (2000), 123–131; Hansen (2002), 289–301; Conrad *EM* 10 (2002), 1174–1184.

2 We are left in no doubt that the Cyclops is a giant or even ogre, but very little is said about his actual appearance: compare the similes used to characterise his counterpart in the *Third Voyage of Sindbad* (Dawood, 130): 'tall as a palm-tree, with red eyes burning in his head like coals of fire; his mouth was a dark well, with lips that drooped like a camel's loosely over his chest'.
3 The deliberate description of the strength of the wine (in ancient Greek practice very strong, but heavily diluted) acts as a broad hint of its importance for the story.
4 This suggests that it is four or five times the strength of ordinary wine.
5 Odysseus' crew see the acceptable side of the Cyclops first: he is a well organised and devoted pastoralist; only in the cannibal phase of his behaviour are we introduced to the heaps of dung left inside the cave, 9.329f. below.
6 A rare misjudgement on Odysseus' part, brought about by a decidedly 'materialist' approach: compare his preoccupation with 'checking' that the Phaeacians have not stolen any of his gifts, 13.215f.
7 This is the problem that precludes killing the Cyclops while asleep. The doorway in the *Thousand and One Nights* version is a metal door of a palace, and is used very carelessly: Sindbad's crew escape but aimlessly return when they can find no hiding-places on the island!
8 The creature in the *Thousand and One Nights* version does not speak.
9 Homer seems to have forgotten that the Cyclops is a son of Poseidon, which ought to indicate some degree of recognition for the latter's brother Zeus.
10 Here the victims are chosen apparently at random; some other versions, including Sindbad, have the ogre feeling the victims for their fatness, and sparing the leanest till last. In most instances of the folktale versions the victims are cooked first, hence their need for a metal roasting-spit.
11 Athene is conspicuously absent as a *deus ex machina* in this episode, in contrast to her role in e.g. the episode of Nausicaa or the showdown with the suitors.
12 The Cyclops seems a stupid ogre at his stupidest here: why should those clearly about to die still offer their thank-offering in the face of the ogre's ingratitude? In oral folktale the powers of the black-and-white enemy are not high. The motif is absent from the *Sindbad* story and from *Dede Korkut* because of cultural attitudes to alcohol in the Muslim world.
13 Oddly again: the Cyclops seems to acknowledge the help of Zeus, despite his previous indifference.
14 The 'Noman' trick is significantly absent from most oral versions, except a small Finnish group (Hackman's type C). The tale-type it embodies does not normally involve a giant, but rather fairies hurt by a spark from the fire, by someone called 'myself'. It offers wordplay on cunning intelligence by the pun between *mētis* and *mē tis*, the oblique negative form, which does occur in the narrative. But *outis* is the form originally given, and the pun would be difficult to grasp.
15 A little awkwardness here; it has been suggested that the stake glows red-hot because the original would have been metal: cf. Page (1955), 9–12.
16 We have not actually been told that he only has one eye (he has two in *Sindbad*, so that 'synchronised blinding' is needed there).
17 The community as hitherto described before the start of the tale proper (9.105–115) is very loose, each Cyclops being a law unto himself.
18 An unusual note of pathos, absent in oral versions; the Cyclops has a rapport with his animal companions, lacking in his relation to humans.
19 This foolhardy gesture does appear in the folk versions. In some a fairy tale feature appears at this point but is missing in the *Odyssey*: the hero, ever set on gifts, equally stupidly falls for the gift of a talking ring from the Cyclops; it acts as a homing device by saying 'Here I am' until the hero saves his life by cutting off the finger to which it is now irremovably attached.
20 Another error of judgement: the Cyclops can now tell his father Poseidon the true name of the perpetrator.

21 Likewise Circe finds in *Od.* 10.325–332 that Odysseus has been predicted to outwit her.
22 Odysseus will pay for the arrogance of this: cf. the comic development in Lucian *Dialogi Marini*, 2.4.
23 As turns out to be the case: Odysseus loses the last of his own crew in book 12, and comes back from Scheria on a Phaeacian ship.
24 There is little hope of determining the earliest history of this tale from the three ancient examples that survive: that in Herodotus set in the Egyptian New Kingdom; Charax of Pergamum in a scholiast on Aristophanes (*Clouds*, 508) and a testimony in Pausanias (9.37.4–8) both set on the Greek mainland. It clearly belongs to a larger trickster cycle, where it is possible for episodes to be inserted or omitted at will. For Herodotus' version, note Asheri-Lloyd-Conshera (2007) *ad loc*. The name Rhampsinitus ('Rameses son of the goddess Neith') is evidently a conflation of several Egyptian rulers of the 19th and 20th Dynasties. Sometimes the modern folktale has an initial motif in which the thieves meet and test one another, instead of being in a predetermined family relationship, which in itself is variable in the ancient examples (two brothers, father and son...). The two Greek versions omit any entertaining pranks and centre attention firmly on the founding of Trophonius' oracle. See also Hansen, 357–371; van der Kooi *EM* 11 (2004), 633–640.
25 Some of the folktale versions are more specific, for example a surface of adhesive pitch.
26 A truncated presentation that does not require public mourning on the part of the mother or spouse.
27 Sometimes the mother's mourning is effected by her being seen to lament for the leakage of wine from the wineskin, without actual theft of the body.
28 An additional trick is for a guard to follow the thief home and mark his door, to which the thief responds by marking all other doors in the street.
29 This action, dismissed as incredible by Herodotus, suggests the consolidation of the folktale before the historian: it has the feel of 'I will give my daughter in marriage to anyone who can catch the thief...'
30 Other Near Eastern versions sometimes include an episode where the royal thief silences criticism of a neighbouring monarch who criticises the king for the marriage. The thief disguises as a guide to the dead and cons the king and queen into thinking they are dead and must dance naked when their coffins open – of course in front of his own master's court. There may be some hint of this in Herodotus' allusion to Rhampsinitus' interest in the world below, but it does not form part of the tale itself. There is further chthonic reference in the two shorter accounts, that the earth swallowed Trophonius (Pausanias), or that he dug a trench and lived in it (Charax). The architectural theme figures in both Greek versions, and is developed in Charax with the appearance of the master-builder Daedalus, constructor of the Cretan Labyrinth; and an accomplice appears in the person of Kerkyon, but seems to add nothing to the overall narrative.

9
TRADITIONAL HEROES, MAGIC OBJECTS

A number of the examples occupy the ground claimed here for fairy tale but often thought of loosely as 'mythology'. The somewhat similar stories of Perseus and Bellerophon deal with a hero betrayed into undertaking an impossible task, but supplied with the means of completing it by divine aid and magic object, and in the case of beheading Medusa lateral thinking with a mirror. Melampus wins kingdom and bride by pursuit and dance with mad maidens; Hippomenes too performs a heroic pursuit, this time with apples in a race. The Jason story also has heroic tasks, this time with the 'girl as helper' for their carrying out. The classical version of *The Two Brothers* is included, though it offers a less distinctive example than its ancient Egyptian counterpart. 'Euthymus and the wolf' makes a hero out of the girl's rescuer, showing that the death of the wolf is an early part of the Red Riding Hood tale. The magic ring of Gyges lacks any heroic motivation, but its property of invisibility fulfils the same function as Perseus' cap.

The Dragon-Slayer: Bellerophon[1]: Apollodorus 2.3.1f. (*ATU* 300)

Bellerophon,[2] son of Glaucus son of Sisyphus,[3] by accident killed his own brother Deliades (others give his name as Piren, others again Alcimenes); and he came to Proetus to receive purification. And <Proetus' wife> Stheneboea[4] had a passion for him, and sent him overtures to make love. He turned her down, and she told Proetus that Bellerophon had sent her an indecent proposal. Proetus[5] believed her and gave him letters[6] for Iobates,[7] with instructions to kill Bellerophon. Iobates read the letters and ordered him to kill the Chimaera, thinking that he would be killed by the beast: for it was not an easy task to capture for many men, let alone one. It had the forepart of a lion, the tail of a dragon and its third part, the middle one, was a goat's, and through it it breathed fire.[8] And it destroyed the land and harried the cattle, for in one creature it had the power of three beasts. And it is also said that this Chimaera was nurtured by Amisodarus, as Homer has said,[9] and that it was the offspring of Typhon and Echidna, according to Hesiod.[10]

(2.3.2) Mounting then his winged steed Pegasus, which had been fathered by Poseidon on Medusa,[11] he was borne aloft and shot down the Chimaera from it. And after this contest Iobates instructed him to fight with the Solymi. And when he achieved this feat as well, he ordered him to fight against the Amazons.[12] And when he had killed them too, Iobates picked out those he considered the finest of the Lycians, and ordered them to ambush Bellerophon and kill him. And when he had killed all of these, Iobates in amazement at his prowess showed him the letter and invited him to stay at his court. And giving him his daughter Philonoe[13] he bequeathed the kingdom to Bellerophon on his own death.[14]

The Dragon-Slayer: Perseus[15]: Apollodorus 2.4.1–5:[16] (*ATU* 300)

(2.4.1) Some say that it was Proetus who seduced Danae, and that the quarrel (between Acrisius and Proetus) started from this; but others say that Zeus changed into gold, and flowing through the roof into the lap of Danae had intercourse with her. And when Acrisius found out later that she had given birth to a child, he did not believe that she had been seduced by Zeus; he threw his daughter with the child into a chest and threw it into the sea. When the chest was washed up on Seriphus, Dictys took up the child and raised him. (2.4.2) And the brother of Dictys, the king of Seriphus Polydectes, fell in love with Danae, but was unable to be with her, as Perseus had already grown to manhood. So he called together his friends, including Perseus, saying that he was collecting contributions for a wedding present for Hippodameia, the daughter of Oenomaus. When Perseus said that he would not refuse to provide even the Gorgon's head, Polydectes asked for horses from the others, but as Perseus could not provide horses he required him to bring him the Gorgon's head instead. But Perseus received guidance from Hermes and Athena and reached the daughters of Phorcys, Enyo, Pephredo and Dino. These were Phorcys' children by Ceto, sisters of the Gorgons, and old women from birth (Graeae). And the three had one eye and one tooth, and took them in turn. Perseus commandeered these, and when they asked for them, he agreed to return them if they would tell him the way to the nymphs. These nymphs had winged sandals and the *kibisis*, which they say was a wallet. And they also had the cap of Hades. When he received guidance from the Phorcides, he returned their tooth and eye, and arriving where the nymphs lived he had the good luck to get what he wanted. He slung on the *kibisis*, put the sandals on his ankles, and put the cap on his head. And with this he saw those he wished to see, but he himself was invisible. And having taken from Hermes a sickle of adamant, he flew off to the Ocean and caught the Gorgons asleep. Their names were Stheno, Euryale and Medusa. Only the last was mortal, hence it was her head that Perseus was sent to fetch. But the Gorgons had heads twined with the scales of dragons, and huge tusks like boars' tusks and brazen hands and golden wings for flying. And those who looked at them they turned to stone. So Perseus stood over them as they slept, while Athena guided his hand, and turning away and looking into a bronze shield through which he saw the Gorgon's reflection, he cut off (Medusa's) head. And when the head was cut off, there sprang from the Gorgon winged horses Pegasus and Chrysaor, the father of Geryon. These the Gorgon conceived by Poseidon. (2.4.3) Perseus, then, put the head of Medusa into the *kibisis* and made his way back; the other Gorgons, raised from their sleep, tried to pursue him, but were unable to see him thanks to the cap, as he was hidden by it.

Perseus then arrived in Ethiopia,[17] whose king was Cepheus, and found the king's daughter Andromeda exposed to feed a sea-monster. For the wife of Cepheus, Cassiopeia, quarrelled with the Nereids over beauty, and boasted that she was superior to all of them. So the nymphs were furious, and Poseidon shared their anger and sent a flood against the country, and a sea-monster. And Ammon gave an oracle that the country would be saved from the disaster if Cassiopeia's daughter Andromeda were put out as prey to the monster, and Cepheus did this, compelled by the Ethiopians, and bound his daughter to a rock. Perseus saw her, and fell in love with her: he promised to Cepheus to kill the monster if he would give him the rescued princess as his wife. When Cepheus swore an oath to this effect, Perseus stood up to the monster and killed it, and freed Andromeda. Phineus plotted against him, the brother of Cepheus originally betrothed to Andromeda, but when Perseus discovered the plot he showed the Gorgon's head to him and his fellow-conspirators, and turned them at once to stone. And when he arrived back in Seriphus and found his mother together with Dictys as a suppliant at the altars because of the violent threats of Polydectes, he went into the palace, called together Polydectes' friends, turned away, and showed them the Gorgon's head. And when they saw it, each of them was turned to stone, in whatever posture he happened to be. And after making Dictys king of Seriphus, he returned the sandals, the *kibisis* and the cap to Hermes, and gave the gorgon's head to Athena.[18] And Hermes returned the objects mentioned to the nymphs, while Athene set the Gorgon's head in the middle of her shield. And some say that Medusa was beheaded at the behest of Athena. For they say that the Gorgon wished to rival the goddess in beauty.

Perseus hurried with Danae and Andromeda to Argos to see Acrisius. But when the latter heard and (still) feared the prophecy, he left Argos and withdrew to the land of the Pelasgians. But Teutamides, king of Larissa, was holding an athletic contest in honour of his father who had died, and Perseus arrived to compete. As he took part in the pentathlon, he threw the discus and hit Acrisius on the foot and killed him.[19] And realising that the oracle was fulfilled, he buried him outside the walls, and not wishing to return to Argos to receive the inheritance of the man he had killed, he went to Megapenthes, son of Proetus at Tiryns, and exchanged kingdoms with him, giving him Argos instead. And Megapenthes ruled the Argives, while Perseus was king of Tiryns and also fortified Midia and Mycenae. (2.4.5) And Andromeda had sons by him: Perses before he arrived in

Greece, whom he left with Cepheus (and from him it is said that the kings of Persia are descended), while in Mycenae his children were Alcaeus and Sthenelus and Eleius and Mestor and Electryon, and a daughter Gorgophone, who was married to Perieres.[20]

The Dancing Princesses[21]: Apollodorus 2.2.2 (*ATU* 306, The Danced-Out Shoes)[22]

Proetus[23] had daughters by Stheneboea: Lysippe, Iphinoe and Iphianassa. And when they grew to woman-hood they went mad, according to Hesiod, because they did not accept the rites of Dionysus, but according to Acusilaus, because they failed to respect the wooden statue of Hera. In their madness they would wander all over Argive territory, and afterwards, passing through Arcadia and the Peloponnese, they would run through desert regions in total disregard for decency.[24] But Melampus,[25] the son of Amythaon and Eidomene daughter of Abas, a seer who first discovered healing through drugs and purifications, promised to cure the girls in return for a third of Proetus' kingdom.[26] When the king refused to agree to pay for the cure in return for so high a price, the girls became still more deranged and <the madness spread to> the rest of the women as well. When the disaster reached epidemic proportions Proetus agreed to pay the amount demanded (Melampus <now> agreed to undertake the cure when his brother Bias <too> should receive a <further> third of the kingdom <in turn>). Proetus was now afraid that if the cure were to be delayed the price would increase still further, and agreed to the cure on these conditions. And so Melampus took the strongest young men with him and pursued the girls from the mountains to Sicyon with shouting and 'a sort of frenzied dancing'. In the course of the pursuit the eldest of the daughters, Iphinoe, lost her life. But the rest had the good luck to return to their right minds thanks to the purifications. Proetus gave the two girls in marriage to Melampus and Bias, and the latter later had a son Megapenthes.

Hippomenes and Atalanta: Ovid *Metamorphoses* 10. 560–680[27] (cf. *ATU* 306)

(560) (Venus speaks:) Perhaps you have heard of a woman who overcame swift men in a footrace? That rumour was not an idle tale, for indeed (Atalanta) used to win races over men; nor could you tell whether she was more outstanding for her speed than for her beauty. When this girl consulted (Apollo) on marriage he replied 'You have no need of marriage, Atalanta: avoid the custom. And yet you will not escape it, and though still living you will lose your own self'. In fear of the divine oracle, she lived unwedded in the woodland shades and put to flight her pressing crowd of suitors with a harsh condition:

> No man is to have power over me, unless he has conquered me in a race: strive against me with your feet: the swift runner will have a wife and a

marriage bed as his prize; death will be the penalty for the slow-footed: let that be the condition for the contest.

(Hippomenes volunteers, and the pair fall in love.) (638) Already the people and her father were pressing for the usual race, when Neptune's descendant Hippomenes sought my (Venus') help with anxious voice: 'I beg the lady of Cythera to be with me in my daring enterprise and assist the flames she kindled!' The ungrudging breeze brought me his persuasive prayers. I confess I was moved, nor did I long delay my help. There is a field which the natives call Tamasenus, the best of the soil of Cyprus, which the ancient elders consecrated to me and ordered to be given as an offering in addition to my temples: in the middle of it shines a tree with tawny leaves and branches crinkling with tawny gold. I happened to be coming from here with three golden apples I had plucked; invisible to all but Hippomenes, I approached him and told him how to use them. The trumpets had given the sign, when both darted forward from their enclosure and moistened the surface of the sand with their swift feet: You might suppose the pair were able to skim the waves without wetting their feet, or cross over the ears of white grain still leaving them standing... (664) Then at last the scion of Neptune launched one of the three tree-fruits: the girl was amazed and in her desire for the shining apple she wandered off from the course and picked up the rolling golden ball. Hippomenes passed her; the seating reverberated with applause. But she made up her delay and the time she had conceded by her swift course, and once more left the youth behind, and again delayed by the throw of the second apple she pursued and overtook him. The final part of the course remained. 'Now', he said, 'goddess who first gave me this gift, be present!' And into the broad plain, so that she should return still more slowly, he threw the shining object with a young man's strength in a sideways direction. The girl seemed to hesitate to go for it; but I forced her to pick it up and made the apple heavier when she had done so; I blocked her both with the added weight and the delay. Nor let my tale be slower than the race itself: he passed the girl, and led off the prize he had won.

The Two Brothers: Peleus and Telamon[28]: Apollodorus 3. 12f. (*ATU* 303, The Twins or Blood-Brothers)

(3.12) Phocus[29] was superior in athletic prowess, and his brothers Peleus and Telamon plotted against him. And Telamon drew the lot and killed him as they were exercising together by throwing a discus against his head, and carried the body together with Peleus, and hid it in some wood. But the murder was discovered and the two were driven away from Aegina by Aeacus. And Telamon came to Salamis, to the court of Cychreus, son of Poseidon and Salamis, daughter of Asopus.[30] Now Cychreus became king of Salamis after killing a snake which was wreaking havoc on the island, and as he had no children, when he died he bequeathed the kingdom to Telamon, who married Periboia daughter of

Alcathous[31] son of Pelops, and when Heracles prayed that he should have a male child, an eagle appeared after the prayer and he called his child Ajax. And he went on expedition with Heracles against Troy, and took as a prize Hesione the daughter of Laomedon, and with her he had a son Teucer.

(3.13) And Peleus fled to Phthia, to the court of Eurytion, son of Actor, and was purified by him, and received from him his daughter Antigone and a third part of his territory. And he had a daughter Polydora who was married to Boreas, son of Perieres. Then he went with Eurytion on the Calydonian boar-hunt, and throwing a javelin at the boar he accidentally hit and killed Eurytion.[32] And so fleeing once more from Phthia to Iolcus he came to Acastus at Iolcus and received purification from him. And he competed also at the games in honour of Pelias, wrestling with Atalanta. And Astydameia, the wife of Acastus, falling in love with Peleus, sent him a message offering to sleep with him. And unable to persuade him, she sent word to his wife that Peleus was about to marry Sterope, Acastus' daughter. And when she heard this she hanged herself. And she told lies about Peleus to Acastus, saying that he had tried to persuade her to sleep with him. But when Acastus heard this he was unwilling to kill the man he had purified,[33] but took him on a hunt on Pelion. There was a hunting-contest, and Peleus cut out the tongues of the animals he had overcome and put them in a wallet, while Acastus' followers took possession of his quarries and laughed at him for being empty-handed. But he produced all the tongues for them, and claimed to have as many quarries as he had tongues.[34] And when he was asleep on Pelion, Acastus abandoned him and returned home, after hiding his sword in the cow-dung. When he got up and looked for his sword, he was caught by the centaurs and was about to die, when he was rescued by Chiron,[35] who sought out his sword and gave it back.

Peleus married Polydora,[36] the daughter of Perieres, by whom he had a son Menesthius – supposedly, though the real father was the river Spercheius. After that he married Thetis, daughter of Nereus, over whose marriage Zeus and Poseidon had been rivals. But when Themis made the prophecy that her child would be mightier than his father they desisted.

Chiron, then, gave Peleus advice to take and keep hold of her while she changed shape, and looking out for her he seized her, and though she changed by turns into fire, water, and a wild animal, he would not let go till he saw her resume her former shape. And he married her on Pelion, and there the gods celebrated their marriage with feasting and singing.[37] And Chiron gave Peleus an ashen spear, Poseidon the horses Balius and Xanthus, immortal steeds.

And when Thetis had a child by Peleus, wishing to make it immortal and without Peleus' knowledge, she would hide it at night in fire to destroy its father's mortal element, while by day she anointed the child with ambrosia. And Peleus kept watch and saw the child writhing in the fire, while Thetis, prevented from carrying out her design, abandoned the infant[38] and went off to the Nereids. Peleus for his part took the child to Chiron, and he fed it on the innards of lions and wild boars and the marrow of bears, and called it Achilles (his former name was Ligyron) because he did not put his lips to his mother's breast.[39]

The Girl Helper in the Hero's Flight: Jason and Medea[40]:
Apollodorus 1.9.23–28 (*ATU* 313, The Magic Flight)

(1.9.23) Having sailed past the Thermodon and the Caucasus (the Argonauts) reached the river Phasis, a river in Colchis. After anchoring the ship Jason arrived at the court of Aeetes, and reciting the instruction from Pelias called on Aietes to give him the fleece, and Aeetes promised to give it to him, if he should yoke the bronze-hooved bulls single-handed. These were a pair of wild bulls in his possession, of enormous bulk, the gift of Hephaestus, which had bronze hooves and breathed fire from their mouths. And when he had yoked them he ordered him to sow the dragon's teeth. For Aeetes had received from Athena half the dragon's teeth which Cadmus sowed in Thebes. And when Jason was at a loss as to how to yoke the bulls, Medea fell in love with him[41]; she was the daughter of Aeetes and Eiduia, daughter of Ocean, and was a witch.[42] And fearing that Jason would be destroyed by the bulls, without her father's knowledge she promised to help him to yoke the bulls[43] and put the fleece in his hands, if he should swear to marry her and take her as a partner on the voyage back to Greece. And when Jason swore the oath, she gave him a drug with which she told him to anoint his shield, spear and body when about to yoke the bulls. For she said that anointed with this he would not be harmed by fire or iron for a single day. And she indicated to him that when the teeth were being sown, armed men would spring up out of the ground against him[44]; she told him that whenever he saw them tightly gathered together, he should throw stones into their midst from a distance, and when they fought each other on this account, he was then to kill them. When Jason heard this and anointed himself with the drug, he arrived at the temple grove and went after the bulls, and although they sent against him a great deal of flame he yoked them. And when he had sowed the dragon's teeth, armed men rose up out of the earth, and when he saw a group of them he threw stones at them unobserved, and while they fought one another he came up and cut them down. And although Jason had yoked the bulls Aeetes still refused to give him the fleece, but intended to burn the Argo[45] and kill the crew. But Medea was one step ahead, and brought Jason by night to the fleece, and after she and Jason had lulled its guardian dragon to sleep, she took the fleece and arrived at the Argo. And her brother Absyrtus also followed her. And in company with them the Argonauts put to sea during the night.

(24) When Aeetes discovered Medea's daring deed he set off to pursue the ship. Medea saw him close at hand, murdered her brother and tearing him limb from limb threw him into the sea. Aeetes gathered the child's limbs and delayed the pursuit, and so he turned back,[46] buried the limbs he had rescued, and called the place Tomi.[47] And he sent many of the Colchians to hunt for the Argo, threatening that if they did not bring him Medea, they should suffer the punishments owed to her; they split up and each band searched in different places.

... (25) And as they sailed past the Sirens, Orpheus held the Argonauts back by singing a counter-chant. Only Butes left the ship and sailed towards them, but Aphrodite snatched him and settled him in Lilybaeum.

And after the Sirens, Charybdis, Scylla and the Wandering Rocks received them, above which they saw a great flame and smoke rising. But Thetis and the Nereids, at the invitation of Hera, brought the ship through.

… (28); they arrived in Corinth, and continued to live happily there for ten years, but afterwards King Creon of Corinth betrothed his daughter Glauce[48] to Jason, who divorced Medea and married her. But Medea called on the gods Jason had sworn by, and finding fault again and again with Jason for his ingratitude, sent to the bride a robe steeped with poisons, and when she put it on both she and her father were consumed by a raging fire, and the children Medea had from Jason, Mermeros and Pheres, she killed; and taking from the sun a chariot drawn by winged dragons she flew off on it to Athens.

Little Red Riding Hood: Euthymus and the Wolf[49]: Pausanias 6.6.7–11 (*ATU* 333)[50]

(7) They say that during his wanderings after the fall of Troy Odysseus was driven with his fleet by the winds to cities in Italy and Sicily, among them Temesa.[51] There one of his sailors got drunk and raped a girl; as a punishment the local people had stoned him to death.[52] (8) Odysseus for his part was unconcerned at the loss and sailed off, but the *daimōn* of the stoned man lost no opportunity to kill the people of Temesa, young and old alike. They were preparing to leave Italy altogether when the Delphic priestess forbade them, but ordered them instead to propitiate the Departed Spirit (Hero[53]) and set aside an enclosure and build a temple,[54] and every year to give him the most beautiful young woman in Temesa as a wife. (9) And so when they carried out the god's commands they were terrorised no longer by the ghost. But Mr. Courage (Euthymus[55]) happened to arrive in Temesa at the very time when it was the custom to propitiate the ghost. He found out what was happening, and felt the urge to enter the temple and see the girl. When he saw her, first of all he was seized with pity for her, then he fell in love with her. And the girl promised to marry him if he would save her.[56] Mr Courage put on his armour and waited for the ghost to attack. (10) And he won the fight and the ghost was driven out of the region; it sank into the sea and was never seen again.[57] Mr. Courage had a prestigious marriage, and the people of Temesa were henceforth free of the ghost… (11) I happened to see a picture[58] and learned the following: (it was a copy of an ancient painting). There was a young man, Sybaris, the river Calabrus and the spring Lyca. In addition there was the ghost's shrine and the city of Temesa, and among them too the ghost that Mr. Courage cast out: his colour was terribly black and he looked utterly fearful, and he was wearing a garment of wolfskin. And the lettering on the picture called him Lykos ('Mr. Wolf').[59]

Gyges and the Magic Ring: Plato, *Republic* 2. 359C–360B (*ATU* 560–562, The magic Ring/Aladdin/The Spirit in the Blue Light)

The sort of power I am talking about would be precisely the sort they say was possessed by [the ancestor of] Gyges[60] the Lydian. For they say he was a shepherd under the then king of Lydia, and that after a great rainstorm and earthquake the ground gave way and there was a chasm in the place where he was grazing his flock. When he saw this he was amazed and went down into it; and they tell the fanciful tale (*mythologousi*) that he saw among other wonders a hollow bronze horse with doors; when he peeped in he saw a corpse inside, which seemed of greater than mortal size, with nothing else but a golden ring on its hand, which he put on before leaving,[61] and when the shepherds had their usual gathering to make their monthly report to the king about his flocks, Gyges appeared there wearing the ring. So sitting beside the others he happened to turn the bezel of the ring towards the inside of his hand. And when this happened (360) he appeared invisible to those sitting beside him, and they spoke about him among themselves as if he were absent. He was amazed at this, and as he continued to fumble with the ring he turned the bezel out again, and by doing so became visible again. And noticing this he performed an experiment with his ring to see whether it had this power, and observed that that was indeed the case: if he turned it inwards, he became invisible, if he turned it outward he became visible.[62] When he realised this, he managed to become one of the messengers who attended the king's court, and he arrived and seduced the king's wife, and with her help he attacked the king and took possession of the kingdom.[63]

Notes

1 For the tale-type as a whole, Röhrich *EM* 3(1981b), 797–820; Hansen, 119–130.
2 On the Chimaera, Ogden (2013), 75–81. The name Bellerophon itself is problematic: 'slayer of Bellerus'? And if so, who was he?
3 The celebrated arch-trickster in Greek tradition: Gantz (1993), 173–176.
4 Anteia in Homer's version: the 'Potiphar's wife' theme: numerous analogues in Hansen, (332–352), including most notably the case of Hippolytus and Phaedra; for an anthology, Yohannan (1968).
5 King of Corinth (Homer's Ephyre), and stepfather of Oedipus.
6 The *sēmata lugra* ('baleful signs') of Homer's version. The celebrated 'Uriah letter' theme, Stith Thompson K978.
7 King of Lycia.
8 The nature of the beast, like the sphinx, suggests a Near Eastern hybrid, appropriate to the Lycian colour of the tale.
9 Amisodorus, Homer *Iliad*, 16.328f.
10 Hesiod *Theogony*, 325–329.
11 Pegasus: first only in post-Homeric versions; it is supplied at the instigation of Athena, (Pindar, *Olympian*, 13.63–92).
12 We have no details of these latter two tasks. There seem to be four tasks rather than three, perhaps suggesting one as part of an alternative tradition.
13 Anonymous in Homer.
14 Apollodorus misses out a negative end to the tale, present in Homer, that Bellerophon is reduced to wandering on the Aleian Plain ('plain of wandering'): Kirk (1990) on *Iliad*, 6.201f.
15 Hartland (1894–1896); Röhrich, *EM* 3 (1981b), 787–829; Hansen, 119–130, 246–251; Ogden (2008).
16 Perseus' adventures offer the hero-tale par excellence: the hero, of secretly divine ancestry, is sent by a wicked king on a deliberately fatal quest. Supernatural helpers provide him with the wherewithal to acquire magic objects/helpers necessary to slay a sequence of monsters and enemies. Often his title is proven by cutting out a

monster's tongue, to be produced when an impostor claims the victory. In fact, as normally in fairy tales, the hero requires little by way of actual valour. He is provided and protected almost throughout by others, whose support is predetermined by his birth.

17 At this point the Dragon Slayer properly begins: some mythographers relocate the exploit to Joppa in Palestine: local tradition still points out Andromeda's fetters (Pausanias, 4.35.9; Josephus, *Bellum Judaicum*, 3.9.3). For the offence by the wife of Cepheus, cf. Niobe's fatal boast offending Leto, which does not however activate a Dragon Slayer account, and Laomedon's offence against Apollo and Poseidon, which does. Cf. also Euthymus and the wolf (above, a very truncated version). Hansen (2002), 123 seems right to see Phineus as a trace of the 'false suitor' motif, but here he has a prior claim.

18 The return of magic objects is rarely reported in hero-tales: the handing over of the Gorgon's head to Athena may be part of her motivation for helping Perseus in the first place.

19 The final motif in the story of Acrisius actually belongs to the much broader folklore theme of vain attempts to elude destiny, central for example to the Oedipus story (*ATU*, 931).

20 Hansen considers six ancient examples of dragon-slayer tales which he tentatively groups in three sub-types, with Perseus and Heracles-Hesione as one type, sited in coastal regions away from the Greek mainland. The criteria are sound, but the sample necessarily too small.

21 Opie and Opie (1980), 245–252; Anderson (2000), 119–122.

22 Köhler-Zülch *EM* 12 (2007), 221–227. The modern tale has the girls attending a secret ball where they dance with corpses, sometimes with their former lovers, in an underworld. This setting is hinted at in an allusion in Pausanias (8.18.7) to the fact that one of the three girls died at a cave in the Aonian mountains above Nonacris, where there is an entrance to the Styx (ibid., 8.18.4).

23 Proetus was the king of Corinth who purified Bellerophon (Apollodorus, 2.3.1).

24 For madnesses of this kind, cf. Plutarch's account of mass female suicides in Miletus, solved only by threatening to expose the naked corpses of the girls, *Moralia*, 249b–d.

25 Melampus is a resourceful trickster figure from Hesiod onwards.

26 The fantasy of kings giving huge portions of their kingdom and executing failed suitors puts the story firmly into the fairy tale repertoire.

27 Only one princess this time, and running rather than dancing. But the magic apples supplied by Aphrodite from the magically leaved tree, and the death penalty for failure, should leave us in little doubt as to the similarity of the two stories.

28 Ranke *EM* 2 (1979), 912–919. Hansen regards the overall tale as too complex for discussion (333f.), and only focuses on Potiphar's wife, but does relate the overall tale, much adapted, to Plautus' *Menaechmi*. The story is one of relatively few tales where we can immediately point to a securely dated Ancient Near Eastern version (Lichtheim 2, 1974, 203–211) quite unequivocally predating by some two millennia the modern popular tale, and conveniently showing how far two such versions can differ, consistent with remaining securely identical.

29 Phocus ('seal'): some modern versions have the brothers eating a golden crab so that one becomes a king, the other fabulously wealthy.

30 Purification for murder is a recurrent opening to *ATU* 303, as it is to *ATU* 300.

31 Her father Alcathous has 'dragon-slaying' credentials in his own right (Hansen, 124f.)

32 For misfortune striking twice in this way (the purified accidentally killing the purifier's son), cf. Herodotus' story of Croesus and Adrastus, 1.34–43.

33 Potiphar's wife: the episode is found as part of the Ancient Egyptian version of the *Two Brothers* tale: see also Hansen, 450f.

34 Cutting out the animal tongues is a defining characteristic of the Dragon Slayer (*ATU*, 300). Note its presence also in Gottfried von Strassburg's version of Tristan, much of which likewise dates from Antiquity (Anderson 2007).

35 Peleus is rescued by the half-man, half-horse Chiron; Bata is rescued by a talking cow in the Ancient Egyptian version.
36 Polydora, 'much-gift' seems to be the equivalent of the treacherous wife in the Bata story, who is endowed by all the gods, and seems to 'prefer the better offer' in the form of the Pharaoh. For the episode, cf. the advice of Eidothea to Menelaus to keep hold of the shape-shifter Proteus, *Odyssey*, 4.414–424.
37 The subject of the celebrated epyllion by Catullus (64).
38 The same is told of Demeter in the *Homeric Hymn to Demeter*, 242–262.
39 The defining motif of Type 303 is actually missing from Apollodorus' version, namely the 'life-token' aspect which will enable one brother to rescue the other (already present in the Ancient Egyptian version).
40 The latter half of the Argonautic expedition is generally recognised as belonging to 'The Girl Helper in the hero's Flight' (Hansen, 151–166; Puchner *EM* 9, 1999, 12–19). The girl falls in love with the hero her father is trying to kill with fatal tasks, gives him magic help to accomplish the tasks, and then obstructs her father's pursuit; a false bride often distracts the hero, but the heroine defeats her. The Theseus-Ariadne story follows the pattern (with no pursuit by Minos), but the forgotten fiancée element is this time more prominent. Hansen makes a good case for Epicaste daughter of Augeas as a similar helper for Heracles' cleansing of the Augean stables.
41 Normally in the folktale tradition the heroine falls in love naturally; in Apollonius the love-affair is managed by Hera and Athena for their own ends. Aeetes plays the part of the ogre: treacherous and cruel rather than a dreadful giant as such.
42 And also of course the niece of the arch-witch Circe.
43 Sometimes all three tasks concern the taming of animals, as in *Dede Korkut*; note also *Culwych* in the *Mabinogion*, faced with the task of sowing a field in a day.
44 What the sown men were remains open to speculation: were they autochthones, 'sons of the soil'? An underground army, or concealed in trenches? Whatever the answer, the same result is faced by Cadmus in dealing with the other half of the teeth (Apollodorus, 3.4.1).
45 Hansen points out a bizarre modern Mexican version, in which the hero is fed three hot breakfasts.
46 Normally the folktale ruses are impossible, taking the form of tossing a magic object behind to produce a barrier (e.g. a comb which turns into an impassable forest), and are normally given three variations. The dismemberment of Absyrtus may be a displacement from the episode much later where the heroine arranges the dismemberment of the hero's uncle Pelias; sometimes this entails dismemberment of the heroine herself.
47 I.e. cutting <*temnō*>.
48 Normally the rival is an ugly pretender who insinuates herself because the hero has broken a taboo (e.g. by kissing his mother), and literally forgets the heroine till his memory has been jogged by a ruse. The ending is usually a happy one, but conspicuously not so in the Greek versions, where Medea's revenge and its consequences are irreversible.
49 *Red Riding Hood* in a very different guise, without the jingling dialogue, the red hood or the grandmother: a young girl is rescued by an athletic hero from a ghost *called* wolf, depicted wearing a wolf-skin, and already punished for rape by stoning (in a previous life), but finally by drowning.
50 Opie and Opie (1980), 119–125; Zipes (1993); Anderson (2000), 92–96; Hansen, 127f.; Kawan *EM* 11 (2004), 854–868.
51 There may be an element of confusion with the Teumessian fox, a Greek mainland legend from Boeotia.
52 A traditional community punishment in antiquity; it is applied in a different way in *Red Riding Hood*, where the wolf's belly is filled with stones, but 'death by stones' is the same in both cases.

53 The term *hero* is morally neutral, as used for example of the suitors in Homer's *Odyssey*.
54 A rather more elevated 'take' on the grandmother's cottage.
55 Euthymus was an actually attested athletic victor, so that Pausanias' version of the story is strictly speaking a local legend. Hansen relates the story to *ATU* 300, as a 'dragon-slayer' narrative.
56 Not now a politically correct rescue: the girl gives herself to the hero under duress.
57 The Grimms' *Red Riding Hood* has a second wolf drowned: it is not clear how sinking in the sea 'kills' the ghost.
58 Only the visual depiction of the story identifies the villain as Lycus ('wolf'). Such paintings were often exhibited in temples as propaganda for a local hero or saint.
59 Paintings sometimes rationalise where stories metamorphose: compare the case of Actaeon depicted visually as wearing a deerskin rather than actually turning into a deer.
60 Proclus defends Plato's reading, of an ancestor of *the* Gyges, but the Gyges of Herodotus, 1.7–14 and Nicolaus of Damascus seems obviously one and the same. In Herodotus we have a scandalising novella blaming King Candaules for antagonising his wife; in Nicolaus a quasi-historical account where Gyges makes improper advances to the future queen and must stage a coup to save his own life.
61 The subterranean treasure looks more like a genuine archaeological possibility than it did when K.F. Smith discussed the tale over a century ago; but the story as presented is still resolutely magical.
62 Plato's narration has a scientist's or logician's precision, while the fantastic detail is left imprecise or ambiguous. The prevailing resemblances are to Aladdin, or to Near Eastern wonder-tale in general.
63 Smith (1901 and 1920); Ranke *EM* 1 (1977), 240–247; Tucker *EM* 5 (1987), 928–933. Anderson (2000), 284–287; (2007), 284–287 (with analogues to the Gawain legend); Marzolph *EM* 14 (2014), 1189–1194.

10
ANIMAL TALES

The most prevalent theme in the following examples is that the animals are helpful to individual men in distress: a friendly dolphin rescues a famous singer from pirates; a household cockerel offers vengeance and moral instruction to his household companion, the poor cobbler; a gnat gives its life to save a shepherd from a snake; a fox-girl secures her son's succession to a kingdom. None of the examples, except the last ('the goose that laid the golden egg') is actually an Aesopic fable, a genre that overlaps surprisingly little with fairy tale. The *testamentum porcelli* is a parody of a Roman will. Helpful animals often figure as subsidiary motifs in larger tales, as for example in the cow that might yield its bones to provide a trousseau tree for Cinderella, or the ants that help Psyche in her grain-sorting task.

Animal Helpers: Arion and the Dolphin: Herodotus 1.23f. (Stith Thompson Motif B550, Animals Carry Men)

(23) The Corinthians say, and the people of Lesbos agree with them, that in the lifetime of (Periander of Corinth) there occurred a very great marvel: Arion of Methymna was brought to Taenarus on the back of a dolphin.[1] This man was the foremost lyre-player of his age; he was the first man known to us to compose and name the dithyramb, and he taught it in Corinth. (24) They say that this Arion, after spending the best part of his time at Periander's court, had a desire to sail to Italy and Sicily, and having made a fortune wished to return to Corinth. Now he set out from Tarentum, hiring a Corinthian ship, because he trusted Corinthians above all others. But on the high seas these men plotted to dispose of Arion and keep his money. When he realised this, he begged them to take his money but spare his life; however, he could not persuade them, but the sailors ordered him either to kill himself, so as to be buried on land, or at once to jump into the sea.

Threatened by this dilemma Arion begged them, since that was their decision, to allow him to take his stance in his full robes on the poop deck and sing to them; and he promised to do away with himself after the song. Now the men were delighted at the prospect of hearing the greatest of singers, and withdrew amidships. Arion then dressed in his full regalia, performed the *orthios nomos* and at the end threw himself into the sea, still wearing all his robes. And the crew sailed on to Corinth, but they say that the dolphin took up Arion and brought him to Taenarus. Arion then made his way to Corinth, still in his robes, and on his arrival told them all that had happened to him. Periander for his part did not believe him, but put Arion under heavy guard and kept a close lookout for the sailors. When they arrived, they were asked if they had any news of Arion, and when they replied that he was safe in Italy and they had left him flourishing in Tarentum, Arion made his appearance to them, just as when he leapt from the ship, and they were terrified and unable to deny their crime now that their guilt had been proven. So say the Corinthians and people of Lesbos alike, and there is a small monument of bronze at Taenarus, depicting a man riding a dolphin.

Arion and the Dolphin[2]: Hyginus *Fabulae* 194 (Stith Thompson Motif B550)

Since Arion of Methymna was a master in the art of the cithara, he was a great friend of Periander king of Corinth. When he had asked the king to allow him to demonstrate his art throughout the state and amassed a great fortune, his servants conspired with a crew of sailors to kill him. But Apollo appeared to him in a dream and told him to perform in his regalia and bardic crown and entrust himself to those who would protect him. When the servants and the sailors wanted to kill him, he begged them that he would sing to them first. And so when the sound of the cithara could be heard along with his voice, dolphins came round the ship, and when he saw them he jumped. They took him up <and brought him to king Periander>. But when he reached land he was eager to be on his way and neglected to push his dolphin back into the sea, so that it died there. When he told Periander his misfortunes the king ordered the dolphin to be buried and for a monument to be erected.[3] After a short time word came to Periander that the ship Arion had travelled on had been brought to Corinth by a storm. When he ordered the crew to be brought to him and asked about Arion, they said he had died and that they had buried him. The king replied: 'tomorrow you will swear an oath at the dolphin's monument'. For that reason he ordered them to be put under guard and told Arion, dressed as when he threw himself overboard, to hide next morning inside the monument. When the king brought them there and told them to swear by the dolphin's spirit that Arion was dead, he stepped out of the monument. They were dumbfounded, wondering by what divinity he had been rescued. Periander ordered them to be crucified at the dolphin monument.[4] Apollo for his part on account of his skill on the cithara placed Arion and the dolphin among the stars.

Micyllus and the Magic Cockerel[5]: Lucian, *The Dream or the Cock*, excerpts) (*ATU* 715/715A, Demi-cock/The Wonderful Rooster)[6]

(1) (The cock speaks for the first time):

My master Micyllus, I thought I would do you a good turn by getting ahead of the night-time as much as I could, so that you could make use of the early hours and get most of your work done early. At any rate if you should finish a single sandal before sunrise, you'll be that further forward towards toiling for your daily bread. But if you prefer to sleep on, I will be quiet and have much less to say than fish do: but see that you don't dream you're rich and go hungry when you wake up.

(2) M.: O Zeus lord of miracles and Heracles averter of ills! What misfortune is this? The cock spoke with a human voice!

C.: Then you consider such a thing a miracle, for me to talk in the same tongue as you?

M.: How can it be anything else? Ye gods, avert this ill-omen from us!

(The cock hears how his master has been humiliated by two grandees in succession)

(8) C.: Tell me first, Micyllus, what happened at Eucrates' house, both what the dinner was like and everything that went on at the drinking-party afterwards...For there is nothing to stop you dining once more, by putting together a dream of that dinner, as it were, and chewing the cud of what you ate in your memory.

(9) M.: I thought I would annoy you by going over all that, but since you want to hear it, this is my story. I had never dined at a rich man's table, Pythagoras,[7] in my whole life, but yesterday I had the good luck to run into Eucrates, and I respectfully addressed him as usual as 'Master', and was ready to go off, so as not to embarrass him by falling in with him in my beggar's cloak. But he said, 'Micyllus, today I am celebrating my daughter's birthday and I've invited a good many of my friends, but since they tell me one of them is ill and is unable to dine with us, you take a bath and come in his place, unless the man I've invited says he can come, for at this moment it isn't clear'. When I heard this I gave him a bow and went off...I thought it an absolute age till my bath, and kept looking at the length of the shadow (on the sundial), and when it would actually be time for it...(Eucrates' friend, the grandee philosopher Thesmopolis, turns up after all). (11) I for my part was getting ready to go off, but Eucrates turned to me and after a good deal of hesitation, he said as he noticed I looked very disappointed, 'You must come in too, Micyllus, and join us for the dinner. For I'll tell my son to dine with his mother in the women's quarters, so that you can have his place'. So I did go in, after coming close to gaping hungrily like the wolf; but I was embarrassed because it looked as if I had driven Eucrates' boy out of the dining-room...

(The second figure to insult Micyllus)

(14)…Take my neighbour and fellow-cobbler Simon, who had a meal with me not long ago, when I boiled up soup at the festival of Cronus with two slices of sausage in it…

C.: I know the man: the snub-nosed little fellow who made off with your earthenware bowl under his arm after dinner – the only one we had. For I saw it with my own eyes.

M.: So he was the one who stole it and then swore by all those gods that he hadn't! But why didn't you cry out and give the word, cockerel, when you saw us being robbed?

C.: I crowed, which was all that I was able to do at the time. But what about Simon, then? For you looked as if you were about to say something about him.

M.: He had a tremendously rich cousin by the name of Drimylus. This man didn't give so much as an obol to Simon – for why should he, when he himself didn't touch the money? But when he died the other day, all that money is Simon's and now the man with the filthy rags, the man licking the pot, happily drives out in his luxurious purple robes, with his servants and carriages and golden goblets and tables with ivory legs, receiving homage from everyone and no longer giving me so much as a glance. The other day for instance I saw him coming towards me and said, 'Hello, Simon', but he was annoyed, and replied 'Tell this beggar not to shorten my name. For I am not called Simon, but Simonides'.

(16ff.) Micyllus now hears about the cock's transformations (Apollo, Euphorbus, Pythagoras, Aspasia…)

M.: But what man or woman did you become after Aspasia?

C.: The Cynic Crates.

M.: What amazing shifts of fortune, in the name of the Dioscuri: a courtesan, then a philosopher!

(20) C.: Then a king, then a pauper, and a little later a satrap, then a horse, a jackdaw, a frog and umpteen other things. It would be a long business to go through them all. But most recently I have often been a cock, for I've taken to this kind of life…

M.: …And so, Pythagoras – but what do you most like being called, so that I shouldn't confuse the conversation by calling you different names at different times?…

C.: It won't make any difference whether you call me Euphorbus or Pythagoras, Aspasia or Crates. For I am all of them.[8] But you would be better to call me what you now see, a cock, so that you do no dishonour to the bird which seems of little account, but has in it so many souls.

(The cock now demonstrates his magic powers to enter his enemies' quarters)

(28) C.: I will cure you, Micyllus. And since it is still night, get up and follow me. For I will take you to Simon's house, and the houses of the other rich men, so that you may see what their quarters are like.

M.: How is that, when their doors are locked? Unless you're going to make me a burglar.
C.: Not at all, but Hermes, since I am his sacred bird, gave me this gift, that if someone took my longest tail-feather, the pliant one that curls round...
M.: You have two like that –
C.: The right one, then; and if I let anyone pull it out and keep it, this sort of man, for as long as I like, is able to open every door and see everything without being seen himself.
M.: I wasn't aware, cockerel, that you were a magician as well. But if you just give it to me, you'll see all Simon's belongings quickly transported over here. For I'll slip in and bring them here instead, and he will once again chew the leather as he stretches it.
C.: That's not to happen, for Hermes instructed me that if the person in possession of the feather did anything of the sort, I was to raise my voice and get him caught.[9]
M.: That's incredible, for Hermes, a thief himself, to grudge that sort of thing to anyone else. But let's go: I'll keep off the gold if I can.
C.: First pluck out the feather, Micyllus...What's this? You've plucked the pair of them!
M.: It's safer that way, cock, and would be less disfiguring to you, so that you won't be limping on one side of your tail.
(29) C.: Very well then. Do we go first to Simon, or one of the other rich men?
C.: No, Let's go to Simon's, since he thinks he ought to have a four-syllable name instead of two syllables, now that he's rich.
M.: And here we are at his door. What do I do next?
C.: Put the feather into the lock –
M.: There we are, then. Heracles! The door has been opened as if by a key![10]
C.: In you go. Do you see him still awake and doing his sums?
M.: Goodness, I do, at a dim, oil-guzzling lamp. He's pale for some reason, cockerel, and all worn out and thin, no doubt from worry; for no-one said he was ill of anything else. Listen to what he says and you'll know why he's like this.
S.: So these seventy talents are quite safe buried under the bed, and no-one else knows. But the other sixteen I think the groom, Sosylus, saw me hiding under the manger; or at least he's always around the stable, not specially concerned otherwise and not fond of work. I've likely been robbed of much more: how else did Tibeios manage to buy the big flat-fish he's supposed to have bought yesterday, or the five drachmas worth of earring he's supposed to have bought his wife? These people are squandering my money, dear, oh dear! But all these cups aren't put away in a safe place either! At any rate I'm scared someone will dig under the wall and snatch them: there are lots of people who're jealous and plotting against me, most of all my neighbour Micyllus!
M.: I'll say! For like you I'll be off with the dishes under my arm!
C.: Quiet, Micyllus, or he'll find out we're here.

172 Animal tales

S.: Anyway it's best to stay awake myself and be on guard. I'll get up every now and then and go round the whole house. Who's that? I see you, you burglar…Oh Lord, You're only a pillar, it's all right. I'll dig up the gold and count it again in case I got it wrong yesterday. But listen again! Someone made a noise; he's coming for me, that's for sure. I'm under siege and everyone's plotting against me. Where's my dagger? If I catch anyone…Let me bury the gold again.

(30) C.: That's the sort of life Simon leads. But let us go and call on someone else, while we still have a little night left…

M.: Poor soul, what a life he leads. I hope my enemies are rich like him! But I want to strike him over the head and go.

S.: Who hit me? Oh dear, I'm being robbed!

M.: Groan and stay awake, and turn yellow like the gold and melt into it. But let's go and visit Gnipho the moneylender, if you like. His house isn't far away either. This door too has opened for us. (31) Do you see him wide awake too with worry, counting up his interest and wearing away his fingers? But soon he'll have to leave it all and turn into a beetle or a gnat or a dog-fly.

M.: I see a miserable fool of a man, living even now a life little better than a beetle's or a gnat's. And he too is worn down with all his sums. Let's go to someone else's.

(32) C.: To see your friend Eucrates, if you like. And look, this door too is open, so let's go inside.

M.: All this was mine a little while ago…

C.: Are you still dreaming about wealth, then? But do you see Eucrates himself underneath his servant, old man that he is…?

M.: Yes, good heavens: I see lewdness and passive posturing and licentiousness unnatural for a man; and in another quarter I see Eucrates' wife in turn underneath the cook…

(33) C.: Well then? Would you want to fall heir to all this as well, Micyllus, and to have everything that Eucrates has?

M.: Certainly not, cockerel, I'd sooner starve! Goodbye to the gold and the dinners! Two obols are riches enough for me, instead of being buggered by the servants![11]

C.: But now dawn is already breaking; let's go home. You'll see the rest, Micyllus, some other time.

The Faithful Gnat: Ps.-Virgil, *Culex*: 174–414 passim[12] (*ATU* 178A, The Innocent Dog)

(174) [A snake] was surveying his surroundings when the huge beast saw before him the guardian of a flock…(179) His mind is afire, his hisses furiously resounding through his mouth … (183) [A gnat], a tiny creature nurtured by the dew terrifies the (shepherd) victim in advance, and through his bites warns him to avoid death. For where the shepherd's eyes were drawn apart and opened his eye-lids,

here the old man's gleaming pupil had been struck by the light dart of nature, when the shepherd leapt up in fury and pounded the creature and sent him to his death, and all his breath was scattered and left his senses. Then he caught sight of the serpent's grim gaze at close quarters; then quickly, pale and scarcely in command of his senses he rushed back, and pulled a sturdy branch from a tree with his hand. What chance or divine force supported him we do not know, but such as to avail to conquer the dreadful spinning limbs of the scaly dragon; and he struck its bones with blow after blow as it fought back and made for him in its foul attack; he struck where the crest surrounds its temples…When through his body there entered a less substantial dream, and his languid limbs were laid to rest by the outpouring of sleep, the effigy of the gnat descended and sang reproaches over the event of his sad death: 'By what deserts am I carried off and forced to face a bitter reward? While your life was dearer to me than life itself, I am carried away by the winds through the void… (214) The Shades compel my remains to swim across the water of Lethe; I am driven off as booty for Charon; I see the doorway ablaze with torches.

(391) The shepherd eagerly sets out to form a place; he decides to mark it out as a circle, turns the hilt of his iron spade to use again and again to dig the grassy earth from the green turf… (411) then on its face he inscribed his praises, and letters form them with silent voice: 'Tiny gnat, the guardian of the flock repays to you who deserve so much the rite of your death in return for the gift of life'.[13]

The Faithful Snake: Pausanias 10.33.5 (*ATU* 178A, The Innocent Dog)

About Amphicleia the natives tell the following tale[14]: a ruler was afraid his enemies were plotting against his baby son, and put him in a vessel and hid it in the ground where he supposed it would be safest. Now a wolf made an attack on the child, but a snake coiled round the vessel and maintained a strict guard. When the child's father returned, he thought the snake was minded to attack the boy and let fly with his javelin, which killed both boy and snake. When he ascertained from shepherds that he had killed the snake who had been the boy's benefactor and guardian, he made a pyre to serve them both. They say that the place is like a burning pyre even today, and the town is called Ophiteia after the snake (*ophis*).

Puss in Boots? Miss Fox: Hyginus *Fabulae* 187 (*ATU* 545A/B, The Cat Castle/Puss in Boots)

Alope[15] is a beautiful girl raped by Poseidon, and she exposes her child with a royal robe[16]; the child is suckled by a mare and found by a shepherd. A dispute arises with a fellow shepherd who is willing to bring up the child but wants the robe, withheld by the original shepherd. When they go to Alope's father, Kerkyon, he immures Alope alive[17] and has the child once more exposed; it is

174 Animal tales

once more reared by the mare, and this time the shepherds recognise the divine protection for the child, now called Hippothoon ('Swifthorse'). Now the evil Kerkyon ('animal tail') kills strangers who fail to beat him in a wrestling match. Theseus does so and Hippothoon petitions him for his ancestral kingdom as a son of Poseidon[18]; as a fellow descendant of Poseidon himself, Theseus grants the request. It is too late to save Alope,[19] but Poseidon changes her body into a spring.

Menas and the Crocodile (Diodorus 1.89): (Stith Thompson Motif B550, Animals Carry Men)

For some say that one of their ancient kings, called Menas, on the run from his own hounds, arrived in his flight at the lake known as the lake of Moeris and then was amazingly taken by a crocodile on his back and ferried to the other side. As he wished to show his gratitude for his rescue, he founded a city nearby which he named Crocodeilopolis. And he gave instruction to the local people to honour these animals and dedicated the lake to sustaining them. And there too he constructed his own tomb as a four-sided pyramid, and built the Labyrinth admired by many.

Piglet's Last Will and Testament (*Testamentum Porcelli*)[20] (cf. *ATU* 200, The Dogs' Certificate; Stith Thompson Motif B270, Animals in Legal Relations)

Here begins the will of Piglet:

Marcus Grunnius Corocotta[21] the Piglet has made his will. As I could not write it with my own hand, I had it taken down from dictation.[22]

Lecuisinier[23] the cook said, 'come here, you who have turned the house upside down, you who have not buried your parents,[24] you who have run away, and today I will take away your life'. Corocotta the piglet said: 'If I have done anything, if I have broken any little pot with my trotters, spare my life and give heed to a suppliant's prayer'. Lecuisiniier replied: 'Off with you, my boy,[25] to the kitchen, and get me my knife, so that I can shed the blood of this piglet'. Piglet was seized by the house-slaves, and led away, on the 16th day before the first day of the month Lamplighting,[26] when there are plenty of cabbages, in the consulship of Ovendone and Peppersprinkle,[27] and when he saw that he was about to die, he asked for an hour's delay and begged the cook to be allowed to make his will. He summoned his parents so as to leave them something from his provisions. These are his words:

To my father, Lardy Hogman,[28] I do hereby bequeath 30 modii of acorns, and to my mother Oldsow[29] the breeder I bequeath 40 modii of Laconian silage, and to my sister Miss Piggie,[30] whose wedding I have been unable to attend, I do bequeath 30 modii of barley. And of my inner parts I give my bristles to the cobblers,[31] my grey cells to those who argue, my little ears to the deaf, my tongue to the lawyers and windbags, my intestines to the sausage-makers, my thighs to the stuffers, my loins to women, my bladder to boys, my tail to girls, my muscles to effeminates, my trotters to messengers and hunters, my nails to robbers. And to the cook whose name I refuse to mention, I bequeath the mortar and pestle which I had brought with me: let him hang his neck with a rope anywhere between Tynside and Timbuctoo.[32] And I wish to have a monument inscribed in gold letters: Marcus Grunnius Corocotta the piglet lived for 999 and a half years; if he had lived another half-year, he would have lived a thousand.[33] Those of you who have been my best friends and my advisers in life, I beg that you treat my corpse with respect, that you may season it with fine condiments of nutmeg, pepper and honey, so that my name may be remembered for all eternity. My lords and kinsmen who have been present to witness the will, order it to be sealed. Baconson signed,[34] Morselman signed, Cumminseed signed, Sausagefellow signed, Porkrinder signed, Applesauce signed, Wedding-pig signed.

Here concludes the will of Piglet made this 16th day before the first days of Lamplighting in the consulship of Ovendone and Peppersprinkle. <May its outcome be> auspicious.

The Goose that laid the Golden Eggs: *Fabulae Aesopicae Collectae* Halm 343b (*ATU* 219E**, The Hen that Laid the Golden Eggs)

Thanks to the lavish devotion of one of his worshippers, Hermes[35] gave him the present of a goose[36] that laid golden eggs. But the man could not wait for the benefits a little at a time, but supposed that the goose was all gold inside, and sacrificed the bird without delay. So it came about that not only did he fail to gain what he expected, but he lost the eggs as well; for inside he found that the bird was all flesh.

Notes

1. The tale of Arion might better be classified as a local legend: it relies on the genuine rapport reported in Antiquity between dolphins and humans, as in Pliny the Younger's report of boys playing with a dolphin (*Ep.* 9.33). On Gellius' and Fronto's versions of Herodotus' account, Anderson in Holford-Strevens and Vardi (2004), 108–111.
2. Hyginus' version now sounds eccentric beside Herodotus' classic telling, but there are two important omissions from the latter that assume importance here. Firstly, Apollo emerges as the protector of a fellow musician, and serves as a 'supernatural helper'. Secondly, there is careful motivation for Arion's final performance: the music is to attract his rescuers.
3. The dolphin monument is here integrated into the action of the story, rather than serving merely as a tailpiece or afterthought as in Herodotus.
4. Compare the fate of Theron in the tale of Callirhoe (above, c. 7).
5. A poor man gets his own back on rich and powerful enemies through the agency of a cockerel whose magic tail-feathers open doors, and whose person conceals a whole range of different identities.
6. Marzolf *EM* 6 (1990), 396–401; Köhler-Zülch *EM* 7(1993), 1069–1083, 1126–1131; Anderson (2000), 107–109.

7 Of whom the cock is a transmigrated form.
8 The folktale version 'half-chick' accommodates all the creatures in its apparently limitless hindquarters, with decidedly coarser peasant humour.
9 In the folktale, the robbery is permitted; but Lucian's diatribe against wealth in effect precludes this particular path to justice.
10 For the magic key motif, Stith-Thompson Motif D1550: 'Magic object opens and closes'.
11 In the folktale, the cock would itself *perform* coarse acts against his master's enemies. Here buggering and the rest is left to the servants, in Graeco-Roman society a particular social disgrace, cf. Juvenal *Satire*, 9.40–46.
12 The story as given here corresponds to the Medieval Welsh legend of Gelert, the hound who is mistakenly killed by Prince Llewelyn: too late he finds that the hound had bloodied himself in killing a wolf to protect the child.
13 The style of the *Culex* is tortuously contrived and loaded with poetic mannerism, in contrast to Pausanias' unvarnished narration of the *ophis*-legend.
14 Pausanias thus accords it the status of a local legend, as is the Welsh tale which gives its name to the type (Bedd-Gelert). Cf. Hansen (2002), 9. But genre-labelling can be unhelpful: the story itself is the same whether it carries a specific historical or geographical setting or not.
15 'She-Fox'. Anderson (2000), 173–176; Köhler-Zülch *EM* 7 (1993), 1126–1131. Culture-areas for this tale diverge, depending on whether the animal is a fox or a cat, the latter less common as a character in the Greek world. The key connection to 'Puss in Boots' amid much diversionary material lies in the helpful animal's providing the royal tokens which secures the kingdom for her protégé.
16 In Western forms of the tale as exemplified by Straparola, Basile and Perrault the cat has to acquire royal or aristocratic costume by trickery (the hero has his clothes stolen while bathing, and royal replacements are provided); here Poseidon provides the connection with water just as directly.
17 The shabby treatment of the cat/fox heroine is part of the tale in both Straparola and Basile, though in only the one instance is the animal actually killed. Rather than having the fox as mother of the hero, a Norwegian example known to Asbjørnsen and Moe, *Lord Peter*, has the cat as a princess transformed by a troll, and so able to marry the hero at the end of the tale.
18 This is proven by the birth tokens; in the early modern versions, the cat has to threaten the inhabitants of the ogre's lands into claiming that they belong to the cat's master.
19 In Basile's *Gagliuso* (2.4) the Cat hero has been promised a golden cage for burial and only pretends to be dead.
20 The *Testamentum Porcelli* is included as a sample of children's literature, though it is not strictly a tale, let alone a fairy tale. But it is cited with disapproval by no less than St. Jerome as occasioning laughter for small boys (in the preface to book 12 of his commentary to Isaiah: *decantant in scholis puerorum agmina cachinnantium* 'hordes of chuckling boys recite it in schools'). It is quite clearly literate entertainment, as it is a parody will, though *ATU* 200 offers a tale of dogs with certificates tucked under their tails. However tiny his offences, the piglet's butcher is unrelenting.
21 The fun begins with the name itself: Corocotta is a pun on *choerococta*, 'roast pig' and corocotta the hyena, perceived as a talking pig rather than a laughing dog (Anderson 1980, 57f.). For a 'historical' reading, Champlin (1987), 174–183; for detailed commentary, Bott (1972). Grunnius = 'Grunter'< grunnire.
22 As indeed one should expect of an upper-class Roman.
23 Lecuisinier = Greek Magirus, a cook.
24 On the face of it an impious act, but they appear as legatees and so are still alive.
25 I.e. a slave.
26 Lamplighting: *lucerninus*, a fictitious month, comically suggesting the start of long winter nights.

27 Ovendone and Peppersprinkle: *Clibanatus* ('baked in a *clibanus*') and *Pipperatus* ('peppered').
28 Lardy Hogman: *Verrinus Lardinus*.
29 Oldsow: *Veturina*.
30 Miss Piggie: *Quirina*, with a similar pun to that in *choerococta*.
31 Some of the uses of the pig's anatomy are less obvious than others; some seem to imply sympathetic magic.
32 Tyneside and Timbuctoo: i.e. diagonally across the Empire: Thebeste was situated in the south-west of the province of Africa, Tergeste on Italy's northeastern border with Dalmatia.
33 For the monument, cf. the pretentious tomb of Trimalchio, Petronius *Satyrica*, 71.5–12. The 1000-year lifespan may conceal a seriously entrenched error, or extraordinary delusions of grandeur.
34 The formulae are authentic, the signatories not so.
35 The god plays a part in a number of 'Aesopic' tales, as a deity of gain and good luck.
36 *ATU* has a hen instead of a goose. Grätz *EM* 5 (1987), 677, 681, n. 17, cf. Rodin *EM* 6 (1990), 374.

11
TINY PEOPLE

Several of the examples will have offered at least a nod to a childhood audience. Both the portrayal of the Nile-dwarves and the pygmies are shown swarming over giants, in the persons of the Nile and Heracles respectively. The infant thieving of the day-old Hermes, like Heracles' defeat of the pygmies, is presented as amusing and good-humoured. 'Artemis and the Three Hairy Giants' (my title) is the closest so far noted to our 'Three Bears', which may however be a modern creation. I can point to no exact modern fairy tale equivalent to the treatment of Smikros.

Dwarves a Cubit High: Philostratus, *Imagines* 1.5
(Stith Thompson Motif F451, Dwarf)

(1) The Cubit-dwarfs play around the Nile, children no bigger than their names, and the Nile is overjoyed, especially as they announce his great floods coming to the Egyptians. At any rate they approach and seem to come to him out of the water as infants tender and smiling, and I think they can also speak. And some of them sit on his shoulders, some hang from his hair, some are sleeping on his arms, others are having fun on his chest. And he gives them flowers, some from his lap, some from his arms, so that they can plait garlands and fall asleep on them, as children who are both holy and fragrant.[1] And the infants climb up one on top of another with their rattles: their sound is a familiar one for the river. (2) But crocodiles and hippopotamuses, which some painters depict on the Nile, lie now in its deep eddies so as not to frighten the children. And symbols of agriculture and sailing show that the river is the Nile, my boy, and for this reason: the Nile makes Egypt navigable by boats; and when the fields have drunk their fill of it, it gives the Egyptians fertile lands; and in Ethiopia, from which it starts, its spirit (*daimōn*) stands over it as a steward; and this spirit sends it in proportion

to the seasons. He is depicted as high as the sky, and he plants his foot on its springs, nodding forward like Poseidon. The river looks towards him and prays for many children.

The Thief in the Cradle: The Birth of Hermes: Philostratus, *Imagines* 1.26 (*ATU* 700, Thumbling)[2]

(1) The figure no more than a child still in swaddling clothes,[3] the one driving the cattle into the cleft in the earth, and the one also stealing the arrows of Apollo – this is Hermes. The god's thefts are sheer delight; for they say that Hermes, when Maia gave birth to him, loved to steal and knew his craft, not of course that the god did this from poverty, but devoting himself to high spirits and good fun. And if you want to watch him one step at a time, first he is born on the peaks of Olympus, right at the top, the seat of the gods… (2) There the Hours are holding Hermes newly born. The painter has shown these too, each at her proper time, and they are wrapping him in swaddling clothes, sprinkling him with the loveliest flowers, so as to let him have baby-clothes of no mean sort. And these ladies are turning their attention to Hermes' mother lying in childbed, but he has given his baby-clothes the slip and is already off and comes down from Olympus. The mountain is delighted with him – for it has a smile just like a man's – and you must imagine that Olympus is delighted that Hermes was born there.

(3) So what was it he stole? The cattle that are grazing on the foothills of Olympus, the ones I mean with the golden horns and whiter than snow – they too are sacred to Apollo – these he is leading, winding this way and that into a cleft in the ground, not so as to kill them, but to make them disappear for a day, until Apollo is anxious about their disappearance, and as if the affair is nothing to do with him, he slips back into his baby-clothes. And Apollo comes to Maia to demand the return of the cattle, while she cannot believe him and thinks the god is talking nonsense. (4) Would you like to know what he is saying? For he seems to me to be indicating by his expression not just a sound but actual words. For he seems to be on the point of saying this:

> Your son, the one you gave birth to yesterday, is doing me an injury. For the cattle I take such a pride in he has thrown into the ground, and I don't know where on earth they are. But he will come to grief and will be thrown even further underground!

But his mother is amazed and does not believe his claim. (5) While the pair are still disputing Hermes stands behind Apollo, and jumps lightly on his back, and quickly undoes Apollo's bow, steals it and slips off, but once he has done so he gives himself away. And that is where the painter has been clear. He dissolves Apollo's anger and has him delighted. His laughter is held in check: it sits over his face as pleasure conquers anger.

Hop O'My Thumb[4]: Hyginus *Fabulae* 4 (*ATU* 327B, The Brothers and the Ogre)

When Athamas, king of Thessaly, thought his wife Ino, the mother of his two sons, had died, he married Themisto, the daughter of a nymph, and had twin sons by her. After that he found out that Ino was in Parnassus, where she had gone for a Bacchic rite. He sent for her and had her brought back and then he concealed her. Themisto found out that she had been found, but did not know who she was. She began to want to kill his sons. She took as her partner in crime Ino herself, whom she took to be a prisoner, and told her to clothe her own (Themisto's) sons in white, those of Ino in black. Ino clothed her own in white, Themisto's in dark clothes. Then Themisto, taken in by the trick, killed her own sons; when she found out, she took her own life. As for Athamas, he killed Learchus, his elder son, on a hunt in a fit of madness; but Ino with her younger son Melicertes threw herself into the sea and became a goddess.

Heracles and the Pygmies[5]: Philostratus, *Imagines* 2.22

(1) As Heracles is sleeping in Libya after killing Antaeus, the Pygmies attack him, with the intention of avenging <the giant>. For they claim to be his brothers, stout-hearted fellows, not athletes nor equal to his prowess in wrestling, but born of the earth and strong men as well, and when they rise out of the earth the sand gives a slight billow. For the Pygmies inhabit the earth like ants and have their provisions stored underground, and their provisions are not obtained from others, but theirs alone and produced by themselves. For they sow and reap and ride on a cart with a tiny yoke, and they say that they use an axe on the stalks of grain,[6] considering these to be trees. But how intrepid they are! These men are making their assault on Heracles, and wish to kill him as he sleeps; and they would not be afraid of him even if he were wide awake. (2) But Heracles lies asleep in the soft sand, since weariness has crept over him in his wrestling, and he draws his breath with all his chest and with his fill of sleep with open mouth, and Sleep in person is standing over him making much, no doubt, of his own part in the fall of Heracles, while Antaeus is lying there; but the painter's art has Heracles breathing and warm, but Antaeus dead and wizened, and leaves him to the Earth.

(3) The Pygmy army is surrounding Heracles[7]: this phalanx attacks Heracles' left hand, while two companies set out against the right hand, since it is the stronger: archers and a host of slingers lay siege to both his feet, amazed at the size of his shin. And those who are advancing against his head – there the king is positioned, as this they take to be his strongest point. And they bring siege-engines as if against a citadel: fire against the hair, a mattock against his eyes, some kind of doors against his mouth and these gates, I suppose, against his nose, so that Heracles may not be able to breathe when his head has been captured. (4) And all these measures against the sleeping figure – but look how he stands up and how he laughs at the danger, and collecting his enemies in a single body, he puts them into his lion-skin and no doubt is carrying them to Eurystheus.

Wine-Girl (Oenoe) and the Pygmies[8]: Antoninus Liberalis, *Metamorphoses* 16 (cf. Stith Thompson Motif F535.5.1, War of Pygmies and Cranes)

(1) Among the men known as Pygmies (i.e. Dwarves) there was a girl called 'Wine-girl'. Her appearance was faultless, but she was disagreeable and conceited. She had no regard for Artemis or Hera, (2) but she was married to Nicodamas, a good, sensible man, and gave birth to a son Mopsus. And all the Pygmies adored her and brought her a great many gifts to celebrate the child's birth. But Hera was angry with Wine-girl for not showing respect to her and turned her into a high-flying crane with a long neck. And she stirred up war between the crane-girl and the pygmies. (3) But Wine-girl, longing to see her child Mopsus, would circle the houses and not leave, while the pygmies put on armour and chased her off. And as a result there is even now a state of war between Pygmies and cranes.[9]

Smikros ('Tiny'): Conon, *Narrationes* 33

Democles of Delphi fathered a remarkable infant called Tiny. On the orders of an oracle, he set sail for Miletus, taking with him the young boy. But in his haste to set sail he abandoned him unintentionally; the boy was 13. A goatherd, son of Eritharses, found Tiny in great distress and took him to his father; and Eritharses, hearing the misadventure of Tiny and his origin, took care of him as of his own child. Now the two children had together captured a swan, but quarrelled: she now appeared as Leucothea and told the children to tell the Milesians that they should give her a cult and organise gymnastic games for children in her honour, because she loved children's competitions. Tiny married the daughter of a noble Milesian: and while she was in labour she had a vision: the sun came in by her mouth and exited by her genitals; this vision, according to the diviners, was a good omen. She gave birth to a son called Branchos, because of her dream, since the sun had passed through her throat (*branchos*); and the child was the loveliest in the world, and Apollo fell in love with him when he found him tending his flocks, where there is set up an altar of Apollo the friend. And Branchos, who received from Apollo the gift of prophecy, gave oracles in the place called Didyma, and to this day it is acknowledged that mong the Greek oracles we know this is the most important after Delphi.[10]

'Artemis and the Three Hairy Giants'[11]: Callimachus *Hymn* 3.66–85

(66) But when any of the young girls is disobedient to her mother, the mother calls upon the Cyclopes against her child – Arges or Steropes. And from inside the house comes Hermes, covered in glowing ashes, and at once he plays the bogeyman to the girl, and she sinks into her mother's lap and covers her eyes with her hands. (72) But still earlier, when you (Artemis) were a little girl, only

3 years old, Leto came holding you in her arms at Hephaestus' invitation, so that he could give you presents on seeing you for the first time. And when Brontes set you on his sturdy knees, you plucked the shaggy hair from his great chest and tore it free by force. And even to this day the middle part of his breast is still hairless, as when mange sits on a man's temples and eats away at this hair.

(80) And so you spoke to them boldly:

> Cyclopes, make a Cydonian[12] bow and arrows and a hollow quiver for my darts. For I too am the child of Leto, just like Apollo. And if I should hunt down a wild beast or a dreadful wild animal, the Cyclopes should eat it.

And you spoke, and they brought your request to fruition.

Notes

1. For Cupids playing children's games, Philostratus *Imagines*, 1.6.
2. Pape *EM* 3 (1981), 349–360. Yolen (1986), 58 ('The two pickpockets') contains a modern analogue of the 'thief in the cradle'. Two pickpockets marry to produce a master pick-pocket. He has apparently an arm injury to make theft impractical. The doctor tests his vision with a pocket-watch. As the baby's arm stretches out to take it, the mid-wife's wedding-ring falls out of the baby's clothes.
3. The subject occurs in vase-painting also: *LIMC* V.1 309ff., on a Hydria from Crete, c. 530BC: the infant Hermes resting on a couch with Maia, Apollo and Zeus in animated discussion; also Apollo's flock hidden in the cave. The most elaborate and literary version is contained in the *Homeric Hymn to Hermes*: commentary by N. Richardson (2010).
4. *Petit Poucet*, first English version in Opie and Opie (1980), 170–178. Meraklis *EM* 3(1981), 360–365. The substitution of the wrong clothes is the identifying element; much of the modern tale, such as the ogre's seven-league boots, does not figure in this early version.
5. A *parergon*, with no more than a comic interlude among the Labours of Heracles. It will have provided the inspiration for the Lilliputians' siege of Gulliver in Part I of *Gulliver's Travels*. Reference to a Pygmy *lochagos* is as early as Epicharmus (Scholiast on Aristophanes' *Peace*, 73). Aristotle already attests to their actual existence (*Historia Animalium*, 8.12.597A7f.: 'not a mythos: there really is a tiny people,…with tiny horses; they live in caves…'. For further testimonia, Hansen on the pygmies against the cranes, 45–49. Stith Thompson, Motif F535.5.1. Pygmies, like *Erōtes*, were regularly depicted both in mythological and everyday scenes in their own right.
6. For this detail, Tom Thumb uses a barley straw as a cudgel against the crows, Opie and Opie, 48.
7. It is not altogether clear whether Philostratus is describing one scene and extending it verbally, or two separate scenes. For visual evidence, *LIMC* 2805 (Marble relief from Rome, villa Albano: 'part of Heracles reclining on his lionskin, cup in hand. A small naked figure has climbed a ladder and stoops into the cup as if to drink'). For Heracles and Erōtes trying to steal his weapons, *LIMC* V.1, 3419–3431; for Heracles and satyrs, *LIMC* V.1, 3230–3238 (various combinations of satyrs robbing him of cloak, quiver, club, bow, lionskin).
8. There is a hint of this story and its doublet where the girl is actually called *gerana* (crane-girl) at *ATU* 709A, a reference to a small number of Indian variants which combine a Snow White-like plot with the idea that the girl has stork parents. The variant given in Ramanujan (1994), 104–110 ('The Kite's Daughter') has a girl rescued

by a kite from infant exposure, and given by the kite to a merchant who already has seven wives. They are jealous when the stork helps her with all the household tasks, for which she is of course not trained, and kill the stork, before the merchant finds out and kills the wives. What skews the resemblance is the classical insistence on the girl's arrogance.
9   On the hostilities of Pygmies and Cranes, Hansen, 45–49.
10 Smikros also appears in a scholiast to Statius' *Thebaid*, 8, 198: again he is a lost child, taken in by a stranger Patron, with whose son he again forms a companionship. He and Patron's son wrap a swan as a gift to Patron: Smikros is married to Patron's master's daughter. We appear to be looking at complementary parts of the same story.
11 This is the closest I can find to anything like the modern favourite *The Three Bears*, Opie and Opie (1980), 260–269, which has not been traced earlier than 1831; but early versions of it have an old crone, not a young girl, upsetting the bears.
12 I.e. Cretan, after Cydonia on the island's northern coast, modern Canea.

12
MISCELLANEOUS TALES

In conclusion a varied sample of tales: *The language of signs misunderstood* underlines the 'wisdom' element in ancient popular storytelling, while the language of animals understood by a human may owe its origins to close observation and actual understanding of animal behaviour. *Pyrrhus and the Old Woman* demonstrates that a well-established medieval and early modern tale could have arisen as an historical anecdote much earlier. 'Herodes Atticus and Heracles Goodfellow' also has an historical basis, although it entails a feat of what the reporter sees as extraordinary perception; the same focus occurs in the story of Smindyrides. I end with a largely unnoticed version of *The Frog Prince*, followed by three puzzling variants related to *Rumpelstiltskin* and one to *Bluebeard*, with the possibility of yet another version of the former's name and the latter's beard!

The Language of Signs Misunderstood[1]: Herodotus 4.131f. (*ATU* 924, Discussion in Sign Language)[2]

(131) ...At last Darius did not know what to do, and the Scythian rulers found this out and sent a herald with gifts for the king: a bird, a mouse, a frog, and five arrows. The Persians asked the bearer the meaning of the gifts; but he replied that his instructions were no more than to deliver the gifts and leave as quickly as possible; he told the Persians to work out what the gifts meant, if they had the wits to do so.

(132) On hearing this the Persians discussed the matter. Darius' opinion was that the Scythians were surrendering to him themselves, their land and their water, arguing that the mouse is a creature found on land and eating the same food as men, the frog lives in water, while the bird most resembles the horse, and the arrows signified that the Scythians were surrendering their military strength. This then was Darius' interpretation; but Gobryas, one of the seven who had

killed the Magian, had a different understanding. His view was that the gifts meant: 'Unless you become birds and fly up to heaven, Persians, or become mice and burrow in the earth, or turn into frogs and jump into the lakes, you will not return home, but will be shot by these arrows'.

Understanding the Language of Animals[3]: Apollodorus 1.9.11f.
(ATU 517, The Boy Who Understands the Language of Birds)

(11) Now Amythaon lived in Pylus and married Eidomene, daughter of Pheres, and had two sons, Bias and Melampus; the latter stayed in the area, and as there was in front of his house an oak tree in which there was a lair of serpents, the servants killed the snakes; but he gathered wood together and burned the bodies, but reared their offspring. And when they reached adulthood they stood beside his shoulders as he slept, and from either side they purified his hearing with their tongues. He stood up in a panic, but understood the voices of the birds flying overhead, and learning from them he foretold the future to men. And he added to this besides the art of divination from sacrifices, and having encountered Apollo at the river Alpheus he was thereafter the finest of prophets.

(12) His brother Bias was wooing Pero the daughter of Neleus; the latter promised to give her to whichever of the many suitors brought him the cattle of Phylacus. These were in Phylace, and they were guarded by a dog which it was impossible for either man or beast to approach. Being unable to steal the cattle, he called on his brother to help: Melampus promised to do so, and prophesied that he would be caught thieving and after being shut up for a year he should get the cattle. And after this promise he went off, and just as he had foretold, he was caught in the act of stealing and was held prisoner in a cell. A little short of a year later, he heard the bore-worms in the hidden part of the roof, one asking how much of the beam had been gnawed through, the other replying that there was very little left. And quickly he asked to be transferred to another cell, and when that had been done, not long afterward the cell collapsed. Phylacus was amazed, and on learning that Melampus was the best of prophets, he freed him and asked him to say how his own son Iphicles might produce children. Melampus promised to tell him provided he should receive the cattle. And having sacrificed two bulls and cut them up, he summoned the birds; and when a vulture arrived, he learned from him that Phylacus once while gelding rams laid down the still bloody knife beside Iphicles. He had been terrified and ran off; he had fixed the knife in a sacred oak, and the bark had grown round the knife and hidden it. So he told him that if he found the knife and scraped off the rust, and gave it to Iphicles to drink for ten days, he would father a child. Melampus found this out from the vulture, found the knife, scraped off the rust, and gave it to Iphicles to drink for ten days, and a son Podarces was born to him. Melampus drove the cattle to Pylos, and receiving the daughter of Neleus he gave her to his brother. And for a while he remained in Messine, but when Dionysus drove the women mad in Argos he healed them for a share in the kingdom and settled there with Bias.

The Emperor's New Clothes: Pyrrhus and the Old Woman[4]: Lucian, *Adversus indoctum* 21 (*ATU* 1620)

They say that even Pyrrhus of Epirus, in other respects a marvellous man,[5] was... so corrupted by flatterers as to believe that he was like the famous Alexander.[6] And yet as musicians say, the two men were two octaves apart, for I have seen Pyrrhus' picture...<Now> when Pyrrhus was in this state of mind and was convinced that this was how he was, there was no-one who did not agree, and everyone went along with him, until at last some old foreign women in Larissa[7] put a stop to his nonsense by telling him the truth. For Pyrrhus showed her pictures[8] of Philip, Perdiccas, Alexander, Cassander[9] and other kings, and asked her who he himself was like, absolutely convinced that she would go for Alexander; but she held back a good while, then said 'Froggy the cook'.[10] And in fact there was a cook in Larissa who did look like Pyrrhus.

'Herodes Atticus and Heracles Goodfellow': Philostratus, *Lives of the Sophists* 2.1.552–554[11] (cf. *ATU* 655, The Wise Brothers)

This is doubtless a true report of a figure of local legend. His name as Philostratus gives it as Agathion 'Son of, little, Goodman', i.e. Goodfellow. The minor feats described suit a 'child of the countryside' and local hero, whom the eminent arbiter of Athenian elegance has taken the credit for discovering. He is also a good-natured giant; and Lucian, not usually complimentary about such phenomena, or always sympathetic to the controversial Herodes, speaks well of the same figure, this time under the name of Sostratus. We need not stress continuity with the figure of Robin Goodfellow associated with peasant gifts of milk and local good-deeds/mischief-making; but the identical name must be allowed to speak for itself.

(552) The figure most people called the Heracles of Herodes was a youth growing his first beard, like a huge Celt,[12] and around eight feet tall. Herodes gives a description of him in one of his letters to Julianus[13]: he says that his hair grew evenly and he had bushy eyebrows, which met together as if they were one, and from his eyes there flashed a brilliant gleam which indicated his impulsive character. He had a hooked nose and a well-developed neck, the result of exertion rather than diet; and he had a chest stoutly built and elegantly slim, and his knees bent outward slightly and gave him a firm stance. (553) And he was dressed in wolf-pelts sewn to form a garment, and he used to take on wild boars, jackals and wolves and mad bulls, and showed the scars of these contests. And some say that this Heracles[14] was a child of the earth[15] in Boeotia, but Herodes says he heard him say that his mother was strong enough to herd cattle,[16] and that his father was Marathon, whose statue is at Marathon, and who is a rustic hero.[17] Herodes asked this Heracles whether he too was immortal, but he said 'I only live longer than mortals'. He asked him also what he ate, and he replied:

I live on milk most of the time, and goats nourish me and herds of cow and brood mares, and from the she-ass I receive a sweet and light kind of milk, but when I apply myself to barley-meal, I take ten quarts at a time, and the farmers of Marathon and Boeotia contribute this feast for me[18]: they call me 'Little Goodfellow' (Agathion)[19] since I seem to bring them luck.

'And as for your speech', said Herodes, 'how were you educated[20] and by what teachers? For you do not seem one of the uneducated to me'. And Little Goodfellow replied,

The interior of Attica is a good school for a man who wishes to engage in conversation; for the Athenians in the city admit as hirelings young men from Thrace and Pontus and from other barbarian nations who flood in, and are corrupted in their speech by them more than they contribute to improving the foreigners' speech. But the interior is uncontaminated by barbarians and so its language is healthy and its dialect sounds the purest of Atthis.[21]

Herodes asked, 'Have you been to a public festival?' Agathion replied,

At Pytho,[22] but I did not mix with the crowd but listened from the vantage-point of Parnassus[23] to the music competitions, when Pammenes won his reputation in tragedy, and (554) the wise Greeks seemed to me to have done no good thing listening with pleasure to the ills of the houses of Pelops and Labdacus[24]; for when myths are not disbelieved they are the counsellors of evil deeds.[25]

Seeing that he had a philosophic disposition, Herodes asked his views on gymnastic contests,[26] and he said,

I despise these, seeing men competing in the pancratium and boxing and running and wrestling, and receiving crowns for this. The athlete who runs should receive a crown for overtaking a deer or a horse, and the man who undergoes training for heavier contests should be crowned for wrestling with a bull or a bear, as I do every day[27]; but fortune has taken away the chance of a great contest, since Acarnania no longer nurtures lions.

Herodes therefore was taken with him and asked him to dine with him. Agathion replied 'I will come to you tomorrow at noon at the temple of Canobus, and you must have the largest bowl in the temple full of milk not milked by a woman'.[28] And he arrived the next day at the time agreed, but when he put his nose to the bowl he said 'The milk is not pure, for the hand of woman hits me'. And with this he went off without touching the milk. So Herodes took up what he said about the woman and sent servants to the cow-sheds to find out the truth, and on learning that that was indeed the case, he realised that there was a superhuman nature about the man.[29]

Sleeping on a Feather: The Oversensitive Sybarite: Aelian, *Varia Historia* 9.24 (*ATU* 1290B*)

Smindyrides of Sybaris fell into luxurious habits[30]; all the Sybarites made it their business to practise luxury and lead an extravagant lifestyle, and especially Smindyrides: at any rate he lay down on rose petals and when he had slept on them he got up complaining that his bed had given him blisters.

The Frog Prince?[31]: Homer, *Odyssey* 6.85–245 extracts (*ATU* Type 440, The Frog King)[32]

(85) And when at last they reached the lovely river-stream,[33] where there were the washing beds that never failed them, and plenty of lovely water welled up to clean even the most soiled garment, there the girls let the mules out from the wagon, and drove them along the river eddies to graze the honey-sweet water-grass. And from the cart they took the clothes in their hands and carried them into the dark river, and vied with one another, rivalling one another in their speed, and trampled them in the pits. But when they had washed them all and cleaned out all the dirt, they spread them in order beside the shore of the sea, where the sea coming against the land would wash the pebbles the cleanest. And they bathed and richly anointed themselves with oil, then they took their meal beside the banks of the river, and waited for the sunlight to dry the clothes, but when the princess and her handmaids had enjoyed their lunch, they threw off their veils and played ball, and Nausicaa the white-armed led their song…

(115) The princess threw the ball in the direction of one of her maids; she missed her maid and it fell into a deep eddy.[34] And the girls let out a great shout. And lordly Odysseus awoke and sitting up he reflected in his mind and heart… (127) With this lordly Odysseus slipped out from under the bushes and with his sturdy hand broke a leafy branch from the thin undergrowth, so as to conceal his manly parts by holding it against his skin… (137) and he seemed a terrifying sight to them, with a filthy layer of brine, and they shrank from him in all directions along the jutting spits of land.[35] Only the daughter of Alcinous (Princess Nausicaa) stood firm, for Athena put courage in her heart and took the fear out of her limbs. (He is not slow to hint at marriage):

> (158) 'That man will be happiest of all in his heart who wins you with his wedding gifts and leads you home with him. For never have I set eyes on such a mortal, neither man nor woman, I am seized with awe at the sight…'.

(223) (Nausicaa)'s maids went apart and spoke to the princess. But lordly Odysseus washed his skin with water from the river <and removed> the brine which was

all over his back and broad shoulders, and from his head he wiped the scurf of the barren sea. But when at least he had washed it all off and anointed himself with oil, and put on the clothes the unwed girl had given him, Athena the daughter of Zeus made him taller to behold and mightier, and sent down from his head the flowing curls, like a hyacinth flower... (237) And the princess was amazed: She spoke to her fair-tressed handmaidens:

> Listen, white-armed maidens, so that I can speak. It is not without the will of all the gods who dwell on Olympus that this man comes among the god-like Phaeacians. Beforehand certainly he seemed to me to be uncouth, but now he is like the gods who dwell in the broad heaven. If only such a man might be called my husband and dwell here, and he might remain here...

The Name of the Helper: Rumpelstiltskin-Type Tales[36]: Parthenius, *Erōtica pathēmata* 27 (*ATU* 500, The Name of the Supernatural Helper)

The story goes that Alkinoe,[37] the daughter of Polybus of Corinth, and wife of Amphilochus son of Dryas, fell passionately in love with a stranger from Samos whose name was Xanthus,[38] ('Goldie') because of the wrath of Athena. For she had hired for wages a spinning-woman called Nicandra, and after this woman had worked for her for a year, had driven her out of the house without giving her full wages; Nicandra had constantly prayed to Athena to avenge her for the unjust loss of her wages. And so she went as far as to leave her home and children she had already had, and sail away with Xanthus. But in the midst of her voyage she realised what she had done, and at once wept floods of tears and cried now for her husband, now for her children. And finally, although Xanthus tried to console her and promised to marry her, she refused to listen and threw herself into the sea.

Dio of Halicarnassus 1.68:

Gold-girl (Chryse) daughter of Pallas brought with her as a dowry to <King> Dardanus the gifts of Athena, the Palladium and the sacred objects of the *megaloi theoi* (she had been instructed in their mysteries).[39] And when the Arcadians fled from the flood in the Peloponnese and settled in the Thracian island, Dardanus there made a temple of these gods, not telling others their secret names, and he performed the rites in their honour that are still practised by the Samothracians.[40]

Lucian, Fugitivi *12–33 (extracts):*

(Philosophy speaks):
(12) But listen, Zeus, to how important they are: for there is a vile tribe of men, and for the most part slaves and serfs, with nothing to do with me (Philosophy)

in their youth for lack of leisure. For they acted as slaves or serfs, or they learned some other trades proper for people of that kind, cobbling or metalworking or having to do with fullers' tubs or carding wool so that it should be easy for women to work, and easy to wind, and easy to lead off whenever they twist yarn or spin their thread.[41] When therefore they were practising such occupations in their youth they did not even know my name...

(Heracles, Hermes and Philosophy go off to Thrace to hunt down three such creatures)

(26) HERMES: ...What must we do now, or how must we track the beasts down?
HERACLES: That is now up to you, Hermes: for you are a crier, so waste no time in making your announcement.
HERMES: That is no problem. But I don't know their names. So you tell me who to name, and their distinguishing marks as well.
PHILOSOPHY: Nor do I know what their names are,[42] for I have never had anything to do with them ever. But from their appetites for possessions, you would not be wrong to call them Gainman or Gainhorse or Goodgain or Muchgain.
(27) HERMES: You are right, but who are these men, and why are they too looking around? But they are coming towards us and want to ask something.
HUSBAND: Would you be able to tell us, gentlemen, or you, madam, if you know three magicians together, and a woman with her hair close-cropped like a Spartan, like a boy and thoroughly masculine?
PHILOSOPHY: Ah, they are looking for our fugitives –
HUSBAND: Why yours? For these are runaway slaves. And I am looking especially for my wife, whom they have kidnapped.
HERMES: You will soon know why we are searching for them; but for now let us make our proclamation together –

> 'If anyone has seen Paphlagonian slaves, one of the barbarians from Sinope, with some kind of name with 'gain' in it, sallow, close-cropped, with a long beard, with a wallet hanging from his shoulder and wearing a tiny cloak, bad-tempered, ill-educated, foul-mouthed, and abusive,[43] he is to give us the information for an agreed reward'.

(28) FIRST SLAVE-OWNER: The description you give does not fit, my man: his name when he was with me was Kantharos (Scarab-Beetle).[44] And he wore his hair long and trimmed his beard, and knew my trade. For he sat in my fuller's shop and cut off 'the excessive nap that makes clothes fuzzy'.

(they now hear of two other scoundrels, (29) and the local hero Orpheus gives them directions):

ORPHEUS: I would show you the house where he lives, but not Scarab-beetle himself, so as not to be insulted by him, for he is far too foul-mouthed: that's the only skill he has mastered.
HERMES: Just show us.

ORPHEUS: Here it is, not far, and I'll be out of here so as not even to look at him.
(30) PHILOSOPHY: One moment, is that not the voice of a woman reciting something from Homer?[45]
HERMES: Indeed it is! But let us hear what she is saying:
WOMAN: 'For I hate that man like the gates of Hades
Who loves gold in his heart, but denies it'.[46]
HERMES: So you must hate Scarab-Beetle!
WOMAN: 'He has insulted any host who has shown him kindness —'[47]
HUSBAND: This verse is about me! He ran off with my wife when I gave him shelter!
(31) FIRST SLAVE-OWNER: ...Got you, Scarab-beetle! Nothing to say now? Come on, let's see what's in your wallet. Lupines, perhaps, or a crust of bread? No, my goodness, but a money-belt of gold!...
(33) HERMES: This is my decree: the woman is to return to Greece to her husband, so that she may give birth to no many-headed monster; ...Then as for this one, he is to be handed over to the pitch-plasterers, so that he may be killed by having his hair pulled out, and with filthy pitch too, the kind women use, then to be brought to Haemus stark naked and stand there in the snow with his feet tied together.[48]
SCARAB-BEETLE: Alas for my miseries. Woe Woe lackaday! (*Ototoi Papapaiax*)

Bluebeard[49]: Apollodorus 3.15.1; Strabo 10.2.9 (*ATU* 312, Maiden-Killer)

(Apollodorus) Procris slept with Pteleon in exchange for a golden crown, and having been found out by Cephalus she fled to Minos,[50] who fell in love with her and persuaded her to sleep with him. But if a woman slept with Minos, it was impossible for her to survive, for, since Minos was in the habit of sleeping with numerous women, Pasiphae bewitched him and when he slept with any other woman, he excreted wild beasts into her crotch, and that was what killed them. So in exchange for Minos' swift dog and unerring javelin, Procris slept with him, after giving him some of Circe's drugs to drink to avoid his harming her. But later, fearing Minos' wife, she returned to Athens (Strabo) <disguised as Pterelas>.[51]

Notes

1 West, *JHS* 108 (1988), 207–211.
2 An eminent or wise man interprets a coded message one way (often in a naively optimistic manner favourable to himself); a social inferior interprets the signs in a more convincing or morally compelling way, showing up the previous interpretation as foolish. S. West adduces a number of authentic or plausible oriental instances where diplomacy or even a love-affair is conducted by means of symbolic gifts, associating it with illiterate or semi-literate cultures where writing would be ineffective. She considers but rejects a folktale connexion only by noting the absence of comparable material in Stith-Thompson's motif index; but the material is accessible through the

Aarne-Thompson-Uther index of complete tales. The point is not symbolic communication as such, but the contrasting interpretations of it, which can be set in a narrative context and thus constitute a tale. Other ancient instances appear in the popularly conceived *Alexander Romance*, in communications between Darius and Alexander (1.36–38), and in the no less popular *Aesop Romance*, where letter-codes concerning a buried treasure are read one way by the slave master Xanthus, then by the wise slave Aesop (*Vita Aesopi*, 79f.) West plausibly suggests that Herodotus' version is a reworking and simplification of a version known to Pherecydes (210). See also Chesnutt and Kawan, *EM* 14 (2014), 1229–1237.

3 Hansen, 462–469; Schmitt, *EM* 10 (2002), 1413–1419. Similar feats are attributed to Apollonius of Tyana, who can conjecture the reason for sparrows' speech at Philostratus, *VA* 4.3 without actually seeing the sparrows.
4 A delusive king believes his flatterer about his royal dignity until someone too humble to be dishonest exposes the truth: Uther, *EM* 7 (1993), 852–857.
5 King of Epirus in the 4th/3rd centuries BCE, whose expansionist foreign policy qualified him as Rome's first foreign enemy.
6 Already termed 'the Great' as early as Plautus, *Mostellaria*, 775.
7 The tale requires a social outcast or innocent to speak up and reveal what everybody thinks. The informant here is female, not a courtier, and from up-country Larissa, so that the lookalike would not himself have been widely known.
8 This scenario touches on a less celebrated variant of the tale, illustrated by *Tyl Eulenspiegel*, 27: a rogue paints a canvas white and pretends it portrays royalty; no-one contradicts him.
9 Alexander's father and two of his lieutenants.
10 Batrachion, 'Littlefrog'.
11 An evidently genuine report of an encounter between a serious intellectual of the high empire and a rustic credited with supernatural powers. Herodes Atticus was a prominent Athenian philanthropist, politician and man of letters embodying the values of the so-called Second Sophistic, and capable of being credited with reasonably objective observation.
12 Celtic speakers in antiquity are spread from Anatolia to the British Isles.
13 Tiberius Claudius Julianus.
14 In a lost work so titled Lucian had called him Sostratus, most likely his real name.
15 A child of the earth: i.e. without a clearly identified human father ('a son of the soil'), and appropriate for a giant.
16 Like the rustic prophetess described in Dio of Prusa *Oration*, 1, 53–58.
17 I.e. a minor supernatural, enjoying longer than human life rather than immortal.
18 An entirely rustic non-meat diet.
19 'Little Goodfellow'.
20 Herodes would have been in search of the purest Attic dialect: Agathion complains of foreign infiltration (one thinks of Aristophanes' ridicule of the speech habits of Scythian policemen).
21 Atthis: the traditional language of Athenian local historians (Atthidographers).
22 I.e. at Delphi in honour of Apollo Pythius.
23 Parnassus: a mountain above Delphi, associated with the seat of the Muses.
24 Pelops: giving the family history of Agamemnon; Labdacus: the Thebans, including Oedipus.
25 Hence Plato's views on censorship of poets and rewriting of myths (*Republic* 376C–394B).
26 On which at least one of the Philostrati had strong views, expressed in *Gymnasticus*.
27 Agathion favours contests where his own strength would be at a premium.
28 This could be regarded as polluted if handled, for example, by a menstruating woman.
29 The story of extraordinarily refined perception touches on the tale of the three experts (*ATU* 655), where one of three youths may detect milk handled by a woman, menstruating or otherwise, wine smelling of a graveyard, or the like.

30 The sensitivity in bed evokes Hans Christian Andersen's *The Princess and the Pea* (*ATU*, 704): she is disturbed by a pea under 20 coverlets, and by her fastidiousness wins the hand of a prince. Book 12 of Somadeva's 11th-century *Katha Sarit Sagara* uses it in a contest to determine the most fastidious of three, but not in a wooing tale. Smindyrides himself is also the centre of a wooing tale (as a suitor of Agariste of Sicyon, daughter of Cleisthenes, in pursuit of whom he deploys a huge retinue, Aelian *Varia Historia*, 12.24); but he is unsuccessful. See also Opie and Opie (1980), 283–287; Uther, *EM* 12 (2007), 10f.
31 Opie and Opie (1980), 238–244; Röhrich, *EM* 5 (1987), 410–424; Anderson (2000), 176–178; Hansen (2002), 145.
32 Commentators on the *Odyssey* have suspected the folktale character of the Nausicaa story: Hainsworth (1988, 291): 'The motif of her impending marriage probably has deep roots in folktale, as if the unknown stranger she assisted were to become her suitor'. Hellanicus married her to Telemachus (*FGrH* 323aF156, Aristotle fragment 506 Rose).
33 The location is important. Princess Nausicaa subsequently notes that the Phaeacians live apart from the familiar world (6.204f.). The action of the *Frog Prince* story often takes place at 'the well at the world's end.' Here the action is located precisely at the edge of the Ocean, where the Phaeacian river meets the sea.
34 The Grimms' version of *The Frog Prince* has the crucial detail of the ball lost in the water, rather than drawing water from the well at the world's end.
35 Homer introduces here a simile, not of a frog, but a lion with flashing eyes; but Odysseus is covered in brine and scurf, has been bedded down under olive bushes with leaves, has come from the water, and advances naked and with an olive branch before him; he is an unaccustomed and unwelcome sight.
36 Opie and Opie (1980), 253–259; Röhrich, *EM* 9 (1999), 1164–1175; Anderson (2000), 138–142.
37 The first tale has the key motif of the woman unable to pay for spinning, with enforced elopement as the penalty for default; but there is no guessing of the name of the man who carries off the defaulter; as in the other two versions, the name given (Xanthus) is connected with the colour of gold
38 'Goldman', cf. Chryse ('Gold-girl') in Diodorus.
39 Chryse is doubly endowed with the wherewithal for spinning: Athena herself is the patroness of domestic skills; while the *Megaloi theoi* are droll, sinister figures, with secret names (which in this instance we do happen to know: they included Axiokerses and Kadmilus, and were associated with gyration (hence modern jingling names like Terry-top).
40 This extract in effect sets up the story, but does not actually tell it. To complete the action we need Chryse to force either the *megaloi theoi* or the king to disclose the secret names to avoid her paying some penalty demanded by them.
41 Rumpelstiltskin's expertise is in spinning yarn into gold.
42 The key link to 'The Name of the Helper': the kidnapped wife cannot be rescued until the helper's name is revealed. It would be reasonable to suspect that the wife has been initially seduced by the villain as part-payment for his magically completing household, or particularly spinning, tasks. Sometimes the villain's bargain is not to ask for the wife's first child, but for herself, as in a Cornish version (Briggs *DBF*, 1.1.217–220).
43 The beard, tiny cloak and bad temper point well to a Rumpelstiltskin-type manikin.
44 Another crucial piece of evidence: this was the secret name of Ra, extracted by Isis thanks to the excruciating pain of the god's foot that she had contrived to poison. Brunner-Traut (1989), 115–120.
45 Occasionally traditional fairy tales incorporate the device of the persecuted female overheard, e.g. Basile 2.8.
46 The Homeric pastiche is drawn from *Iliad* 6, 181f., freely adapted.
47 *Iliad*, 3.354, slightly adapted.

48 Once more punishments are summary and severe: in one Grimm version of Rumpelstiltskin, the manikin stamps the earth hard enough to split himself in two.
49 Opie and Opie (1980), 133–141; Puchner, *EM* 8 (1996), 1407–1413; Anderson (2000), 97–100.
50 Minos is doubly qualified as a 'Bluebeard' figure. As the powerful king of Crete he was a sea-king, who might reasonably be presented as the colour of the waves; and he acquired the magic purple lock of Nisus of Megara (Ovid, *Met.* 8.85–95) (though Ovid's own version has him refuse it).
51 Only Strabo appears to give the elusive name. It is important, as the version given by the Grimms (*Fitcher's Bird*, 46) also contains escape from Bluebeard in some kind of avian disguise (*pteron* = wing).

APPENDIX 1

THE SLEEPING BEAUTY[1]
(*ATU* 410, THE PETRIFIED KINGDOM)

There has never been a problem in recognising that this story is well represented in the early modern period: it appears in Catalan and in French, and then in Basile (*Pentamerone*, 5.5) as *Sun, Moon and Talia*:

> It is foretold that lady Talia will be in danger from a splinter of flax: her parents remove all such material from the palace. But she sees an old lady spinning, and dies when flax gets under her finger-nail. Her father leaves her in the palace in a wood; after some time a king appears; unable to wake her, he rapes her and she gives birth to two children called Sun and Moon. They succeed in waking her, and she is revisited by the king. He succeeds with difficulty in stopping his original wife from making him eat the two children, and she is duly punished in a fire she had prepared for Talia.

This is clearly enough 'our' Sleeping Beauty, though readers of more modern tellings will recognise that the second half has undergone a good deal of expurgation, where it appears at all. The longest ancient 'take' can be pieced together from two Homeric passages and an extract of Pausanias:
(*Iliad*, 24.602–612)
> (Niobe's) 12 children perished in her palace, six daughters and six sons in their prime: these Apollo slew with arrows from his silver bow, in anger at Niobe, and Artemis delighting in shafts killed her daughters, because Niobe compared herself to Leto of the fair cheeks, saying that Leto had only borne two, while she herself had borne many[2]; but the two, though there were only two, killed all those others. For nine days long they lay slaughtered, nor was there anyone to bury them, for the son of Cronus turned the people to stone.[3]

196 Sleeping Beauty (Homer, Pausanias)

(Pausanias, 2.21.10)
> They say that Niobe's daughter's original name was Meliboia, but when Amphion's children were shot down by Artemis and Apollo, she and Amyclas alone survived, since they prayed to Leto. Meliboia however turned so green from fear, and remained green for the rest of her life, that from Meliboia her name was changed to Chloris.[4]

(*Odyssey*, 11.281-284)
> Chloris, the most beautiful lady, whom long ago Neleus[5] wooed with countless gifts and married for her beauty, was the youngest daughter of Amphion, the son of Iasus. In those days he held sway at Orchomenos over the Minyai.

Here we have most of the story: the mother's transgression and the goddess' revenge, with the whole kingdom immobilised. Chloris turns the colour of vegetation rather than being surrounded by it. The marriage to Neleus is ominous, as his name itself means 'cruel'. One thinks of the rape of the sleeping girl in Basile; this time he woos her conventionally, and there is no long sleep as such. We might note that Basile's name for the Sleeping Beauty is Talia: now Greek Thalia means 'the growth in plants' (<thallo) and so is consistent with the name Chloris. Basile has her children as Sun and Moon.[6] The mother of Sun and Moon in Hesiod (*Theogony*, 371-374) is given as Theia,[7] who should therefore be equivalent to Thalia; her extended form Pasithea in Homer is said to be *the bride of Sleep* (*Iliad*, 14.265-271). Both Thalia and Pasithea are said to be Graces.[8] These various connexions leave much unexplained,[9] but Basile's connexion of Talia with the birth of Sun and Moon guarantees the link of much of the detail with the *Sleeping Beauty* story.

A short episode in *Cupid and Psyche* affords a still more concise 'take', under different names:
Apuleius *Met.* 6.21 1-3.

> With these words she opened the box: in it she found no objects, no beauty, but an infernal sleep, truly Stygian, which immediately was uncovered by the removed lid: it entered her and poured through her into all her limbs with a thick cloud of sleep, and took hold of her as she collapsed on the very pathway. And she lay motionless and nothing other than a sleeping corpse... Cupid ran up to his dear love Psyche, carefully wiped off the sleep and replaced it in its original box, and awoke her with a harmless prick of his arrow.

Only the length of the sleep and the immobilising of the kingdom are missing here. All in all there is enough mythographic material to show that there was at least one *Sleeping Beauty* story in Antiquity:

> Niobe offends the goddess Leto by her boasting; as part of her punishment most of her family are killed, and the kingdom turned to stone. Her one surviving daughter Meliboia is spared, but turned the colour of blooming vegetation and renamed Chloris, a synonym of Thalia (<thallo). She is wooed by a suitor Neleus whose name means 'cruel'.

The fact that the story can fit in as an episode to that of *Cupid and Psyche* will suggest further lines of enquiry. So will the story of the grace Pasithea, offered by Hera as a Bride of Sleep (*Il.*, 14.267–269).

Notes

1 Opie and Opie (1980), 102–118; Anderson (2003), 92f.; Neeman, *EM* 12 (2007), 13–19.
2 Modern Sleeping Beauties tend to offer rather more trivial insults, as when the bad fairy in Perrault takes exception to her inferior cutlery!
3 This detail offers us the scenario of the immobile kingdom once the girl is put to sleep; but normally in modern fairy tales the kingdom recovers when the girl is awakened by the prince, whereas Niobe's lithification is forever.
4 Here she is not surrounded by greenery, but literally turns green. It is to be assumed that she would have been lithified with all the rest in *Iliad*, 24 above.
5 On the face of it this is the normal 'prince'; but in fact Neleus means 'cruel', and this detail accords with the details in Basile's early modern version, where the girl is raped and the prince panders to the wishes of his previous, now jealous, wife…
6 Perrault's two children are similarly Morning and Dawn.
7 M.L. West ad loc. can offer no explanation for the name.
8 The names and numbers of Graces are fluid, as noted by Pausanias, 9.35.1.
9 Notably how Hyperion as father of the Sun and Moon in Hesiod fits into the picture.

APPENDIX 2

SOME FRAGMENTARY HINTS

Aside from tales either fully told or summarised we have a small number of tantalising hints of what might appear to be familiar tales. Clearest among these is *qui fuit rana nunc est rex* ('the man who was once a frog is now king', Petronius, 77.6), as clear an allusion as we could hope for to 'The Frog Prince'. Horace offers *neu pransae Lamiae vivum puerum extrahat alvo* (*Ars Poetica*, 340) ('Do not let (the *fabula*) drag the boy alive from the belly of the Lamia who has eaten him'), which we might relate to the notion of bringing someone alive from the wolf's stomach in *Red Riding Hood*, or some similar tale. *Lamiae turres et solis pectines* ('the Lamia's towers and the combs of the sun', Tertullian *adversus Valentinianos*, 2) was tentatively offered by Bolte and Polivka as a hint of *Rapunzel*, with the towers serving as the castle where the ogress imprisons the heroine, and the combs of the sun as part of the obstacle-flight intended to catch the fugitive; but they might also be drawn from separate tales. *Cum Incuboni pilleum rapuisset, thesaurum invenit* ('after he stole the goblin's cap, he found the goblin's treasure', Petronius, 38.8) seems to imply a story where the hero has forced the *incubo* (goblin, devil) to reveal where treasure is hidden in exchange for the return of his cap. The fairy-tale preoccupation with royalty produces Persius *Satura*, 2.37: *Hunc optet generum rex et regina* ('let the king and queen wish for this man as their son-in-law'). Ibid., 37f. *Puellae/hunc rapiant* ('let girls snatch this other fellow away') probably alludes to Hylas and the nymphs. And ibid., 38 *quidquid calcaverit hic, rosa fiat* ('whatever this fellow may trample, let it turn into a rose') might allude to Orpheus' powers over nature. Basile's heroine Marziella (*Pentamerone*, 4.7) is given by a fairy the power to produce violets and lilies from her footprints, in a version of *The Kind and Unkind Girls*.

BIBLIOGRAPHY

I Texts and collections

(t = text, tr = translation, c = commentary, unless already self-evident from the title)

Aelian (1997), *Historical Miscellany (Varia Historia)*, (ttr) N.G. Wilson, Cambridge, MA: Harvard University Press.
Aesopica (1952), B.E. Perry, (t), Urbana: University of Illinois Press.
Afanas'ev, A. (1945, repr. 1970), *Russian Fairy Tales*, (tr) N. Guterman, New York: Pantheon Books.
Anderson, G. (2007), *The Earliest Arthurian Texts*, (ttrc), Lewiston, NY: Edwin Mellen.
Antonius Diogenes (1959–1977), *Wonders beyond Thule (Ta Hyper Thoulēn Apista)* in Photius *Codex* 166, (ttr) R. Henry, Paris: Les Belles Lettres.
Apollodorus (1921), *The Library*, (ttr) J.G. Frazer, Cambridge, MA: Harvard University Press.
Apollonius Paradoxographus (1877), *Rerum Naturalium Scriptores Graeci Minores* I, (t) O. Keller, Leipzig: Teubner.
Apollonius Rhodius (1989), *Argonautica* Book III, (tc) R. Hunter, Cambridge: Cambridge University Press.
────── (1993), *Jason and the Golden Fleece*, (tr) R. Hunter, Oxford: World's Classics.
Apuleius (1990), *Cupid & Psyche*, (ttrc) E.J. Kenney, Cambridge: Cambridge University Press.
Aristophanes (1968), *Clouds*, (tc) K.J. Dover, Oxford: Oxford University Press.
────── (1994), *Frogs*, (tc) K.J. Dover, Oxford: Oxford University Press.
Asbjørnsen, P.C., and Moe, J. (1970), *East o' the Sun and West o' the Moon: Fifty-Nine Norwegian Folk Tales*, (tr) G.W. Dasent, New York: Dover Publications.
Ashliman, D.L. (1987), *A Guide to Folktales in the English Language*, New York: Greenwood.
Augustine of Hippo (1965), *City of God* XVI–XVIII, (ttr) E.M. Sanford with W.M. Green, Cambridge, MA: Harvard University Press.
Babrius and Phaedrus (1965), B. E. Perry, (ttr), Cambridge, MA: Harvard University Press.
Basile, G. (1932), *The Pentamerone of Giambattista Basile*, I–II, (tr) N.M. Penzer (from Benedetto Croce's Italian version), London: John Lane, The Bodley Head.

Betz, H.D. (1986 rev. 1992), *The Greek Magical Papyri in Translation, Including the Demotic Spells*, Chicago, IL: University of Chicago Press.
Boggs, R.S. (1933), *The Half-Chick Tale in Spain and France* (FFC 111), Helsinki: Academia Scientiarum Fennica.
Böklen, E. (1910, 1915), *Sneewitchenstudien*, I–II, Leipzig: J.C. Hinrich.
Bolte, J. and Polivka, G. (1913–1932), *Anmerkungen zu den kinder-und Hausmärchen der Brüder Grimm* I–V, Leipzig: Dieterich'sche Verlagbuchshandlung.
Book of Dede Korkut (1974), (t) G. Lewis, Harmondsworth: Penguin Classics.
Brednich, R. (1999), 'Meleager', *EM* 9: 547–552.
Briggs, K. (1970), *A Dictionary of British Folktales in the English Language* I–II, London: Routledge.
Brunner-Traut, E. (1989), *Altägyptische Märchen*, 8th edn., Düsseldorf: Eugen Diederichs Verlag.
Callimachus (2015), *The Hymns*, (ttrc), S.A. Stephens, Oxford: Oxford University Press.
Celoria, F. (1992), *The Metamorphoses of Antoninus Liberalis: A Translation with a Commentary*, London: Routledge.
Charax of Pergamum in Jacoby, *FGrH* 103F5.
Chariton (1989), *Callirhoe*, (ttr) G.P. Goold, Cambridge, MA: Harvard University Press.
——— (2004), *de Callirhoe Narrationes Amatoriae*, (t) B.P. Reardon, Leipzig: Teubner.
Charon of Lampsacus in Jacoby, *FGrH* 262F12 a.
Chessnut, M. (2014), 'Die Drei Wünsche', *EM* 14: 1076–1083.
Christiansen, R. (1958), *The Migratory Legends* (FFC 175), Helsinki: Academia Scientiarum Fennica.
Conrad, J. (2002), 'Polyphem', *EM* 10: 1174–1184.
Cox, M. R. (1893), *Cinderella*, London: Folklore Society.
Dalley, S. (1989), *Myths from Mesopotamia*, (tr), Oxford: Oxford University Press.
Dawkins, R.M. (1951), *Forty-five Tales from the Dodekanese* (ttr), Cambridge: Cambridge University Press.
Dio of Prusa (1932–1951), (ttr) H.L. Crosby I–V, Cambridge, MA: Harvard University Press.
Diodorus Siculus (1931–1967), (ttr) C. Oldfather et al. I–XII, Cambridge, MA: Harvard University Press.
Diogenes Laertius (1925), *Lives of Eminent Philosophers*, (ttr) R.D. Hicks, I–II, Cambridge, MA: Harvard University Press.
Dover, K.J. (1993), *Aristophanes Frogs*, (ttrc), Oxford: Oxford University Press.
Drascek, D. (1999), 'Mann von Galgen', *EM* 9: 175–179.
Duggan, A., and Haase, D. (eds.) (2016), *Folktales and Fairytales: Traditions and Texts from Around the World*, 2nd edn., 4vv, Santa Barbara, CA: Greenwood.
Eumelus (2000), *Early Greek Mythography* I, (ttr) R.L. Fowler, Oxford: Oxford University Press.
Grimm, J., and Grimm, W. (1857), *The Complete Fairy Tales of the Brothers Grimm*, (tr) J. Zipes, (the last collection, with forty additional tales), New York: Vintage.
Hainsworth, J. B. (1988), (with A. Hoekstra and S. West), *A Commentary on Homer's Odyssey I*, Oxford: Clarendon Press.
Hansen, W. (1996), *Phlegon of Tralles' Book of Marvels*, (trc), Exeter: University of Exeter Press.
——— (1998), *Anthology of Ancient Greek Popular Literature*, (tr), Bloomington: Indiana University Press.
——— (2002), *Ariadne's Thread: A Guide to International Tales Found in Classical Literature*, Ithaca, NY: Cornell University Press.

——— (2017), (tr) *The Book of Greek and Roman Folktales, Legends and Myths*, Princeton, NJ: Princeton University Press.
Herodotus (1966), *Ph.-E. Legrand* I–XI, (ttrc), Paris: Les Belles Lettres.
——— (1996), A. de Selincourt, (tr), revised J. Marincola, Harmondsworth: Penguin Classics.
——— (2007), Asheri, D., Lloyd A., Corcella A., *A Commentary on Herodotus I–IV*, Oxford: Oxford University Press.
——— (2015), N.G. Wilson I–II, (t), Oxford: Oxford University Press.
Hesiod (1966), *Theogony*, (tc) M.L. West, Oxford: Oxford University Press.
——— (2008), *Theogony and Works and Days*, (tr) M.L. West, Oxford: Oxford University Press.
Hoffner, H. A. Jnr (1990), *Hittite Myths* (tr), Atlanta, GA: Society of Biblical Literature.
Homer, (1985–93), *Iliad*, (c) G.S. Kirk et al., I–VI, Cambridge: Cambridge University Press.
——— (1989), *Odyssey* IX–XVI, (c) A. Heubeck and A. Hoekstra, Oxford: Oxford University Press.
——— (1998), *Odyssey* I–VIII, (c) J.B. Hainsworth, A. Heubeck, and S. West, Oxford: Oxford University Press.
——— (1994), *Odyssey* VI–VIII, (ttrc) A.F. Garvie, Cambridge: Cambridge University Press.
Husson, G. (1970), *Lucien, Le Navire ou Les Souhaits*, Paris: Les Belles Lettres.
Hyginus (1933), (tc) H.J. Rose, *Fabulae*, Leiden: Sijthoff.
——— (1992), (t) G. Viré, *de Astronomia*, Stuttgart: Teubner.
——— (1993), (t) P.K. Marshall, *Fabulae*, Stuttgart: Teubner.
Joseph et Aséneth (1968), (ttr) M. Philonenko, Leiden: Brill.
Kandler, H. (2007), 'Siebenschläfer', *EM* 12: 662–666.
Kawan, C. (1996), 'Maedchen: Das umschuldig verleumdete', *EM* 8: 1402–1407.
——— (2004), 'Rotkäppchen', *EM* 11: 854–868.
——— (2007), 'Sneewitchen', *EM* 12: 129–140.
Kenney, E. (1990), *Apuleius, Cupid and Psyche*, Cambridge: Cambridge University Press.
Köhler-Zülch, I. (1993), 'Der gestiefelte Kater', *EM* 7: 1069–1083.
Lichtheim, M. (1973–1980), *Ancient Egyptian Literature* I–III, (t), Berkeley: University of California Press.
Longus (1987), *Poimenika*, (t) M.D. Reeve, Leipzig: Teubner.
——— (2004), *Daphnis and Chloe*, (ttrc) J.R. Morgan, Warminster: Aris and Phillips.
Lucian, (1913–67), *Works*, (ttr) A.M. Harmon, K. Kilburn, and M.D. Macleod, Cambridge, MA: Harvard University Press.
Marzolf, U. (1990), 'Halbhänchen', *EM* 6: 396–401.
Meraklis, M (1981), 'Daümling und Menschenfresser', *EM* 5: 360–365.
Maximus of Tyre (1994), *Dissertationes*, (t) M.J. Trapp, Leipzig: Teubner.
——— (1997), *The Philosophical Orations*, (tr) M.J. Trapp, Oxford: Oxford University Press.
Nonnus, *Dionysiaca* (1940–42), (ttr) W.H.D. Rouse, I–III Cambridge, MA: Harvard University Press.
Ovid (1970), *Metamorphoses VIII*, (tc) A.S. Hollis, Oxford: Oxford University Press.
——— (2004), *Metamorphoses*, (t) R.J. Tarrant, Oxford: Oxford University Press.
Pape, W. (1981), 'Daümling', *EM* 3: 349–360.
Parkinson, R.B. (1997), (tr) *The Tale of Sinuhe and Other Ancient Egyptian Poems 1940–1640 BC*, Oxford: World's Classics

Parthenius (1999), (ttrc) J.L. Lightfoot, *The Poetical fragments and the* Erōtika Pathēmata, Oxford: Oxford University Press
Pausanias (1918–1935), (ttr) W. Jones, I–V, Cambridge, MA: Harvard University Press
―――― (1971), *Pausanias' Guide to Greece*, (tr) P. Levi, I–II, Harmondsworth: Penguin Classics.
Perrault, C. (1957), *The Fairy Tales of Charles Perrault*, (tr) G. Brereton, Harmondsworth: Penguin Classics.
Petronius (1975), *Cena Trimalchionis*, (tc) M.S. Smith, Oxford: Oxford University Press.
―――― (2011), *Satyrica*, (c) G. Schmeling, Oxford: Oxford University Press.
Philonenko, M. (1968), (ttr) *Joseph et Aséneth*, Leiden: Brill.
Philostratus (1922), *Lives of the Sophists*, (ttr) W. Cave Wright, Cambridge, MA: Harvard University Press.
―――― (1931), *Imagines*, (ttr) A. Fairbanks, Cambridge, MA: Harvard University Press.
―――― (1968), *Eikones*, (ttrc) K. Kalinka and O. Schönberger, Munich: Artemis.
―――― (2005), *Apollonius of Tyana* I–III, (ttr) C.P. Jones, Cambridge, MA: Harvard University Press.
―――― (2016), *Lives of the Sophists*, (t) R.S. Stefec, Oxford: Oxford University Press.
Phlegon of Tralles (1996), *Book of Marvels*, (trc) W. Hansen, Exeter: University of Exeter Press.
Pliny the Elder (1938–63), (ttr) H. Rackham and W.H.S. Jones, I–X, Cambridge, MA: Harvard University Press.
Pliny the Younger *Epistulae* (1963), (t) R.A.B. Mynors, Oxford: Oxford University Press.
―――― (1966), *The Letters of Pliny*, (c) A.N. Sherwin-White, Oxford: Oxford University Press.
Plutarch (1927–2004), *Moralia*, (ttr) F.C. Babbitt et al. I–XVI, Cambridge, MA: Harvard University Press.
(Pseudo-Virgil) *Culex* (2002), (ttr) G.P. Goold in *LCL* Virgil, vol. 2, Cambridge, MA: Harvard University Press.
―――― (2002), (ttrc) M.G. Iodice, Milan: Oscar Classici Greci E Latine.
Ramanujan, A.K. (1994), *Folktales from India*, New York: Pantheon.
Reardon, B.P. (1989), *Collected Ancient Greek Novels*, (tr), Berkeley: University of California Press.
Richardson, N. (1974), *Homeric Hymn to Demeter*, (tc), Oxford: Oxford University Press.
―――― (2010), *Three Homeric Hymns*, (tc), Cambridge: Cambridge University Press.
Röhrich, L. (1981a), 'Dankbarer Toter', *EM* 3: 306–322.
―――― (1981b), 'Perseus', *EM* 3: 787–829.
―――― (1999), 'Name des Unholds', *EM* 9: 1164–1175.
Rodin, K. (1990), 'Hahn, Huhn', *EM* 6: 374.
Rölleke, H. (1987), 'Fürchten lernen', *EM* 5: 584–593.
Schönbeck, H.-P. (1981), 'Circe', *EM* 3: 57–59.
Schwartz, H. (1988), *Miriam's Tambourine: Jewish Folktales from around the World*, (tr), Oxford: Oxford University Press.
Schwartz, J. (1963), *Lucient de Samosate, Philopseudes et de Morte Peregrini*, Paris: Les Belles Lettres.
Strabo (1917–1932), *Geography*, (ttr) H.L. Jones I–VIII, Cambridge, MA: Harvard University Press.
Tales from the Thousand and One Nights (1973), (tr) N.J. Dawood, Harmondsworth: Penguin Classics.
Testamentum Porcelli (1922), (t) F. Bücheler, pp. 268f. of his 6th edition of Petronius, Berlin.

——— (1972), (ttrc) N. Bott, Zurich: Aku-Fotodruck.
Till Eulenspiegel: His Adventures (1995), (tr) P. Oppenheimer, Oxford: World's Classics.
Wehse, R. (1981), 'Cinderella', *EM* 3: 39–57.
——— (1996), 'Liebhaber blossgestellt', *EM* 8: 1056–1063.
Xenophon of Ephesus (1978), *Ephesiaca*, (t) A.D. Papanikolaou, Leipzig: Teubner.
——— (1989), (tr) in Reardon, above: 125–169.
Yolen, J. (1986), (tr) *Favourite Folktales from Around the World*, New York: Pantheon.
Zipes, J. (1987), (tr) *The Complete Fairy Tales of the Brothers Grimm*, New York: Vintage.
——— (1989/2016), (tr) *Beauties, Beasts and Enchantment: Classic French Fairy Tales*, 2nd edn., New York: Crescent Moon Publications.
——— (1993), (tr) *The Penguin Book of Western Fairy Tales*, New York: Penguin.
——— (2002), (tr) *The Great Fairy Tale Tradition: From Straparola and Basile to the Brothers Grimm*, New York: Norton.

II Secondary literature

Aarne, A. and Thompson, S. (1961), *The Types of the Folktale*, Helsinki: Academia Scientiarum Fennica. See also H.-J. Uther below.
Ackermann, H.C. and Gisler, J.-R. (eds.) (1981–1997), *Lexicon Iconographicum Mythologiae Classicae* I–VIII, Zurich: Artemis.
Anderson, G. (1980), 'The Cognomen of M. Grunnius Corocotta', *AJPh* 101: 57f.
——— (2000), *Fairytale in the Ancient World*, London: Routledge.
——— (2003), 'Old Tales for New: Finding the First Fairy Tales', in Davidson, H.E. and Chaudhri, A., *A Companion to the Fairy Tale*, Cambridge: D.S. Brewer.
——— (2004), 'Aulus Gellius as a Storyteller', in Holford-Strevens, L. and Vardi, A. (eds.), *The Worlds of Aulus Gellius*, Oxford: Oxford University Press.
Aptowitzer, V. (1924), 'Asenath, the Wife of Joseph: A Haggadic Literary-Historical Study', *Hebrew Union College Annual* 1: 239–306.
Baraz, Y. (2012), 'Pliny's Epistolary Dreams and the Ghost of Domitian', *TAPA* 142. 105–132.
Ben-Amos, D. (2010), 'Straparola: The Revolution that Was Not', *AJF* 123: 426–446.
Bettelheim, B. (1976), *The Uses of Enchantment: The Meaning and Importance of Fairy Tales*, London: Thames and Hudson.
Bieler, L. (1933), 'Psyches dritte und vierte Arbeit bei Apuleius', *Archiv für Religionswissenschaft* 30: 242–270.
Binder, G., and Merkelbach, R. (eds.) (1968), *Amor und Psyche*, Darmstadt: Wissenschaftliche Buchgesellschaft.
Blécourt, W. de (2012), *Tales of Magic, Tales in Print: On the Genealogy of Fairy Tales and the Brothers Grimm*, Manchester: Manchester University Press.
Bolton, J.D.P. (1962), *Aristeas of Proconnesus*, Oxford: Oxford University Press.
Bottigheimer, R. (2002), *Fairy Godfather: Straparola, Venice, and the Fairy Tale*, Philadelphia: University of Pennsylvania Press.
——— (2009), *Fairy Tales: A New History*, New York: State University of New York Press.
——— (2014), *Magic Tales and Fairy Tale Magic*, London: Palgrave Macmillan.
Bremmer, J. (1983), *The Early Greek Concept of the Soul*, Princeton, NJ: Princeton University Press.
——— (2002), *The Rise and Fall of the Afterlife*, London: Routledge.
Canepa, N. (ed.) (2019), *Teaching Fairy Tales*, Detroit: Wayne State University Press.
Casson, L. (1974), *Travel in the Ancient World*, Baltimore: Johns Hopkins University Press.

Champlin, E. (1987), 'The Testament of the Piglet', *Phoenix* 41: 174–183.
Clodd, E. (1898), *Tom Tit Tot*, London: Duckworth.
Dasen, V. (1993), *Dwarfs in Classical Antiquity*, Oxford: Oxford University Press.
Davidson, H.E. and Chaudhri, A., (eds.) (2003), *A Companion to the Fairy Tale*, Cambridge: Derek Brewer.
Dégh, L. (1969), *Folktales and Society: Storytelling in a Hungarian Peasant Community*, Bloomington: Indiana University Press.
Dundes, A. (ed.) (1982), *Cinderella: A Casebook*, Madison: University of Wisconsin Press.
——— (ed.) (1989), *Little Red Riding Hood: A Casebook*, Madison: University of Wisconsin Press.
Dundes, A. and Edmunds, L. (1995), *Oedipus: A Folklore Casebook*, 2nd edn., Madison: University of Wisconsin Press.
Edmunds, L. (1985), *Oedipus: The Ancient Legend and Its Analogues*, Baltimore, MD: Johns Hopkins University Press.
——— (1990), *Approaches to Greek Myth*, Baltimore, MD: Johns Hopkins University Press.
Fehling, D. (1977), *Amor und Psyche*, Wiesbaden: Franz Steiner.
Felton, D. (1999), *Haunted Greece and Rome: Ghost Stories from Classical Antiquity*, Austin: University of Texas Press.
Gantz, T. (1993), *Early Greek Myth: A Guide to Literary and Visual Sources*, Baltimore: Johns Hopkins University Press.
Glenn, J. (1971), 'The Polyphemus Folktale and Homer's *Kyklopeia*', *TAPhA* 102: 133–181.
Goldberg, C. (1984) 'The Historic-Geographic Method: Past and Future', *Journal of Folklore Research* 21: 1–18.
Hackman, O. (1904), *Die Polyphemsage in der Volksüberlieferung*, Helsinki: Frenckellska Tryckeri-Aktiebolaget.
Halliday, W.R. (1933), *Greek and Roman Folklore*, New York: Cooper Square Publishers.
——— (1933), *Indo-European Folk-Tales and Greek Legend*, Cambridge: Cambridge University Press.
Hansen, W. (ed.) (1998), *Ancient Greek Popular Literature*, Bloomington: Indiana University Press.
——— (2002), *Ariadne's Thread: A Guide to International Tales in Classical Literature,* Ithaca, NY: Cornell University Press.
Harper, N.N. (1977), 'The Witch's Flying Ointment', *Folklore* 88: 105.
Hartland, E.S. (1894–96), *The Legend of Perseus: A Study of Tradition in Story, Custom and Belief,* London: David Nutt.
Holford-Strevens, L. and Vardi, A. (eds.) (2004), *The Worlds of Aulus Gellius*, Oxford: Oxford University Press.
Hynes, W.J. and Doty, W.G. (2003), *Mythical Trickster Figures: Contours, Contexts and Criticisms*, Tuscaloosa: University of Alabama Press.
Jason, H. and Kempinsky, A. (1981), 'How Old Are Folktales?' *Fabula* 22: 1–27.
Jones, S.S. (1983), 'The Structure of Snowwhite', *Fabula* 24: 56–71.
——— (1990), *The New Comparative Method: Structural Analysis of the Allomotifs of 'Snowwhite'*, Helsinki: Suomalainen Tiedakademia.
——— (1995), *The Fairy Tale: Magic Mirror of the Imagination,* London: Routledge.
Jorgensen, J. (2012), Review of Bottigheimer 2009, *Journal of American Folklore* 125: 518–510.
——— (2017), Review of Bottigheimer 2014, *Journal of Formalized Reasoning* Oct. 14th.
Kakridis, J. (1949), *Homeric Researches*, Lund: C.W.K. Gleerup.
Keller, O. (1877), *Rerum Naturalium Scriptores Graeci Minores* I, Leipzig: Teubner.

Krohn, K. (1926), *Die folkloristiche Arbeitsmethode*, Oslo (tr. R. Welsch as *Folklore Methodology*, Austin: University of Texas Press, 1971.
——— (1931), *Übersicht über einige Resultate der Märchenforschung*, (FFC 96), Helsinki: Academia Scientiarum Fennica.
Lüthi, M. (1976), *Once upon a Time: On the Nature of Fairy Tales*, Bloomington: Indiana University Press.
Mackensen, L. (1923), *Der singende Knochen* (FFC 49), Helsinki: Academia Scientiarum Fennica.
McKay, K.J. (1962), *Erysichthon, A Callimachean Comedy*, Leiden: Brill.
Megas, G. (1967), 'Die Sage von Alkestis', *Laographia* 25: 158–191.
Mundy, C.S. (1956), 'Polyphemus and Tepegöz', *Bulletin of the School of Oriental and African Studies* 18: 279–302.
Nicolaisen, W.F.H. (1993), 'Why Tell Stories about Innocent Persecuted Heroines?', *Western Folklore* 52: 61–71.
Ogden, D. (2007), *In search of the Sorcerer's Apprentice,* Swansea: University of Wales Press.
——— (2008), *Perseus*, London: Routledge.
——— (2013), *Dragons, Serpents, & Slayers in the Classical and Early Christian Worlds: A Sourcebook*, Oxford: Oxford University Press.
Opie, I. and Opie, P. (1974/1980), *The Classic Fairy Tales*, Oxford (pagination follows the Granada re-issue), St. Albans.
Page, D. L. (1955), *The Homeric Odyssey*, Oxford: Oxford University Press.
——— (1973), *Folktales in Homer's Odyssey*, Cambridge, MA: Harvard University Press.
Philip, N. (1989), *The Cinderella Story*, Harmondsworth: Penguin Classics.
Propp, V. (1968) *Morphology of the Folktale*, 2nd edn., Austin: University of Texas Press.
Radin, P. (1956), *The Trickster*, New York: Knopf Doubleday.
Ranke, K. (1934), *Die Zwei Brüder: eine Studie zur vergleichenden Märchenforschung* (FFC114), Helsinki: Academia Scientiarum Fennica.
——— (1977–2015), *Enzyklopädie des Märchens*, I–XV, Berlin: De Gruyter.
Reardon, B.P. (1982), 'Theme, Structure and Narrative in Chariton', *Yale Classical Studies* 27: 1–27.
Reitzenstein, R. (1912), *Das Märchen von Amor und Psyche bei Apuleius*, Leipzig: Teubner.
Röhrich, L. (1962), 'Die mittelälterlichen Redaktionen des Polyphem-Maerchens (*AT* 1137) und ihr Verhältnis zur ausserhomerischen Tradition', *Fabula* 5: 48–71.
Rooth, A.B. (1951), *The Cinderella Cycle*, Lund: CWK Gleerup.
Scobie, A. (1977), 'Some Folktales in Graeco-Roman and Far Eastern Sources', *Philologus* 121: 7–10.
——— (1979), 'Storytellers, Storytelling and the Novel in Graeco-Roman antiquity', *Rheinisches Museum für Philologie* 122: 229–259.
——— (1983), *Apuleius and Folklore*, London: Folklore Society.
Smith, K.F. (1902), 'The Tale of Gyges and the King of Lydia', *American Journal of Philology* 23.3: 261–282.
——— (1920), 'The Literary Tradition of Gyges and Candaules', *CPh* 41: 1–37.
Stramaglia, A. (1999), *Res Inauditae, Incredulae: Storie di Fantasmi nel Mondo Greco-Latino*, Bari: Levante.
Swahn, J.-Ö. (1955), *The Tale of Cupid and Psyche*, Lund: C.W.K. Gleerup.
Swain, S. (2000), (ed.) *Dio Chrysostom: Politics, Letters and Philosophy*, Oxford: Oxford University Press.

Tatar, M. (1987), *The Hard Facts of the Grimms' Fairy Tales*, Princeton, NJ: Princeton University Press.
———— (1999), *The Classic Fairy Tales*, New York: Norton.
———— (2015), *The Cambridge Companion to Fairy Tales*, Cambridge: Cambridge University Press.
Terpening, R.H. (1985), *Charon and the Crossing*, Lewisburg: Bucknell University Press.
Thompson, S. (1946), *The Folktale*, Berkeley: University of California Press (repr. 1977).
Thompson, S. (1954–1958), *Motif-Index of Folk Literature* I–VI, Bloomington: Indiana University Press.
Tolkien, J.R.R. (1947) *On Fairy-Stories* (expanded edition with commentary and notes eds. V. Flieger and D.A. Anderson, 2008), London: Harper Collins.
Trenkner, S. (1958), *The Greek Novella in the Classical Period*, Cambridge: Cambridge University Press.
Uther, H.-J. (2004), *The Types of International Folktales: A Classification and Bibliography* I–III, FFC 284–286, Helsinki: Academia Scientiarum Fennica (revision of Aarne-Thompson above).
Von Hendy, A. (2002), *The Modern Construction of Myth*, Bloomington: Indiana University Press.
Walsh, P.G. (1970), *The Roman Novel*, Cambridge: Cambridge University Press.
Warner, M. (1994), *From the Beast to the Blonde: On Fairy Tales and their Tellers*, New York: Farrar Straus Giroux.
———— (1998), *No go the Bogeyman: Scaring, Lulling, and Making Mock*, London: Chatto.
———— (2014), *Once Upon a Time: A Short History of Fairy Tale*, Oxford: Oxford University Press.
West, S. (1974), 'Joseph and Asenath: A Neglected Greek Romance', *Classical Quarterly New Series* 24: 70–81.
———— (1988), 'The Scythian Ultimatum', *JHS* 108: 207–211.
Wright, J.R.G. (1971), 'Folktale and Literary Technique in *Cupid and Psyche*', *Classical Quarterly* NS 21: 273–284.
Yohannan, J.D. (1968), *Joseph and Potiphar's Wife in World Literature*, New York: New Directions.
Ziolkowski, J.M. (2007), *Fairy Tales from before Fairy Tales: The Medieval Latin Past of Wonderful Lies*, Ann Arbor: Michigan University Press.
Zipes, J. (1979), *Breaking the Magic Spell: Radical Theories of Folk and Fairy Tales*, Austin: University of Texas Press.
———— (1993), 'Spinning with Fate: Rumpelstiltskin and the Decline of Female Productivity', *Western Folklore* 52: 43–60.
———— (1993), *The Trials and Tribulations of Little Red Riding Hood*, New York: Routledge.
———— (ed.) (2000) *The Oxford Companion to Fairy Tale*, Oxford: Oxford University Press
———— (2002), *The Brothers Grimm: From Enchanted Forests to the Modern World*, New York: Palgrave Macmillan.
———— (2006), *Why Fairy Tales Stick: The Evolution and Relevance of a Genre*, New York: Routledge.
———— (2008), 'What Makes a Repulsive Frog so Appealing? Memetics and Fairy Tales', *Journal of Folktale Research* 45.2: 109–143.
———— (2012), *The Irresistible Fairy Tale: The Cultural and Social History of a Genre*, Princeton, NJ: Princeton University Press.

GLOSSARY OF SOURCES IN GREEK (G) OR LATIN (L)

Antoninus Liberalis, (G) mythographer, 2nd c. CE
Anon. *Testamentum Porcelli*, 4th c. CE?
Appendix Perottina, (L) Additional fables by Phaedrus transcribed by Niccolo Perotti
Aelian, (G) miscellanist, 2nd /3rd c. CE
Aesop, (G) supposed author of (anonymous) fables, 6th c. BCE?
Antonius Diogenes, (G) novelist, 1st/2nd c. CE?
(Ps.-)Apollodorus, (G) mythographer, 1st/2nd c. CE
Apollonius paradoxographus, (G) writer on wonders, 2nd c. BCE?
Apuleius, Latin novelist and man of letters, 2nd c. CE
Aristophanes, (G) comic dramatist, 5th/4th c. BCE
Augustine of Hippo, (L) theologian and scholar, 4th/5th c. CE
Callimachus, (G) poet and scholar 4th/3rd c. BCE
Charax of Pergamum, (G) historian, 2nd c. CE
Chares of Mytilene, (G) historian, 4th c. BCE
Charon of Lampsacus, (G) historian, 5th c. BCE
Conon, (G) mythographer, 1st c. BCE/CE
Dionysius of Halicarnassus, (G) writer on rhetoric and historian, 1st c. BCE
Dio of Prusa, (G) belletrist and philosopher. 1st/2nd c. CE
Diodorus Siculus, (G) historian, 1c. BCE
Diogenes Laertius, (G) biographer, 3rd c. CE
?Eumelus, (G) archaic poet, 8th c. BCE
Herodotus, Greek historian, 5th c. BCE
Homer, Epic poet 8th c. BCE?
Hyginus, (L) mythographer, 2nd c. CE?
Longus, Greek novelist, 2nd/3rd c. CE
Lucian, Greek satirist and belletrist, 2nd c. CE

Nonnus, Greek poet, 5th c. CE
Ovid, (L) poet, 1st c. BCE/CE
Parthenius, (G) poet and scholar, 1st c. BCE
Pausanias, (G) scholar and periegete, 2nd c. CE
Philostratus, (G) sophist and biographer 2nd/3rd c. CE
Philostratus, (G) author of descriptions of artworks 2nd/3rd c. CE (may be identical with the previous entry)
Phlegon of Tralles, (G) miscellanist 1st/2nd c. CE
Photius, (G) Greek scholar and prelate, 9th c. CE
Plato, (G) philosopher, 5th/4th c. BCE
Pliny the Elder, (L) polymath, 1st c. CE
Pliny the Younger, (L) statesman and epistolographer, 1st/2nd c. CE
Plutarch, (G) biographer and moralist, 1st/2nd c. CE
Servius, (L) commentator on Virgil, 4th c. CE
Strabo, (G) geographer 1st c. BCE/CE
Suda (G) Byzantine Dictionary 10th c. CE
Xenophon of Ephesus, (G) novelist, 2nd c. CE?

INDEX OF TALE TYPES

ATU 178A The Innocent Dog 172–173
ATU 200 The Dogs' Certificate 174–175, 176n20
ATU 219E★★ The Hen that laid the Golden Eggs 175
ATU 300 The Dragon-Slayer 155–158, 164n30, 164n34, 166n55
ATU 303 The Twins or Blood-Brothers 159–160, 164n30
ATU 306 The Danced-out Shoes 158–159
ATU 307 The Princess in the Coffin 78–80
ATU 313 The Magic Flight 161–162
ATU 326A Soul Released from Torment 70–73
ATU 327A Hansel and Gretel 91–93, 116–117
ATU 327B The Brothers and the Ogre 180
ATU 332 Godfather Death 73–74
ATU 333 Little Red Riding Hood 162
ATU 366 The Man from the Gallows 74–76
ATU 410 The Petrified Kingdom 195–197
ATU 425B Son of the Witch (Cupid and Psyche) 17, 45
ATU 440 The Frog King 188–189
ATU 480 The Kind and Unkind Girls 125–126, 140n2, 198
ATU 500 The Name of the Supernatural Helper 189–191
ATU 505 The Grateful Dead 106
ATU 510A Cinderella 2, 3, 6, 8, 9, 55–63
ATU 517 The Boy who understands the Language of Birds 185
ATU 545A/B The Cat Castle/Puss in Boots 3, 12, 14, 173–174, 176n15

ATU 560–562 The Magic Ring/Aladdin/The Spirit in the Blue Light 162–163
ATU 570★ The Rat-Catcher 103–104
ATU 571B Lover Exposed 99–101, 119n11
ATU 655 The Wise Brothers 150, 152
ATU 700 Thumbling 179
ATU 709 Snow White 1, 5, 9, 14, 55, 63–66, 68n33, 69n41
ATU 750A The Three Wishes 99
ATU 750B Hospitality Rewarded 108–111
ATU 766 The Seven Sleepers 82
ATU 779E The Dancers of Kolbeck 112–115
ATU 780 The Singing Bone 118
ATU 882 The Wager on the Wife's Chastity 127–140
ATU 883A The Innocent Slandered Maid 126–127, 141n6
ATU 899 Alcestis 11, 15n20, 80–81, 85n57
ATU 924 Discussion in Sign Language 184–185
ATU 950 Rhampsinitus 11, 150–152
ATU 960A The Cranes of Ibycus 99, 106
ATU 1137 The Ogre Blinded (Polyphemus) 143–150
ATU 1187 Meleager 101–103
ATU 1620 The Emperor's New Clothes 7, 8, 13, 186

Christiansen Migratory Legends:
ML 3020 The Sorcerer's Apprentice/Inexperienced Use of the Black Book 70, 76–78, 85n41
ML 3061 The Pied Piper 14, 103–104, 120n26

Stith Thompson Motif-Index:
B270 Animals in Legal Relations: *Testamentum Porcelli* 174–175
B550 Animals carry Men 167–168, 174
D1427.1 Pied Piper of Hamelin 103–104
D1550 Magic object opens and closes 176n10
D2063.1.1 Tormenting by sympathetic magic 101–103
E155.1 Slain Warriors revived Nightly 82–83
E721.1 Soul wanders from body in sleep 81, 91
E721.1.2.3 Soul of sleeper prevented from returning by burning the body 81, 91
F452 Dwarf 178–179
F535.5.1 War of Pygmies and Cranes 4, 181
F647 Marvellous sensitiveness 188, 193n30
G263.1 Witch transforms Lovers into Animals 87–91
H1010 Impossible Tasks 105
J2072.1 Short-sighted Wish 107–108
K978 Uriah Letter 163n6
K1371.1 Lover steals Bride from Wedding with Unwelcome Suitor 111–112
N721 Runaway Horse carries Bride to her Lover 111–112

Unclassified:
'Artemis and the Three Hairy Giants' 178, 181–182
Snow White's Revenge 105
The Fairy Lover 80

INDEX

Note: Page numbers followed by "n" denote endnotes.

Aarne-Thompson-Uther index of tales (ATU) 2, 4
Adversus indoctum (Lucian) 186
Aelian 55: *Varia Historia* 56–57, 108, 188
Allegory of Prodicus 8
Amatoriae Narrationes 118
Andersen, Hans Christian: *The Princess and the Pea* 193n30
Animal tales 12–13; *Culex* 172–173; *The Dream or the Cock* (Lucian) 169–172; *Fabulae* (Hyginus) 168, 173–174; Herodotus 167–168; *Testamentum Porcelli* 174–175, 176n20
Antoninus Liberalis 6, 96; *Metamorphoses* 105, 181
Antonius Diogenes 82–83
Apollodorus 45, 80–81, 103–104, 159–162, 185, 191
Apollonius Rhodius 80; *Argonautica* 12
Appendix Perrotina 106–107, 111–112
Aptowitzer, V. 67n16, 67n22
Apuleius: *Cupid and Psyche* 2–4, 6, 8, 9–10, 17–47, 47n2, 196, 197; *The Golden Ass* 91
Aristeas of Proconnesus 81
Aristophanes: *Frogs* 93; *Wasps* 6
Augustine of Hippo: *City of God* 91

Babes in the Wood 3
Basile, G. 9, 176n16, 176n17, 195; *Gagliuso* 176n19; *La Gatta Cenerentola* 8; *Lo cunto de li cunti* 3

Beauty and the Beast 9
Bolte, J. 2
Book of Dede Korkut 8, 85n57
Bottigheimer, R. 4, 15n21

Callimachus: *Hymns* 115–116, 123n85, 181–182
Chaereas and Callirhoe (Chariton) 127–140
Charax of Pergamum 152, 154n24
Chariton: *Chaereas and Callirhoe* 127–140
Charon of Lampsacus 80
Cicero: *de Divinatione* 106
Cinderella 9, 10; *Daphnis and Chloe* (Longus) 60–63; Hyginus de Astronomia 56; Strabo and Herodotus 55–56; *Varia Historia* (Aelian) 56–57, 108, 188
City of God (Augustine of Hippo) 91
Conon: *Narrationes* 181
Contes de fées (D'Aulnoy) 3
Cranes of Ibycus 106
Culex 172–173
Cupid and Psyche (Apuleius) 2–4, 6, 8, 9–10, 17–47, 47n2, 196, 197

Daphnis and Chloe (Longus) 60–63
D'Aulnoy, Madame: *Contes de fées* 3
de Divinatione (Cicero) 106
Diodorus 45
Diogenes Laertius 82
Dionysiaca (Nonnus) 45–47
Dio of Halicarnassus 189

212 Index

Dio of Prusa 8, 87; *Oration 1* 93–96
The Dream or the Cock (Lucian) 169–172

The Emperor's New Clothes 7, 8, 13, 186
Enzyklopädie des Märchens (Ranke) 4
Epimenides 82, 86n59, 86n68, 86n76
Erōtes 13, 182n5
Erōtica pathēmata (Parthenius) 189–191
Eumelus 80

Fabulae (Hyginus) 168, 173–174, 180
Fabulae Aesopicae Collectae (Halm)
  117–118, 175
Frogs (Aristophanes) 93
Fugitivi (Lucian) 13, 189–191

Gagliuso (Basile) 176n19
The Golden Ass (Apuleius) 11, 14, 91
Grimms 1, 2, 4, 9, 14: *Kinder-und Hausmärchen* 3

Hadrian of Tyre 11
Halm: *Fabulae Aesopicae Collectae* 117–118, 175
Hansen, William 4, 14
Hermotimus of Clazomenae 81–82
Herodotus 55–56, 126–127, 150–152, 167–168, 184–185
Histoires ou contes du temps passé (Perrault) 3
Homer: *Odyssey* 5, 7, 87–91, 99–101, 143–150, 188
Hyginus: *Fabulae* 168, 173–174, 180
Hyginus de Astronomia 56
Hymns (Callimachus) 115–116, 123n85, 181–182

Ibycus 106
Imagines (Philostratus) 178–180
international tale 2, 8, 9, 11
Ivory Snow-White 65–66

Kakridis, J. 119n4
Kinder-und Hausmärchen (Grimms) 3
King John and the Abbot 2
King Little-Fist 65–66

La Gatta Cenerentola (Basile) 8
Le piacevoli notti (Straparola) 3
Letters (Pliny the Younger) 72–73
L'héritier, Marie-Jeanne 3
Life of Apollonius of Tyana (Philostratus) 91–93
Little Red Riding Hood (Perrault) 6, 162
Lives of the Sophists (Philostratus) 186–188
Lo cunto de li cunti (Basile) 3

Lucian: *Adversus indoctum* 186; *The Dream or the Cock* 169–172; *Fugitivi* 13, 189–191; Phalaris 116–117; *Philopseudeis* 70–78

magic tales 2, 4, 14
Metamorphoses: Antoninus Liberalis 105, 181; Ovid 4, 5, 65–66, 107–108, 110–115, 125–126, 158–159
Moralia (Plutarch) 74, 106

Narrationes (Conon) 181
non-magical folktale categories 1
Nonnus: *Dionysiaca* 45–47

Odyssey (Homer) 5, 7, 87–91, 99–101, 143–150, 188
Opie, I. 182n4
Opie, P. 182n4
Oration 1 (Dio of Prusa) 93–96
Ovid: *Metamorphoses* 4, 5, 65–66, 107–108, 110–115, 125–126, 158–159

Parthenius: *Erōtika Pathēmata* 189–191
Pausanias 152, 162, 173
Peri Thaumasiōn (Phlegon of Tralles) 78–80
Perrault, Charles 2, 10, 14, 17, 176n16, 176n17; *Histoires ou contes du temps passé* 3; *Little Red Riding Hood* 6, 162
Phaedo (Plato) 5, 84n26
Phalaris 116–117, 124n108
Philip, N. 68n29
Philopseudeis (Lucian) 70–78
Philostratus: *Imagines* 178–180; *Life of Apollonius of Tyana* 91–93; *Lives of the Sophists* 186–188
Phlegon of Tralles: *peri Thaumasiōn* 78–80
Photius *Codex* 166 82–83
Piglet: *Testamentum Porcelli* 174–175, 176n20
Plato: *Phaedo* 5, 84n26; *Republic* 162–163
Pliny the Younger: *Letters* 72–73
Plutarch: *Moralia* 74, 106
Polivka, G. 2
The Poor Man of Nippur 9
The Princess and the Pea (Andersen) 193n30
Propp, Vladimir 1

Ramanujan, A.K. 182n8
Ranke, Kurt: *Enzyklopädie des Märchens* 4
Republic (Plato) 162–163
Rip van Winkle 11, 70, 86n68
Rose de la Force 3

Schwartz, H. 67n16
Servius on *Aeneid* 103–105

The Sleeping Beauty 14, 195–197
Smith, K.F. 166n61
Snow White 1, 5, 9, 10, 55; *Metamorphoses* (Ovid) 65–66; Xenophon of Ephesus 63–64
The Sorcerer's Apprentice 11, 70, 85n41
Strabo 55–56, 98n48, 103–104, 191
Straparola 4, 6, 176n16, 176n17: *Le piacevoli notti* 3

Tale of Two Brothers 4–5, 8, 9
Testamentum Porcelli (Piglet) 174–175, 176n20

Thompson, Stith 1, 3–4
Tolkien, J.R.R. 1, 2
The Types of International Folktales (Uther) 3

Uther, H.-J.: *The Types of International Folktales* 3

Varia Historia (Aelian) 56–57, 108, 188

Xenophon of Ephesus 10, 55, 63–64

Zipes, Jack 7

For Product Safety Concerns and Information please contact our EU
representative GPSR@taylorandfrancis.com
Taylor & Francis Verlag GmbH, Kaufingerstraße 24, 80331 München, Germany

www.ingramcontent.com/pod-product-compliance
Lightning Source LLC
Chambersburg PA
CBHW071354290426
44108CB00014B/1545